Author, Publisher, Entrepreneur

Guy Kawasaki • Shawn Welch

Also by Guy Kawasaki

The Art of Start

Rules for Revolutionaries

The Macintosh Way

Selling the Dream

How to Drive Your Competition Crazy

Hindsights

The Computer Curmudgeon

Database 101

Reality Check

Enchantment

#APETheBook

You can follow *APE* news using the hashtag #APETheBook on social-media networks. Because of rapid advancements in self-publishing, this book is updated as often as necessary. This is the Austen version of *APE*. To see what has changed or been added since this version was printed, visit APETheBook.com/updates.

NONONINA PRESS
APE: Author, Publisher, Entrepreneur—How to Publish a Book
Guy Kawasaki and Shawn Welch

Copyeditor: Rachelle Mandik
Cover Design: Holly Thomson
Interior Design: Shawn Welch

Published in the United States by Nononina Press
ISBN 978-0-9885231-0-4

Version 1.1 (Austen)
Printed by Lightning Source LLC

[About the Authors]

Friendship is born at that moment when one person says to
another: "What! You too? I thought I was the only one."

C. S. Lewis

Guy Kawasaki is the author of eleven previous books, including
What the Plus!, Enchantment, and The Art of the Start. He is also the
cofounder of Alltop.com and the former chief evangelist of Apple.
Kawasaki has a BA from Stanford University and an MBA from
UCLA, as well as an honorary doctorate from Babson College.

Shawn Welch is the author of three previous books, including *From
Idea to App, iOS 5 Core Frameworks,* and *iOS 6 for Developers.* He
is also the developer of several iOS apps. Previously he worked as a
senior media editor for Pearson Education. He also helped pioneer
many of Pearson's earliest efforts in iPad solutions. Welch has a BS
from Kansas State University.

[Contents]

A great book should leave you with many
experiences, and slightly exhausted at the end.
You live several lives while reading.

William Styron, interview with George Plimpton, 1958

[Author]   1

[Publisher]   77

[Entrepreneur]   253

[Preface]

The best way to become acquainted with
a subject is to write a book about it.

Benjamin Disraeli

This fried my brain. In 2011, a large tech company wanted to buy five hundred copies of the ebook version of my book *Enchantment* to use for a promotion. Penguin, my publisher, doesn't sell ebooks directly, so it referred this lead to Apple.

Apple told the company to buy five hundred gift cards, scratch off the back, and then enter individual gift codes one at a time into iTunes. At that point, the company gave up on Apple and tried Amazon and Barnes & Noble. An employee of the company ended up making five hundred individual credit-card purchases.

I'm not a novice author. My publisher didn't treat me like dirt. I had an agent, he got me a large advance, and the people at Penguin moved heaven and earth to make *Enchantment* a *New York Times* and *Wall Street Journal* bestseller. But the traditional publishing system could not handle an order for five hundred copies of an ebook.

Shortly after this experience, I had dinner with a friend named Halley Suitt Tucker, who told me to read *Be the Monkey* by Barry Eisler and Joe Konrath so that I could understand the advantages of self-publishing. This book sold me on the concept. I was ready to rock and roll. I thought self-publishing would be easy: write in Microsoft Word, upload to Amazon, and cash checks. Maybe the process works like this for novels, but publishing a nonfiction book with subheads, bulleted lists, and pictures is like swimming with alligators.

Over several weeks I asked five knowledgeable people about the best way to self-publish an ebook, and I got eight answers—two of which directly conflicted with each other. Fortunately, I hooked up with Shawn Welch via Google+ (you'll hear more from him later). He helped me understand the complexities of publishing an ebook, and he ended up designing and producing *What the Plus!*

But what happens if an author doesn't have a **Shawn**? Then self-publishing is a mystifying, frustrating, and inefficient task.

Why self-publish, then?

The answer is that self-publishing enables you to determine your own fate. There's no need to endure the frustration of finding and working with a publisher. You can maintain control over your book and its marketing, receive a greater percentage of revenues, and retain all rights and ownership.

A successful self-publisher must fill three roles: **Author, Publisher,** and **Entrepreneur**—or **APE**. These roles are challenging, but they are not impossible—especially if people who have done it before explain it to you. And that's what Shawn and I will do in the book you are now reading. Our goal is to help you succeed as a self-publisher as quickly and easily as possible.

[How to Read This Book]

Though thoroughly reconceived, the 16th edition continues the *Manual's* tradition as an authority for generations of readers seeking answers to all things related not only to the written word but also to the myriad and evolving ways in which words and ideas are shared and published.

**From *"The History of The Chicago Manual of Style,"*
The Chicago Manual of Style Online**

Twenty years ago I took *The Chicago Manual of Style* with me on a vacation and read it from cover to cover. I can't tell you that I memorized it, but it did make using the book more efficient for all these years.

Shawn and I hope that *APE* serves a similar function in your writing career. The process of publishing a book can take a year, and we hope you'll write more than one book. This means you may return to *APE* again and again.

Self-publishing is a vast subject, so *APE* is a long book. Our advice is to blast through *APE* the first time to see the big picture. Later you'll understand the importance of topics that didn't make sense or weren't relevant the first time through. Then you can return to *APE* as a reference.

You'll learn that publishing is a parallel, not serial, process that requires simultaneous progress along multiple fronts. A traditional publisher has the luxury of throwing multiple people at these parallel activities. A self-publisher doesn't have multiple people.

Self-publishing is akin to launching a start-up. Entrepreneurs must create a product, test it, raise money, recruit talent, and find customers at the same time. Also, we cover the same topic from different angles because of the parallel-processing nature of self-publishing.

Here are some details about *APE* to make reading easier and more valuable:

- **Voice.** Overall, the book's voice is mine (Guy's). The pronoun "I" refers to me. The pronoun "we" refers to Shawn and me—that is, to our collective opinion or advice. This might break some conventions, but we think it makes the book easier to understand—and it was easy to convince our editorial board (me) that it was the right thing to do.

- **Hyperlinks.** *APE* contains approximately four
  hundred hyperlinks. If you're reading the ebook
  version, you can click on the links. Since you're
  reading the print version, refer to the link library on
  APETheBook.com. Hyperlinks are indicated using a
  triple dagger[†††] symbol.

  On the website, we also provide tools and
  templates to make *APE* a more useful resource.

- **Prices and percentages.** The day we release *APE*,
  it will be wrong. There's no way around this. We'll
  revise it, but it will still not be 100 percent accurate.
  We quote prices and percentages to give you a rough
  idea of what things cost and the deals you'll get, but
  you must check for updated information from the
  companies we mention.

Now, let's get started on your self-publishing adventure.

[Acknowledgments]

I would maintain that thanks are the highest form of thought;
and that gratitude is happiness doubled by wonder.

G. K. Chesterton, *A Short History of England*

Our thanks to all these folks who helped us create *APE*. First, there's Halley Suitt Tucker, without whom I might not have started self-publishing at all. Then there are all the people who contributed their time, expertise, and passion in generous and valuable ways: Noelle Chun, Inder Comar, Carlos dos Santos, Joel Friedlander, Marylene Delbourg-Delphis, Scott Dougall, Robert Duffy, Gretchen Dykstra, Sarah Evans, Erin Fetsko, Peggy Fitzpatrick, Leslie Gordon, Nitin Gupta, Sloan Harris, Bradley Horowitz, Gina Weakley Johnson, David Kazzie, Andrew Keith, Rachelle "MCAT"

Mandik, Tess Mayall, Will Mayall, Karen McQuestion, Bill Meade, Maria Murnane, Katie Murphy, Sara Peyton, Carol Porter, Gina Poss, Alan Rinzler, Lindsey Rudnickas, Susan Ruszala, Ray Sabini, Holly Thomson, Bojan Tunguz, and Val Swisher.

Oh the wonders of social media and the kindness of people we met via Google+, Facebook, Twitter, and LinkedIn. All these folks provided ideas, editing, and edification. Jeff Altman, David Anderson, Jeff and Rhonda Angcanan, Arin Basu, Roane Beard, Lici Beveridge, Paula Biles, John E. Bredehoft, Ellen Britt, Flora Morris Brown, PhD, Matt Campbell, Stuart L. Canton, Subhro Bikash Chakraborty, Kenken Clarin, Joshua Cohen, Ryan Delk, Doug Detling, Errette Dunn, Brandy D. Ellis, Kristen Eckstein, Chris Edwards, Scott Engel, Jon D. Evans, Connie Feil, Urs Frei, John Gallagher, Bob Garrett, Terrie Gray, John Heckendorn, Lisa Kalner Williams, Thomas Denis Keating, Donald Kennedy, Karen Lattari, Kimberly Lau, David Lawrence, Robert Light, Bruna Martinuzzi, Eileen McDonnell-Gross, Martina G. McGowan, D. Borje Melin, Chris Melck, Linda Michels, Claudia Neumann, Alan Northcott, Crystal Ponti, Karl Raats, Maciej Rajk, Dan Redler, Matthew Robinson, Presse-Service Karin Sebelin, Silvino Pires dos Santos, Bob Soltys, Martha Spelman, Keith Spiro, Jirapong Supasaovapak, Rachel Thompson, and Wendy Wright.

Author, Publisher, Entrepreneur

[Author]

But you must be sure that your imagination and love are
behind it, that you are not working just from grim resolution,
i.e., to make money or impress people.

Brenda Ueland, *If You Want to Write*

Writing is the starting point from which all goodness (and crappi-
ness) flows. This section explains the theory and practice of writing
a book. Writing a book isn't an easy process, and neither is it always
enjoyable, but it is one of life's most satisfying achievements.

CHAPTER 1

Should You
Write a Book?

To me a book is a message from the gods to mankind;
or, if not, should never be published at all.

Aleister Crowley, *The Confessions of Aleister Crowley*

Why People Read Books

The purpose of this chapter is to help you decide whether you should write a book. Over the years, dozens of people have asked me what I think of their idea for a book. My response is always the same:

> Imagine you're in a Barnes & Noble bookstore (let's hope there are still bookstores when you read this) or you're on the home page of Amazon. You see novels by Isabel Allende, Jonathan Franzen, Daniel Silva, Anne Lamott, and Lee Child. Over in nonfiction there are books by Stephen Jay Gould, Malcolm Gladwell, and Clayton Christensen. And maybe there are a few vanity tomes by the CEOs of large, well-known companies.

In this sea of choices, why should anyone give a shii-take about your book?

Many would-be (and some published) authors cannot answer this question because they're focused on a different one:

How will I benefit from writing a book?

Their answers to this other question include: "It's good for my visibility." "To make money." "It will help me get speaking gigs and consulting engagements." "It's good for my company." "It will make me a thought leader." Any of these reasons may be true for the author, but they are not relevant for readers. Think about this:

How often do you peruse Barnes & Noble or Amazon while wondering how you can help an author achieve his or her personal goals?

Your answer, like mine, is probably "never." I'm happy for authors to earn lots of royalties, but that's not why I buy their books. I'd bet the same is true for you, too. Let's examine the good and bad reasons to write a book.

Good Reason 1: Enrich Lives

The first good reason to write a book is to add value to people's lives. Both writer and reader benefit when a book enables gains in the following arenas:

- **Knowledge.** Science books explain how the world works. Business books explain management techniques. History books explain events of the past. Books like these spread knowledge and expertise. Example: *The Elements of Style* by William Strunk Jr. and E. B. White.
- **Understanding.** Both novels and nonfiction can help people understand themselves and others. They can provide tools and techniques to foster greater awareness and comprehension of their lives. Example: *Light in August* by William Faulkner.
- **Entertainment.** Novels entertain people by providing adventure, fantasy, and out-of-the-ordinary role-playing. Some people want to be heroines. Some people want to be spies. I want to be a Navy SEAL. To each his own. Example: *The Lord of the Rings* by J. R. R. Tolkien.
- **Laughter.** Some books brighten people's lives with humor, mirth, or sarcasm. For me, there's Fran Lebowitz's *Social Studies* and Alice Kahn and Whoopi Goldberg's *Multiple Sarcasm.* Another popular example: *Stuff White People Like* by Christian Lander.

Stop reading and answer this question: Will your book add value to people's lives? This is a severe test, but if your answer is affirmative, there's no doubt that you should write a book.

Good Reason 2: Intellectual Challenge

At the tender age of forty-eight I took up ice hockey even though I had never skated before (there are no frozen ponds in Hawaii). Canadians will tell you that I was forty-five years too late, eh? I would never make money or earn a college scholarship by playing hockey. My motivation was the joy of learning the world's most enchanting sport.

The second good reason to write a book is the same reason I play hockey: to master a new skill, not to make money. I found an extreme example of this in writing. Ernest Vincent Wright wrote a novel that did not contain any words with the letter "E."[†††] It's called *Gadsby—50,000 Word Novel Without the Letter "E."* You can download a PDF if you don't believe me.[†††]

According to the book's introduction, Wright was tired of hearing "it can't be done; for you cannot say anything at all without using E, and make smooth continuity, with perfectly grammatical construction." He used a typewriter with the "E" key tied down so that he could not inadvertently use the letter. (Hat-tip to Andrew Keith for pointing me to this book.)

Here is a great passage from the introduction of Wright's book:

> People as a rule will not stop to realize what a task such an attempt actually is. As I wrote along, in long-hand at first, a whole army of little E's gathered around my desk, all eagerly expecting to be called upon. But gradually as they saw me writing on and on, without even noticing them, they grew uneasy; and, with excited whisperings amongst themselves, began hopping up and riding on my pen,

---

looking down constantly for a chance to drop off into some word; for all the world like seabirds perched, watching for a passing fish! But when they saw that I had covered 138 pages of typewriter-sized paper, they slid onto the floor, walking sadly away, arm in arm; but shouting back: "You certainly must have a hodge-podge of a yarn there without us! Why, man! We are in every story ever written hundreds of thousands of times! This is the first time we ever were shut out!"

In my book (pun intended), a book should be an end, not a means to an end. Even if no one reads your book, you can write it for the sake of writing it. Memoirs, for example, fit in this category. And the number of people who want to read a book of such a pure origin may surprise you.

Good Reason 3: Further a Cause

The third good reason to write a book is to evangelize a cause. A cause seeks to either end something bad (pollution, abuse, bigotry) or perpetuate something good (beauty, peace, affection). *Silent Spring* by Rachel Carson is an example. Her cause was the environment, and her book resulted in the ban of DDT and catalyzed the start of the environmental movement.

To write such a book, you must go beyond *explaining* something to *promoting* a point of view and action. Note: an appropriate cause is seldom your personal wealth. A good cause is a much higher calling. Also, you can further a cause with fiction as well as nonfiction, so this applies to novelists, too.

The acid test for this kind of book is, "Do you feel a moral obligation to write the book?"

Good Reason 4: Catharsis

Way back in 1987, I wrote my first book, *The Macintosh Way*. At the time I was running a small software company, but it was not operating the way I thought it should. I wrote this book because I knew there had to be a better way to do business.

This experience taught me the fourth good reason to write a book: Writing is therapeutic. It helps you cope with issues that seem gargantuan at the time. The process of expressing yourself about a problem, editing your thoughts, and writing some more can help you control issues that you face.

Bad Reason 1: Popular Demand

There are also bad reasons to write a book. The first one is popular demand: "Lots of people tell me I have a good story." Or, "Lots of people tell me that I'm a good writer." Let's dissect this. Exactly how many is "lots"? Divide that number by a hundred to estimate how many people will *buy* your book. Then divide that number by four to estimate how many people will actually *read* your book.

Have you ever told friends or relatives that they should open a restaurant because they were great cooks? How about telling a funny person she should be a comedienne? If you have, did you truly intend that they go into the food business or start calling comedy clubs? Maybe people were making polite conversation or flattering you when they said you should write a book, but these are not reasons enough.

The exception to this rule is if a *writer or author* tells you that you should write a book, which is the equivalent of a restaurateur or comedian telling you to get in the business. This is because they know how much work is involved—as well as the exhilaration of finishing and publishing a book. For example, Percy Bysshe Shelley encouraged his wife, Mary Shelley, to finish a short story that she'd written at the suggestion of Lord Byron (yes, *the* Lord Byron). This short story became Frankenstein.††† (Hat-tip to Carlos dos Santos for this story.)

Bad Reason 2: Money

The second bad reason to write a book is to make a lot of money. The average number of copies that most books sell, according to street wisdom, is a few hundred. You may believe that publishing a book will boost your speaking and consulting opportunities too—but only if your book is good and your marketing is great.

Sure, you hear about people who self-published their books and made millions of dollars, but the reason you hear about them is that they are rare, not commonplace. A more realistic and healthier approach is to believe that making money is a possible outcome, but not the purpose, of writing a great book. May you be so fortunate as to experience both.

Summary

Writing is often a lonely and difficult process, so take a moment to reflect on the good reasons and bad reasons to write a book. We still encourage you to do it, because it is one of the most rewarding experiences in life, but few things worth doing are easy.

CHAPTER 2

A Review of Traditional Publishing

The girl doesn't, it seems to me, have a special perception or feeling which would lift that book above the "curiosity" level.

A publisher's rejection of *The Diary of Anne Frank*, in *Rotten Rejections* by André Bernard

Resisting Change

This chapter provides an understanding of how traditional publishing works so that you can fully appreciate self-publishing. In the beginning, rich and powerful people employed scribes to copy text. Access to the printed word was restricted and undemocratic. For example, few people could read the *Book of Kells*, an illustrated book of the four Gospels of the New Testament, because there was only one copy.[†††]

Traditional publishing has a long history of resisting change. Here are two illustrative stories. First, France prohibited authors from selling their own books until August 30, 1777. The only people who were allowed to sell books were members of the bookselling guild. (Source: *The Enlightenment and the Modernization of Authorship: Self-Publishing Authors in Paris (1750–91)* by Marie-Claude Felton. Hat-tip to Donald Kennedy for this story.)

Second, when Robert de Graff introduced $0.25 paperback books in 1939, publishers scoffed at his idea.[†††] (Historians can make the case that Aldus Manutius pioneered the paperback concept when he created the *octavo* format four hundred years earlier.) One publisher sold de Graff the paperback rights to its books with this explanation: "We feel we ought to give it a chance—to show it won't work here."

At the time, people paid $2.50 or more for hardcover books. De Graff's paperbacks had to sell in large quantities for him to drive down costs, so he could not depend on the five hundred bookstores in America. Instead, he used magazine distributors to reach newsstands, drugstores, and mass-transit stations.

Do you see a pattern? For readers and writers, the democratization of publishing wrought good news and, typically, denial by traditional publishers. Readers gained access to more books at lower costs and now have the ability to make instant purchases, sync across devices, and carry thousands of titles on their tablets. Writers gained control of their own fate. They did not have to kowtow to publishers and then wait a year before their works hit bookstore shelves.

Traditional Publishing

In the days before desktop publishing and self-publishing, it was tough to get a book published. Shawn and I have done it sixteen times, and while the process got easier, it was never efficient or optimal. Publishing a book in the traditional way takes twelve to eighteen months—authors and readers can't wait this long anymore.

In case you aren't familiar with traditional publishing, these are the key players in the process:

- **Agents.** Agents help their clients identify editors and craft book proposals. Then the agents pitch editors to acquire the book. An agent's compensation is approximately 20 percent of the royalties that the author receives.

  Big traditional publishers won't even accept a pitch or manuscript from an author without an agent. Authors who have convinced an agent to represent them have cleared a significant hurdle in the filtering process of publishers of any size.

- **Editors.** Editors decide which books to acquire. Then they act as internal advocates for the authors. They also edit the overall content of a manuscript at a high level and write much of the marketing materials. In other words, they are the gatekeepers, evangelists, and psychiatrists for authors.

- **Editorial assistants.** In the old days, proposals formed towering stacks (called "slush piles" by industry insiders) on the desks of editorial assistants all over New York. Editorial assistants scanned the proposals for those that looked "interesting" and passed those on to editors.

These days many editors give their assistant access to their e-mail for screening, so even if you send an e-mail to an editor, editorial assistants are often the first point of contact. If you'd like insight into what editors and their assistants are thinking when they read proposals, check out SlushPile Hell.[†††]

Editorial assistants also ensure the completion of dozens of details necessary for a book to get out the door. These details include contracts, permissions, cover copy, blurbs, and marketing materials.

- **Copyeditors.** Copyeditors go through a manuscript line by line, letter by letter, and correct hundreds of mistakes. These mistakes range from spelling and grammar all the way to incorrect facts, changes in character names, and gaps in plots. Whereas an editor focuses on the big picture of a book, a copyeditor sweats the details of every line of text.

- **Designers.** This is a catch-all term for several roles. Typically, there is at least a cover designer and book-interior designer. Most authors never even meet these designers, but they can make or break a book's success with their efforts.

- **Publicists.** A publicist is the "vice president of marketing" for a book. She interacts with the sales force, editor, book reviewers, bloggers, and resellers. She, not the editor, typically controls the marketing budget for the book. The editor is supposed to produce something great. The publicist is supposed to make it sell.

The relationship between author and publicist is usually the most contentious one in publishing because no author has been happy with his publicist in the history of mankind. (No publicist has been happy with her author in the history of mankind either, though.) In the "Entrepreneur" section of *APE*, you'll learn how to fill the role of publicist, and you'll have no one to blame but yourself.

The Fantasy of Traditional Publishing

Now that you understand who the players are in traditional publishing, we'll explain the process. Anyone who hasn't been through the process believes the following fantasy:

- If you're a nonfiction writer, you craft a book proposal and e-mail it to ten publishers who are interested in your genre and three agents who know publishers interested in your genre. If you're a fiction writer, you write your entire novel and go through the same process.
- Editors immediately read your proposal or draft. Astounded by your book's bestselling potential, a few call you to buy the rights to the book. Or, if the recipient is an agent, he calls you to beg for the honor of representing you.
- Within a week you come to terms with a publisher— or the agent comes to terms with you and begins to pound his Rolodex for the perfect publisher. In any case, after another week or two, you have several deals with six-figure advances that enable you to concentrate on writing.

- Your editor is totally simpatico with your goals for the book. You are completing each other's sentences. Meanwhile, the publisher's legal department has drafted a contract that you find acceptable.
- You work steadily and rapidly toward completing the book. Progress is good because you are able to carve out large blocks of time to write without the distraction of making a living or taking care of kids. (A big enough advance can fix anything.)
- Six months later, you submit your final manuscript draft to the editor. The editor drops everything and begins to read it. For the first time in his career, he has only a handful of changes, suggestions, or concerns, and he sends it back to you in less than two weeks.
- A graphic designer has created ten designs for the cover. You like three of them, but you adore one in particular, which you select.
- Three months later, the publisher launches the book. The publicist has no problem booking you on *Good Morning America,* the *Today* show, and *Oprah.* The *New York Times, Washington Post,* and *USA Today* are set to publish reviews the day your book hits the street. Arianna Huffington wants an exclusive Google+ Hangout on Air with you. Everyone's biggest concern is whether there are enough trees to cut down to make paper for your book.
- The day after the book hits bookstores, James Cameron calls you to buy the film rights.

Now take a break for four minutes and thirty-eight seconds and watch a YouTube video called "So You Want to Write a Novel" to see if you are a typical author.[†††]

Figure 02.01. A scene from "So You Want to Write a Novel."

The Reality of Traditional Publishing

Maybe the publishing process is fast, smooth, and easy if you're Danielle Steele, Bill Clinton, Isabel Allende, or Malcolm Gladwell. By contrast, this was the real-world experience of Karen McQuestion, the author of *A Scattered Life*:

- She queried agents 187 times for the first six books that she wrote. She eventually signed with two agents for two different books at two different times.

- She directly queried editors 131 times. Her agents queried editors an additional 40 times.
- All the editors had good things to say about her books, but none of them made an offer.

The reality of what most authors experience with traditional publishers is much closer to McQuestion's experience than any fantasy you've conjured. From our observations as authors and Shawn's tour of duty working for Pearson Education, here's the reality of working with a traditional publisher:

- You spend three to six months knocking on the door of dozens of publishers and agents but rarely achieve success. You might not even get rejection notices. This is not because publishers don't want to personally inform you about their decision. Most of the time it's because they're busy babysitting the authors they have already signed.
- Let's say that you strike gold, and you find an editor who wants to publish your book. You face two to three months of contract negotiation. And your advance, if you're lucky, is in the $5,000 to $10,000 range.
- It takes you twelve months to finish writing. You believe you could have finished faster if you had gotten an advance large enough so you could do nothing else but write. But deep down inside you know that your lack of self-discipline and inexperience with the writing process were the real problems.

- Your editor takes two to three months to read your draft, and he wants it substantially changed. You need at least a month to fix everything he wants, even though you agree with practically nothing he wants.

- Microsoft Word's spelling and grammar checker indicates that your manuscript is perfect, but the copyeditor has found hundreds of mistakes. You didn't even know what a serial comma is, much less why the copyeditor added it two hundred times.

- You hate all three cover designs that the art department has created. However, your editor told you that if you want the book to come out on time, it's too late to design more covers.

- A month after you "finish writing" and implement all of the changes from the editors, your publisher tells you that you need to rephrase what you thought were perfectly crafted sentences. There are a few dozen changes to make to fix loose lines, widows, and orphans—whatever those are.

- Twelve to eighteen months after you listened to your friends who told you, "You should write a book," it's now in stores. Unfortunately, your publicist is getting little PR traction because you're an unknown author, and Mark Zuckerberg released his book, *F Is for Facebook: The Gospel According to Mark*, the same week that you released yours.

After three months of haranguing anyone you can get on the phone at your publisher, you come to two realizations. First, you're the primary person responsible for the marketing of your book. Second, publishers don't use marketing to *cause* books to sell well—they help books that are *already* selling well to sell even better. To use a pyromaniac analogy, publishers are accelerants, not sparks.

Traditional Publishing and False Rejection

Publishers have a tough job because it's difficult to separate the diamonds from the dirt. However, they have made some terrible decisions by rejecting great works of literature. This doesn't mean a traditional publisher has made a mistake if they reject your book. But rejections do not necessarily mean that you should give up.

Before self-publishing became so easy, persevering meant continuing to pound on traditional publishers' doors until you found one that accepted your book. Now at least you have the self publishing alternative as long as you don't give up altogether because of rejections.

My theory is that rejection is like the flu: the way to prevent its devastating effects is to receive a small dose (aka a vaccine) so you can build resistance in advance. Here is a small dose of rejections of famous authors compiled by Michelle Kerns of the *Examiner*.[†††]

We're not providing these examples to prove that publishers are clueless. Rather, we want to expose you to rejection so that if it happens to you, you won't automatically think that your book isn't good.

Author	Title	Rejections
William Golding	*Lord of the Flies*	Twenty rejections by publishers.
Stephen King	*Carrie*	"We are not interested in science fiction which deals with negative utopias. They do not sell."
John le Carré	*The Spy Who Came in from the Cold*	"You're welcome to le Carré—he hasn't got any future." (One publisher passing le Carré to another.)
Joseph Heller	*Catch-22*	"I haven't the foggiest idea about what the man is trying to say... Apparently the author intends it to be funny—possibly even satire—but it is really not funny on any intellectual level."
George Orwell	*Animal Farm*	"It is impossible to sell animal stories in the USA."
John Grisham	*A Time to Kill*	Twelve rejections by publishers and sixteen by agents.
Jack Kerouac	*On the Road*	"His frenetic and scrambled prose perfectly express the feverish travels of the Beat Generation. But is that enough? I don't think so."
Thor Heyderdahl	*The Kon Tiki Expedition*	Twenty rejections by publishers.

The beauty of self-publishing is that it enables authors to find out if people like their book without a traditional publisher. If today's self-publishing technology existed when these authors sought publishers, perhaps their books would have reached readers sooner.

October 12, 1988

Guy Kawasaki
ACIUS, Inc.
20300 Stevens Creek Blvd. Suite 495
Cupertino, CA 95014

Dear Guy:

Thanks so much for sending me THE REWARD IS THE REWARD.

This is a wonderful manuscript but, as you suspected, one that I find too specialized for our general market. Unfortunately, Kenzi Sugihara in Bantam Computer Publishing feels the same way.

I am, however, a great admirer of your ideas and work. When you do write a general interest book, I hope you would be willing to let me consider it.

Sincerely,

Harriet Rubin
Executive Editor

Figure 02.02. Rejection is part of the life of an author. This is a copy of one of the rejection letters I received for my first book. I renamed it *The Macintosh Way*, and Scott Foresman published it.

A Model for the Future

Traditional publishers are in a period of gloom and doom. Sales are flat, and margins are decreasing. Large, once proudly independent companies such as Random House and Penguin, are clinging together. However, there are some publishers who are embracing the new electronic realities of publishing. O'Reilly Media is one example.[†††] Let's take a look at its approach to publishing:

- **Direct sales.** O'Reilly sells books directly to people from its website. It doesn't try to preserve a multi-tiered distribution model that doesn't necessarily serve customers better.
- **Multiple formats.** O'Reilly provides ebooks in PDF, EPUB, MOBI, DAISY, and Android APK formats as well as printed-on-paper.
- **DRM-free.** O'Reilly publishes ebooks that are free of digital rights management (DRM). (More about DRM in chapter 20: "Self-Publishing Issues.")
- **Easy access.** Customers can download their O'Reilly books in as many formats as many times for as many devices as they want.
- **Syncing.** People can sync their O'Reilly books to Dropbox (a cloud-based storage service) accounts. (More about Dropbox in chapter 5: "Tools for Writers.")
- **Online subscription.** O'Reilly created the Safari Books Online brand, which provides online subscription access to books, videos, and interactive learning tools.[†††]
- **Community.** There is also a question-and-answer forum as well as a community forum for O'Reilly customers.[†††]

- **Conferences.** O'Reilly conducts conferences around the world about the topics in its books.[†††]
- **Multimedia.** O'Reilly offers webcasts by authors as well as online educational courses and certification.[†††]

O'Reilly is the way of the future: multiple formats, DRM-free, and expanding the definition of publishing to include multimedia learning, community forums, and face-to-face conferences.

(Hat-tip to Jason Epstein for pointing out O'Reilly Media as an example.)

Summary

Traditional publishing is under siege by many forces, and it is not appropriate for many writers. Self-publishing, on the other hand, is the best thing that has ever happened to writers. As Marilyn Monroe said, "Sometimes good things fall apart so better things can fall together."

CHAPTER 3
The Self-Publishing Revolution

The only really necessary people in the publishing
process now are the writer and reader.

Russell Grandinetti, Amazon

Cause and Effect

This chapter explains the advantages and disadvantages of self-publishing and why self-publishing is such a big deal. Technology has enabled publishing to take three big leaps:

- **Publishing 1.0:** In 1440, Johannes Gutenberg created the printing press and more people could read the Bible. Whereas woodblock printing was capable of 40 pages per day, a Renaissance-era printing press churned out 3,600 pages per day. This caused a rise in literacy and threatened the literate elite. Believe it or not, in 1637, England restricted the number of print shops.

- **Publishing 2.0:** Three companies—Apple, Aldus, and Adobe—enabled anyone with a Macintosh, laser printer, and PageMaker to print newsletters, newspapers, and books. Until desktop publishing entered the picture, the best case for solo writers unaffiliated with a publisher was a typewriter and a photocopier or duplicator.

- **Publishing 3.0:** Amazon, Apple, and Barnes & Noble enabled writers to create and sell books electronically as well as print paper copies on demand. Anyone with a computer, phone, or tablet could read these books. The imprimatur of a large publisher meant less and less. "Buzz" about a book meant more and more.

The problem *isn't* that traditional publishers are dumb or evil. There are plenty of smart and nice people in the industry—probably more than most industries because a love of reading motivated their career choice.

The problem is that traditional publishing grew up in a world with limits and logistics such as shelf space, access to printing presses, editing and production expertise, and shipping of physical books.

In the old, constrained world, somebody had to select, print, and distribute what was worthy of royalty, shelf space, and killing trees. That somebody was an employee of a traditional publisher; he served as a filter, finisher, and arbiter of taste. Several thousand traditional publishers added this kind of value for hundreds of years.

Shelf space for ebooks, however, is infinite, and anyone who can use a word processor can write and publish a book. These changes don't mean that books are better—no more than a democratic political system guarantees better leaders—but at least the system is more accessible.

The Three Ds of Self-Publishing

Even if you like the heft, smell, and feel of printed books, the advantages of ebooks are here to stay. While printed books may never die (an ebook of Annie Leibovitz's photographs won't cut it), we're not going back to a time when there are no ebooks.

Companies such as Amazon and Apple, along with programmers and geeks, have produced three fundamental curve jumps in publishing:

- **Democratization.** Anyone with a computer and a word processor can publish a book, and anyone with a computer, tablet, or smart phone can read a book. Writing and reading are no longer the provinces of the rich, famous, and powerful.
- **Determination.** Authors can determine the success of their books, and readers can determine the quality of what they read. There's no one else to blame for a poor publishing experience if you're an author and for a poor reading experience if you're a reader.
- **Disintermediation.** Entities that do not add value wither and die. The distribution of books from authors to readers is more direct, immediate, and inexpensive than ever. Gatekeepers must add value or face their demise.

If you're going to succeed in self-publishing, you need to believe in these changes at the core of your existence.

Advantages for Authors

Enough about the big picture of publishing, let's get down to the nitty-gritty details of the advantages of self-publishing for authors:

- **Content and design control.** Unless you're already a successful author or a huge celebrity, control of your book is an illusion when you're working with a traditional publisher. When you self-publish a book, you control what's in it, how long it is, and how it looks. On the other hand, if you don't like your book, you have no editor or editorial board to blame.
- **Longevity.** Traditional publishers stop marketing a book when the month-long introduction ends or it stops selling—whichever comes first. There is little input from the author. As a self-publisher, you control this decision. By using a print-on-demand vendor and publishing an ebook, you can keep your book in print forever—or at least as long as it takes for readers to discover your book.
- **Revisions.** Traditional publishing can take months to fix errors because publishers print revisions only after they've sold the current inventory. When you self-publish a book, you can revise it immediately with online ebook resellers and even change the version that's being printed on demand.
- **Money.** Traditional publishers pay authors 10 to 15 percent of proceeds of the sales of a book to distributors. Amazon, by contrast, pays a 35 percent or 70 percent royalty. Apple pays 70 percent, and

Barnes & Noble pays 65 percent. Self-publishing also enables authors to sell directly to customers—reaping the profits that distributors and retailers would have gotten.

- **Direct connection.** Self-publishing enables authors to maintain closer connections to their readers if they sell books directly. This is a powerful advantage if authors and readers want to interact and if authors want to sell future works to their readers.

- **Price control.** Authors exercise little control of the pricing of their books when working with traditional publishers. Self-publishing enables you to change the price of your book whenever you want. All you have to do is go to your account with Kindle Direct Publishing, iBookstore, Nook, and/or Kobo and input the changes.

- **Time to market.** A traditional publisher takes nine to twelve months to get a printed book to market, and it will not release the ebook version earlier than the printed version. By using a print-on-demand company, you can get your book to market in a couple of weeks. You can get an ebook through Kindle Direct Publishing in forty-eight hours.

- **Global distribution.** Traditional publishers use a wait-and-see attitude toward global distribution of a new book. They wait to see if the book sells well in the local market and if other publishers want to buy foreign rights. Self-publishing enables you to achieve global distribution of your ebook on day one. Kindle Direct Publishing, for example, will sell your ebook to customers in one hundred countries from the start.

- **Control of foreign rights.** When a traditional publisher sells the foreign rights of your book, it takes a percentage of the sale. If you self-publish and sell these rights, you'll make more money because you're not sharing revenue with a traditional publisher. You must weigh this advantage, however, against the difficulty of finding (or being found by) a foreign publisher, negotiating a contract, providing artwork, and collecting royalties.

- **Analytics.** Unless you're bugging your traditional publisher for information, the most you'll learn about your sales is your twice-a-year royalty statement. (Shawn's lucky; he gets a royalty statement four times a year from his traditional publisher.) If your traditional publisher subscribes to BookScan, it can provide retail point-of-sale sales results for your printed book.[†††] BookScan, however, does not include ebook sales, and it only tracks approximately 75 percent of retail print-book sales.

  Most online ebook resellers provide real-time or near real-time sales results, and many print-on-demand printers can provide similar information. This enables you to gain insight about how your sales and marketing promotions are doing. Also, when you conduct experiments with pricing, you can see the results immediately.

  We should also tell you that members of Amazon's Author Central[†††] can view BookScan numbers without an affiliation with a traditional publisher.

- **Deal flexibility.** Traditional publishers only sell to resellers except for bulk sales of printed books to large organizations. Anything outside of this—for example, selling five hundred copies of the ebook version of *Enchantment*—is difficult for traditional publishers. As a self-publisher, you can cut any kind of deal with any kind of organization. For example, you could sell a site license for your book to a large company for all its employees.

The Disadvantages of Self-Publishing for Authors

You may be thinking, "There's got to be a catch," and there is. While the advantages of self-publishing are many, there are disadvantages, too:

- **Advance.** There are only two kinds of authors: those who have a big advance, and those who want a big advance. A six- or seven-figure advance is a thing of beauty. It enables you to focus on writing, hire a nanny, and buy a MacBook Air. It's also proof that the publisher is serious about your book. And if your advance is large enough, you can cope with a publisher who can't directly sell five hundred copies of your ebook.

  The problem is that as a self-publisher, you not only won't get an advance, you also are responsible for all the costs of publishing your book, such as editing, cover design, layout design, and production.

- **Editing.** Self-publishing can be a lonely path. In particular, you might not have an editor who is a mentor, advisor, and psychiatrist. Don't kid yourself—a good editor will make your book better. You can get all kinds of feedback from friends and relatives, but this isn't as good as what you can get from a professional editor.

- **Team.** In addition to an editor, a traditional publisher throws many people at your book at the same time. You may not have 100 percent of their attention for a long period of time, but you do get help. These folks can include an editorial assistant, technical editor, copyeditor, art director, publicist, and sales force. As a self-publisher, you'll still need to do what they would have done—or hire independent contractors.

- **Marketing muscle.** We'll address how to gain marketing muscle on your own, but it's unlikely you'll have as much as a traditional publisher. This is important if you want big-name publications, blogs, radio shows, and television shows to review your book. If you make your book a success, then you can attract these organizations later, but it's nice to have them pushing your book from the start.

- **Prestige.** After the creation of desktop-publishing tools in the mid-1980s, there was a flood of self-published books. In those days, "self-published" meant that you couldn't find a real publisher because your book was crappy. The stigma and suspect nature of self-publishing are far less than in those days, but they still exist.

- **Distribution.** As long as people are flying from airports and shopping in Costco, books printed on paper will sell. Publishers use a sales force to get books into these outlets. You won't have a sales force working for you, so the probability of seeing your book in the San Francisco airport is low.

- **Foreign rights.** Traditional publishers have established relationships around the world with other publishers so they can help you get your book translated for other markets within a year of first publication. It's much more difficult for authors to do this by themselves, although, as we mentioned, you can simultaneously ship your untranslated ebook version into dozens of countries on day one.

Plan C

Plan A for many authors is to write a pitch, get an agent, sign a publishing deal, receive an advance, and write a bestseller. Plan B, when Plan A doesn't happen, is to self-publish. You may achieve success with Plan B and write happily ever after, but there is also Plan C.

In this scenario, you implement Plan B and use your sales results to prove to a publisher that people like your book. Then you sell the rights to your book to the publisher (fully cognizant of the frustration you'll encounter but salved by an advance for it, plus some prestige). In software terminology, you can think of the self-published version of your book as a paid beta test.

Maria Murnane[†††] is an example of Plan C. She's a PR person who moved to Argentina from Silicon Valley. Part of her income in Argentina came from playing professional soccer (I'm not making this up). While not practicing or playing soccer, she wrote a novel called *Perfect on Paper,* which fictionalized her trials and tribulations as a single professional in Silicon Valley.[†††]

After a four-week search, Murnane found an agent who "loved" her book. Then she spent six months revising it for the agent. Her agent submitted the book to seven big traditional publishers, all of whom rejected it. Eventually even her agent fired her—via this e-mail:

> I do feel that we're going in circles about this at a point. We are coming upon a year, which should be the term of our agreement. There are still some publishers (Red Dress among them) that you are free to approach with the book as it is, and because we haven't exhausted the possibilities, you may yet find your match with another agent. I think at this point it would be best to terminate the agreement and allow you to explore your options. I just don't think there's more I can do for you with this novel.

Undaunted, Maria revised her book for another five months. Then she took it to a writers' conference, where more people turned it down. Finally Maria's father convinced her to self-publish the book. Being the PR person she is, she undertook her own marketing program and earned more than one hundred five-star reviews on Amazon and sold more than one thousand copies. This might not seem like a big number, but keep reading.

Around the same time, Amazon launched Amazon Publishing, and it negotiated the rights for Maria's book. Since then the book has sold in the low six figures and has enabled Maria to live in New York as a writer. She has published two additional books: *It's a Waverly Life* and *Honey on Your Mind.*[†††]

Maria's example provides three valuable lessons: First, rejection doesn't necessarily mean your book isn't good. Second, rejection doesn't necessarily mean you should give up. Third, you may have more than one book in you, so you can use each book to build your customer base and get closer to success.

Plan C is an attractive alternative to relying on only Plan A or Plan B. It has the advantages of self-publishing (speed to market and freedom of content and style) and the advantages of traditional publishing (lucrative advances, foreign-rights sales, and prestige).

This is why AmazonEncore, an imprint of Amazon Publishing, is pure genius.[†††] It acquires successful books from self-published authors and adds Amazon's clout to take them to the next level. It is, if you will, an institutionalized Plan C. (More on Amazon Publishing and AmazonEncore in chapter 21: "How to Navigate Amazon.")

Artisanal Publishing

In the past, writers who were rejected by traditional publishers resorted to publishing their own books—this was called "vanity publishing." Many people attached a stigma to these books and, truthfully, the stigma was justified because many early self-published books were not properly edited and produced.

However, one generation's stigma is another generation's opportunity. When was the last time you decided to read a book because of who published it? What influences you more: the name of the publisher or reader ratings and reviews?

You need to get over feeling stigmatized if you can't find a traditional publisher. Perhaps these publishers have done you a favor by forcing you to think different [sic] and think outside the hardcover. The story of John Audubon may help allay your doubts.

Audubon created his epic work, *The Birds of America*, in the late 1820s. At the time, New York publishers already included such houses as the Harper Brothers, G. P. Putnam, Charles Scribner, and John Wiley. However, Audubon self-published his book using a subscription model, five illustrations at a time: one large bird, one medium bird, and three small birds. Each subscription consisted of 435 plates.

Until the mid-nineteenth century, most authors published their books at their own expense—Walt Whitman, for example, self-published (and typeset!) *Leaves of Grass.* Self-publishing could change from stigma to bragging point—maybe we could change the term to "artisanal publishing" and foster the image of authors lovingly crafting their books with total control over the process.

What would you rather read: a mass-produced or artisanal book?

Finally, you'll love this: during Audubon's time, the New York publishers based much of their business on pirating the works of Charles Dickens, Emily Brontë, and Thomas Babington Macaulay. So today's gatekeepers are yesterday's pirates. It was not until 1846 that George Palmer Putnam instituted the royalty system that's still in place today. Before then, publishing was mostly self-publishing.

Summary

The advantages of self-publishing far outweigh the disadvantages for most authors. You can use self-publishing as the end goal or a means to a traditional publishing deal. Keep in mind the concept of *artisanal publishing* as a new, cool form of publishing—you heard the term here first!

CHAPTER 4
The Ascent of Ebooks

A revolution is not a bed of roses. A revolution is a struggle to the death between the future and the past.

Fidel Castro, January 5, 1961

Publishing Spring

This chapter explains the impact and consequences of ebooks. In 2012, "publishing spring" occurred for the publishing industry when tablets reached critical mass and grew beyond an early-adopter fad and Christmas gift. Revolutions occurred in Arab countries and were called Arab Spring, and a similar revolution happened in publishing.

If you want evidence, look at how people are reading in Starbucks or on airplanes (any class). Amazon, Apple, Samsung, Barnes & Noble, and Google are selling e-readers and tablets ranging from $69 to $750 to make this trend continue. And Amazon says it sells more ebooks than printed books in the United States and the UK.

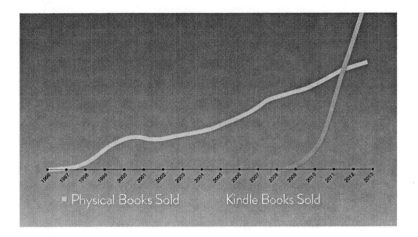

Figure 04.01. Sales of physical versus Kindle books by Amazon.

However, interpret this chart carefully: Amazon says that it sells more ebooks than printed books. This doesn't mean that ebooks outsell printed books in totality. (More on this later in this chapter.)

The Advantages of Ebooks for Readers

I used to buy twenty printed books per year, but since the day Apple shipped the first iPad in April 2010, I've bought five. Four were gifts, and one was *The Chicago Manual of Style*. And I buy forty ebooks per year. People love ebooks because of these advantages:

- **Immediate gratification.** When you finish an ebook, you can buy another one in seconds. You don't have to drive to a store, hope that you find something you like, and then drive home before you can start reading it. I often buy a book while my plane is boarding at the gate. When I'm on planes with wireless connectivity, I even buy books while flying.

- **Privacy.** People around you cannot see what you are reading. Maybe you're an S&M fan, so you're reading a book about Microsoft Windows or *Fifty Shades of Grey*. With ebooks, there's no external cover to reveal your literary tastes. For all people know, you're reading *War and Peace* or Mitt Romney's new autobiography, *But 47 Percent Is Less Than a Majority*.

- **Vast selection.** The cost of storing digital files is trivial, so publishers can provide their entire selection as ebooks. For new books, this is a no-brainer. There are costs to scanning old books, but the process is doable, and Google is doing this anyway. With ebooks, the term "out-of-print book" may become an oxymoron.

- **Buy once, read many.** A physical book is in only one place at a time. If you're not at that place, you can't read it. I can read the same book on any of two tablets, two smart phones, and two computers. Each one can sync to the "farthest page read."

- **Highlighting, annotating, and bookmarking.** Ebook reading apps enable you to highlight text, annotate your thoughts, and bookmark important pages. Then you can search for these "dog-eared" pages later. Highlights, annotation, and bookmarks sync across devices, so you could highlight a passage on one device and see it on others. You can also share these actions with other readers. This can make reading both more efficient and fun.

- **Backlighting.** You can read an ebook in the dark on backlit tablets such as an iPad, Kindle Paperwhite, or Nexus 7 without disturbing people around you. I like to read in bed and fall asleep without having to turn off the lights.

- **Dictionary and Wikipedia access.** If you don't understand a term or concept, ebook readers have integrated dictionaries and Wikipedia. This means that it's easy to get clarification about things you don't understand.
- **Weight.** My Nexus 7 is ⅜ of an inch thick and weighs less than a pound. These figures remain the same whether there are one or a hundred books on it. By contrast, a hundred hardcover books would weigh more than a hundred pounds and create a stack ten feet high.
- **Battery life and environmental costs.** Some tablets run for ten hours without recharging. Some Kindle devices can run for weeks. (The Electric Power Research Institute calculates that it costs $1.36 per year to charge an iPad.) I don't know the total environmental impact of manufacturing, charging, and recycling tablets, but ebooks don't require killing and shipping as many trees.
- **Adjustable text size.** Do you need reading glasses? I sure do. Ebooks enable you to change the font size until it's something you can read more easily. Shawn doesn't appreciate this feature yet, but his day will come.
- **Listen to the book.** Most Kindle devices support text-to-speech, so they can read a book to you while you're on a treadmill or a bike. You can switch between listening and reading and stay in sync on multiple devices. Finally, if you buy the Audible version and ebook version, you can listen to the book as you read it.[†††]

- **Listen to music while reading.** What's more idyllic than to simultaneously read a book and listen to music with the same device? With many tablets, you can do this. This is the trifecta of bliss: a collection of good books, your music, and no one bothering you.
- **Color graphics.** Color photographs and graphics can appear anywhere and in any quantity in an ebook. Color printing, on the other hand, is expensive. Even when an author can convince a traditional publisher to print graphics in color, these images are usually grouped in one place. Many tablets are still monochrome, but millions of Kindle Fire, iPad, Samsung, and Nexus 7 tablets are color.
- **Flexibility.** You can transfer documents such as Word and PDF files to tablets to read them. Therefore, a tablet is a flexible, central library for material from all sources, not only authors and publishers.
- **Zero loss.** It's more difficult to lose an ebook, because you can download it again. Even if you loan an ebook to someone, you can always get it back.
- **Lower price.** Ebooks usually cost 40 percent ($5 to $10) less than their paper versions. The magic price points for self-published ebooks are $0.99, $2.99, and $9.99. Amazon also lets you loan Kindle ebooks to others for fourteen days and borrow books if you're an Amazon Prime customer who owns a Kindle device.[†††] (Amazon Prime is a membership program that costs $79 per year. It provides free two-day shipping to the forty-eight contiguous states; up to seven-day shipping to Alaska, Hawaii, and Puerto Rico; and other benefits.)

- **Rich multimedia content.** iPad owners can read books with graphics, photos, links, movies, animations, and user-interaction elements such as self-assessment quizzes. Apple calls these "Multi-Touch" books. Check out Michelle Obama's *American Grown*, published by Random House, to see what you can do.[†††]

The Disadvantages of Ebooks for Authors

For the first five months, *What the Plus!* was only available as an ebook. I promoted it to millions of people on Google+, Twitter, and Facebook, and I sold approximately 15,000 copies and gave away another 20,000 copies. Amid all this action, I received four requests for a printed version. There are several ways to look at this:

- Printed books are dead.
- My experience is a single data point for an author with geeky readers.
- Only a handful of people asking for a printed version doesn't mean only a handful would have bought it.

No matter what the interpretation, there are still good reasons to print your book:

- **Revenue.** In 2011 approximately $27 billion worth of books sold in the United States. Only $2.1 billion of this was in an electronic format. Much as I love ebooks, printed books are more than 90 percent of the action, except in the adult fiction category.

Sales of the printed form of *Enchantment* outnumber the ebook version by two to one. The percentage of printed-book sales will decline, but it will take a long time, if ever, to reach zero. Why leave any revenue on the table? (The "Publisher" section of this book explains revenue numbers and debunks a popular myth about ebooks outselling printed books.)

- **Distribution.** Availability causes impulse purchases. If you want Target, Walmart, and airport bookstores to sell your book, usually a traditional publisher must publish it, because you won't have access to these resellers.

    If my books are for sale after a speech, 20 percent of the audience buys one. There's no way that 20 percent of the people would have gone home and purchased my book online in ebook or printed format. However, many people have asked me to sign an iPad that contains my ebooks.

    (A service called Kindlegraph[†††] enables an author to "autograph" ebooks by inserting a personalized message and digitized signature. It claims that 3,500 authors of more than 15,000 ebooks have signed up for the service. Still, this isn't as compelling as seeing an author and getting an autograph on a printed book.)

- **Libraries.** If you want to reach people who cannot afford to buy a book, much less a tablet, then printing your book is necessary because most libraries still focus on physical books. You can't blame them, because many traditional publishers make it onerous for libraries to lend ebooks.

For example, HarperCollins enables libraries to loan an ebook twenty-six times, and then the libraries need to buy another copy. According to a blog post on "A Newbie's Guide to Publishing," libraries have to pay three to five times more for ebooks than consumers do.[†††] For some reason, traditional publishers believe they can restrict-access their way to survival.

- **"Proof."** The ability to hold your book in your hand and show it to your friends and relatives is a powerful feeling. The fact that a publisher agreed that your book is worth publishing is important too. Printed books provide more "proof" that you're a writer than an ebook file on a computer or a tablet does. Also, a physical book is a more meaningful gift compared to a PDF or promotional code to many people.

The Myth of the Dominance of Ebooks

If you follow the publishing business, you'll see news reports along the lines of "Ebooks Now Outselling Printed Books." As a self-publisher, you need to know the entire story.

I spent several hours deciphering a report called "BookStats 2012—An Annual Comprehensive Study of the U. S. Publishing Industry" from the Association of American Publishers and the Book Industry Study Group.[†††] Here's what I figured out:

- Approximately two thousand companies submitted data to the study. This data accounted for $16 billion in sales in 2011. The Book Industry Study Group then extrapolated this number to arrive at a total market size of $27 billion. All numbers are United States only.
- The $27 billion represented the wholesale revenues of publishers, not the retail revenues of resellers who sold the books to people.
- Here is a breakdown of how much each type of book accounted for:

Type of book	Description	Percent of market	Revenue in dollars
Trade	Adult fiction, adult nonfiction, juvenile fiction, and juvenile nonfiction	51 percent	$14 billion
Textbook	Higher-ed and K-12	34.5 percent	$9.5 billion
Professional	Business books	13 percent	$3.1 billion
Scholarly	Research and journals	.73 percent	$.2 billion
Other		.8 percent	$.2 billion

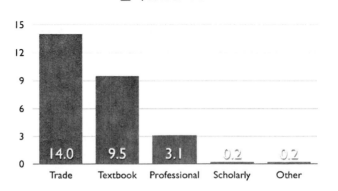

Figure 04.02. Breakdown of 2011 US book sales.

- The revenue of ebooks accounted for 30 percent, or $2.1 billion, of the adult-fiction category. $2.1 billion amounts to double the revenue from 2010 to 2011. Ebooks kicked butt in this category.
- At 30 percent market share, ebooks were the most popular format for adult fiction. Mass-market softcover was second at 29.5 percent. Hardcover and softcover books accounted for 36 percent. So while it is true that ebooks outsell all other formats for adult fiction, they only led mass-market softcovers by 0.5 percent. If you compare all printed formats of adult fiction (mass-market softcover + hardcover + softcover), printed books outsold ebooks 70 percent to 30 percent.
- The $2.1 billion of ebooks sold in the adult-fiction trade-book category represent 97 percent of all ebook sales.
- Zooming out of adult fiction, 79 percent of all trade books were still the printed format.
- Zooming out of trade books to the entire US publishing industry, if $2.1 billion was 97 percent of ebook sales, then 100 percent was $2.16 billion. And the $2.16 billion of ebooks was only 8 percent of the $27 billion US publishing industry.

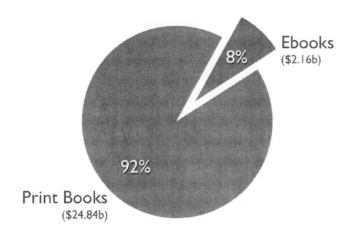

Figure 04.03. The big picture of the formats of books.

Again, these figures represent a snapshot of the US publishing business in 2011. The trend is that ebooks will eventually overtake all forms of publishing except Annie Leibovitz coffee-table books.

In the meantime, if you're a writer of adult fiction, you're in the sweet spot of ebooks. But don't assume, no matter what kind of book you're writing, that ebooks are outselling printed books in general.

Come to think of it, the "Arab Spring" analogy is apt: there were revolutions in several countries, but this doesn't mean that everyone is living under democratic conditions in those countries now.

Summary

Ebooks and tablets are rearranging the publishing landscape. Right now, only about 10 percent of publishing revenue comes from ebooks, but the technical advantages of electronic publishing are enormous. This doesn't mean that printed books will disappear anytime soon, but for a novice self-publisher, ebooks are probably the way to go.

CHAPTER 5

Tools for Writers

Actually, as the artist gets more into his thing, and as he gets
more successful, his number of tools tends to go down. He
knows what works for him. Expending mental energy on
stuff wastes time.

Hugh MacLeod, *Ignore Everybody*

In Our Humble Opinion

This chapter helps you select the tools to write your book.
Admittedly, Shawn's and my recommendations are subjective, but we've written sixteen books over a twenty-five year
period, so at least there is a basis for our prejudices.

Computer

In our book (again, pun intended), you should use a Macintosh.
No computer makes you more creative and productive, because a
Macintosh becomes part of you whereas you need to overcome other
operating systems.

In particular, we recommend a MacBook Air[†††] because it's thin,
light, and sexy, so you won't mind carrying it with you, and therefore
you can write all the time. We have never met anyone who regretted
buying a Macintosh.

(Disclosure: as many people know, I fell in love with Macintosh early in my career when I worked for Apple as a software evangelist. Additionally, Shawn has written three books on iPhone and iPad development and regularly speaks on the subject.)

We're not suggesting that you *must* buy a MacBook Air, but if there was ever a justification, this is it. If you don't want to buy a MacBook Air, at least ensure that your computer has these characteristics:

- Weighs fewer than three pounds, so you won't hesitate to take it with you everywhere you go.
- Runs a recent version of Microsoft Word so you can share your files and work with vendors. (More on this later in this chapter.)
- Lasts at least five hours on batteries, so that when you enter the writing "zone" you won't have to stop for lack of a charged battery.

Word Processor

We recommend that you use Microsoft Word[†††] to write your book. It is a bazooka, and you might think you only need a flyswatter, but there are three good reasons to embrace our recommendation:

First, Word is the de facto standard among designers, editors, resellers, PR consultants, and beta testers. You can "save as" Word from other word processors, but this innocent act can cause catastrophes. And if any vendor other than Apple's iBookstore tells you that it won't accept Word files, you should find another vendor.

Second, Word can track the changes and comments of people who have reviewed your manuscript. Reviewers can type their comments into your manuscript directly, or they can write comments in the margins in balloons. Either way, when you open your manuscript, their comments are highlighted. You turn this feature on by going to the Tools menu and launching "Track Changes" and then "Highlight Changes" and "Track changes while editing."

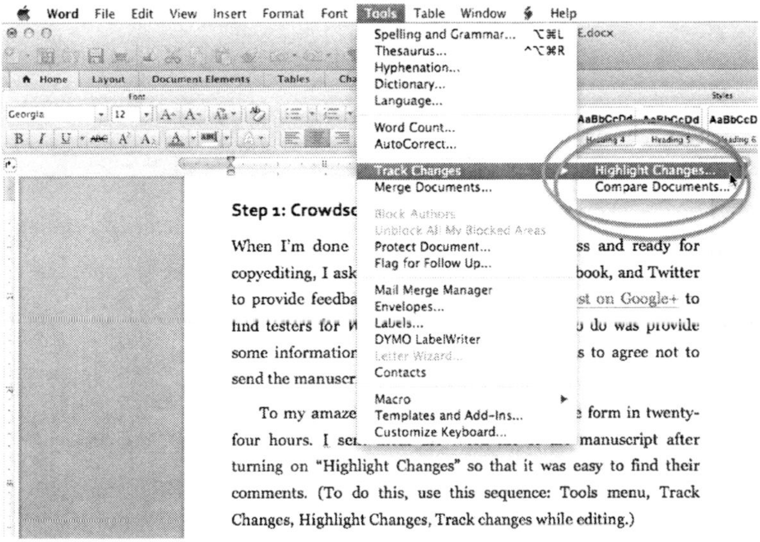

Figure 05.01. Turning on Highlight Changes.

Figure 05.02. Using Word to track changes.

Third, Word enables you to assign styles to format your manu-script.[†††] (Access this feature by selecting "Styles" from the Format menu.) Using styles introduces a structure that will set you free to focus on writing. Here's the gist of styles:

- A style should control the formatting of every para-graph of your book. This includes the font, font style (bold, italics, etc.), size, spacing, justification, inden-tation, and margins. The more you maintain the discipline of using styles, the faster and easier the publishing stage will go.

- The style of one paragraph should invoke the style of the paragraph after it. For example, suppose your book contains a "Heading 3" followed by a "NormalFirst" followed by a "Normal" paragraph. After you type in the "Heading 3" paragraph, pressing Return invokes the "NormalFirst" style.

After you type in the "NormalFirst" paragraph, pressing Return invokes the "Normal" style. Word's ability to do this makes it easier to keep your document consistent.

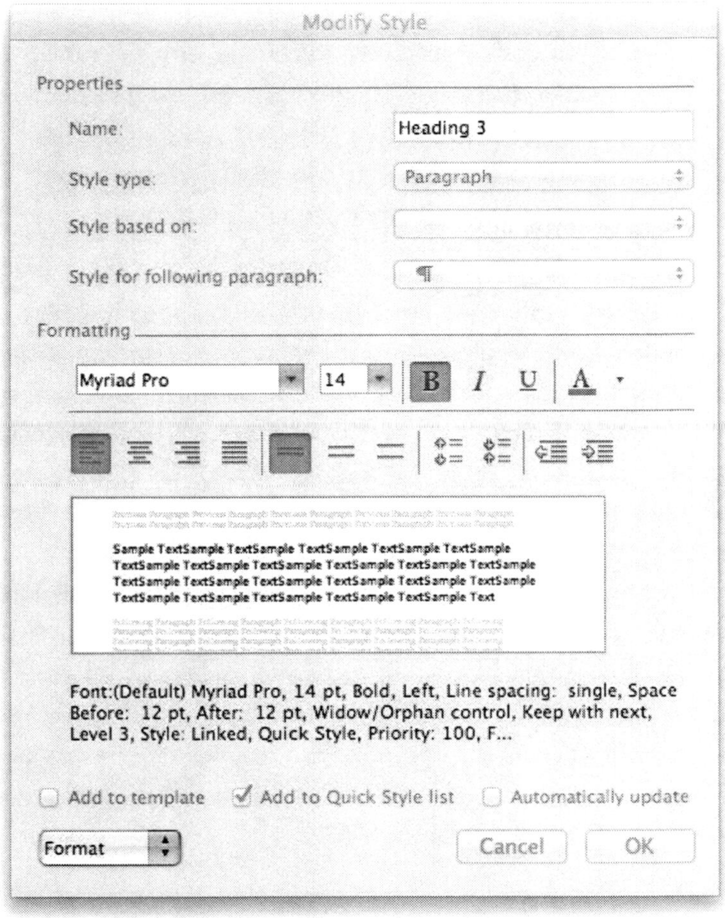

Figure 05.03. Modifying Word styles.

- When you want to change the format of a paragraph, change the paragraph's style, not that particular paragraph. By doing this, you'll ensure that every paragraph with the same style changes in the same way, and the change automatically ripples through the entire document.

- If you don't want every paragraph with the same style to change, you should create and assign a new style to that paragraph. Then you can use the new style in other places. If you properly format your manuscript, you'll rarely use a style just once.

The styles feature is a powerful tool to keep you organized. It's far, far, far better to apply styles as you write your manuscript instead of trying to format a fifty-thousand-word document after the fact. You might be thinking, "I'm pretty organized. I'll write my manuscript and not worry about Word styles." Wrong. Using Word styles becomes essential when you or your designer converts your manuscript to various ebook formats.

Admittedly, you will need to pound Word into submission—there is no other way to describe the process—but it's worth the trouble. To help you get started, we have provided a Word template at APETheBook.com. This template includes all the styles we used when writing the manuscript for *APE*. For more information about using Word as an author, read *Perfect Pages: Self Publishing with Microsoft Word* by Aaron Shepherd.[†††]

Other Word Processors

You may have a friend or relative who uses alternatives to Word, and she may recommend that you use it instead of Word if for no other reason than saving the $119.99 that Word costs for a single license on a Mac. If you're lucky, she may even offer to help you write your book with it.

However, after you write your book, many people, sites, and services will need to work with your file. That's when you may regret your initial decision of bypassing Word. Also, your friend or relative may know how to use another word processor but not the intricacies of the final stages of the publishing process. Then the blind will be leading the blind.

With these caveats and cautions, if you still don't want to use Word, here are several other products:

- **OpenOffice Writer.** This word processor is part of the OpenOffice productivity suite, which also includes spreadsheet, database, presentation, and graphics applications.[†††] Because it is an open-source product, you can download these applications for free and use them in any way.

   Millions of people use this software, and thousands of people, not only programmers, are working on improving it.[†††] There's also an offshoot of OpenOffice called **LibreOffice,** which some people consider to be better than OpenOffice.[†††]

- **Pages.** Apple's answer to Word is Pages.[†††] It is simpler and more elegant than Word but lacks many of Word's features (admittedly, you won't use most anyway). However, many entities and people that you will exchange files with are not routinely using Pages—especially if they are using Windows computers. Pages can export as the Word format, but, again, don't trust exporting to perfectly preserve formatting. We warned you.

- **Scrivener.** This is not so much a word processor as a "writer's studio" that is a "powerful content-generation tool for writers that allows you to concentrate on composing and structuring long and difficult documents."[†††] It focuses on outlining, structuring, taking notes, and tracking research sources, and you can use it in conjunction with Word. I pride myself in having an organized mind, but my mind isn't this organized.

- **LaTeX.** This is a "document preparation system," not a word processor.[†††] Its output is usually high-quality technical and scientific publications. The philosophy of LaTeX is that authors should not worry about the appearance of a document and should focus on writing it. Then, at the end, designers will take care of appearances. If you like to see how your book will look when it's finished while you're writing it, LaTeX isn't for you. You may also have difficulties finding an affordable designer who is familiar with LaTeX.

- **Google Docs.** If you have an anti-Microsoft obsession, there's always Google Docs.[†††] However, it's not designed for book-length documents, so your obsession will cause a great deal of compromise. Google Docs is useful for sharing an outline or short sections to obtain feedback, but we wouldn't write a book using it.

Many organizations claim that their product imports and exports files to the Word file format with no loss of information and formatting. This is impossible. During the beta testing of *APE*, several people sent files that I couldn't open or that didn't display their comments. Who were they? People who used LibreOffice and Pages.

Not even Word, much less other products, exports the Word format properly every time. During the beta testing, several people entered spaces betweenwords [*sic*] more than four hundred times because of errors that they saw in the copy of the manuscript that they were reading. Who were they? The ones who read the manuscript using Word 2007 (Shawn and I used Word 2011).

The worst time to discover incompatibilities and figure out workarounds is the final stage, when you're rushing your book to market. You may think you're very clever by avoiding the cost of buying Word, but like they said in the old Fram Oil Filter ad: "You can pay now or you can pay later."

Utilities

Disorganization is the enemy of good writing, so you need a system for storing tidbits of information and maintaining backups. There are many services that perform these functions, but to save you time, here are our recommendations:

- **Evernote.** If you have any OCD tendencies, Evernote is your dream come true.[†††] It enables you to store your digital tidbits such as notes, ideas, website clippings, e-mails, and documents. You can access your information from other computers, smart phones, and tablets. Optical character recognition (OCR) is built into Evernote, so you can upload a scanned document and then search for text within it later. (Disclosure: I advise for Evernote.)

- **Fujitsu ScanSnap S1500M.** This scanner makes Evernote even more useful.[†††] Anytime you want to keep a document that's printed on paper, you can scan it with a ScanSnap S1500M, and it will magically appear in your Evernote account.

- **Dropbox.** Nothing can make you feel dumber than losing your manuscript file. Dropbox enables you to create a folder on your local hard disk that constantly synchronizes with the Dropbox site and your computer, smart phone, and tablet. If you make changes when you're offline, the next time you go online, your local copy overwrites the Dropbox copy on your other computers and other devices.[†††]

  Since Shawn and I wrote this book using a shared folder in Dropbox, the working manuscript was available to his MacBook Air, iMac, and iPad as well. I also shared access to this folder with a handful of beta testers so that they could always grab the latest, greatest copy.

  If your manuscript file gets corrupted or someone accidentally deletes it, Dropbox enables you to download past versions of the file for every revision that is synced. I had to do this several times during the writing of *APE*.

- **YouSendIt.** During the self-publishing process, you'll have to send your manuscript to editors, designers, and readers.[†††] When the file gets large, some people's e-mail servers will reject it. YouSendIt provides a way to transfer large files. You upload one copy to its servers and then send a link to people who want to download it. Novels are usually small enough to e-mail, but if you're writing a book with many charts, graphs, and pictures, you may encounter this problem.

You can set a time or quantity limit of downloads with YouSendIt. I used it to enable hundreds of beta testers to download the draft of *APE*, a 30 MB Word file. YouSendIt provides a real-time count of the number of downloads, and as soon as the limit is reached, it stops any more people from downloading it.

Summary

Let's just cut to the essentials: write with Microsoft Word on a MacBook Air, and use Evernote, Dropbox, and YouSendIt. Let's start writing!

CHAPTER 6

How to Write Your Book

There is no shortcut to awesome.

Zoe Winters[†††]

How to Start

This chapter helps you understand the process of writing a book. Many authors and instructors have tackled this subject. My favorite book on the subject is *If You Want to Write* by Brenda Ueland.[†††] It changed my life by empowering me to write even though I didn't consider myself a writer. I'm not sure that anyone can tell you how to write a book, but here's what works for me.

- **Start with a story.** What is the "story" of your book? What's compelling you to write it? The story of *APE* is that I found it so hard to self-publish a book that I wanted to explain the process so others would not experience the same pain. Many great companies, products, services, and books start with a story. You can learn more about starting with a story by reading *Made to Stick* by Chip and Dan Heath.[†††]

- **Refine your story to a pitch.** In Silicon Valley we use the term "elevator pitch." It means explaining what a company does in thirty seconds—the length of time you have someone captive in an elevator.

- **Create an outline or storyline.** I don't begin writing until the outline is complete (though it usually changes while I write the book). This takes me as long as two months, but once I have an outline, the rest is filling in the details and editing. Microsoft Word has built-in outlining. Go to the View menu and select "Outline" to access this feature.

  Many authors find an outline too constricting, but an outline sets me free. If you can't write an outline, perhaps your thoughts are insufficiently organized.

- **Do the research.** I buy (an author who doesn't buy books is a hypocrite) and skim the leading books in a genre to familiarize myself with prior writing. (I bought thirty-two books for the background research for *Enchantment*.) I do this while creating an outline. This kind of research applies as much to fiction as nonfiction writers—and be sure to credit your sources.

- **Vomit it out.** Once my outline and research is complete, I call the next stage "vomiting." I try to write as much as possible as quickly as possible before I forget anything or lose trains of thought. I know full well that most of the writing will change, and I'll throw away a lot of it, but this is OK for now.

- **Postpone the self-criticism.** Starting your book is only the first five miles of a twenty-six-mile marathon that's one-third of a triathlon (authoring, publishing, and entrepreneuring). You will spend weeks refining what you spewed forth. If you're harsh on yourself now, you might convince yourself that your book isn't good enough to finish.

- **Do not write to impress others.** Authors who write to impress people have difficulty remaining true to themselves. A better path is to write what pleases you and pray that there are others like you. Your first and most important reader is *you*. If you write a book that pleases you, at least you know one person will like it.

- **Do not use ghostwriters.** This is the first book that I've coauthored with anyone. Shawn has much more expertise with publishing tools than I do, so he fills a big gap in my capabilities. I have used researchers (for example, Noelle Chun for this book) to collect information, and people contributed guest chapters to *What the Plus!* But I have never used a ghostwriter—that is, someone who is writing as if he were me.

  I have a hardcore attitude: a "self-published, ghostwritten book" is wrong because the concept behind self-publishing is that you have knowledge or emotions that you want to express. When people read a book—particularly a self-published one—they have the right to expect that it's the person's writing, not cleaned-up dictation or slapping a name on a book that someone else wrote.

- **Read.** Stephen King said it best: "If you don't have the time to read, you don't have the time or the tools to write." If you want to become a good writer, become a good reader of your genre for competitive analysis and other genres to expand your mind. I read approximately forty books a year.

I'll give you a power tip about the early stages of a book. After I've taken my best shot at an outline, I place a copy on Google Docs and invite a few million close friends to read it and send me feedback.[†††] This is called crowdsourcing feedback. I do not allow comments in the Google Docs document because there are usually too many. Instead, people write in the comments area of the post.

Some people think I'm nuts to distribute the outline, because someone could steal my idea. But this works for me for four reasons: (1) I'm not paranoid; (2) I'm confident—if seeing my outline enables someone to write a better book than mine, I'm doomed anyway; (3) having done this with several books, I know that total strangers often provide the best ideas; and (4) this is a great way to begin to build buzz for the book.

Another benefit of crowdsourcing feedback is that the people who participate gain a sense of shared ownership of your book. They have "invested" in it, so they want it to succeed. This is a valuable development that will help you when you finally have to market your book.

How to Continue

If you thought starting a book was hard, wait until you try to finish one. As I said, writing a book is a marathon, not a sprint, and it's a marathon without people handing you cold water and cheering you on. Here's what to do to keep going:

- **Control your doubts.** Every author doubts himself. The issue isn't whether you doubt yourself but whether you let doubt prevent you from finishing your book. This is my twelfth book. I'm not sure it will sell, but I have learned to power through my doubts because I know that every author has them.

- **Remember the value you're adding to peoples' lives.** In your darkest, most frustrated hours, remember the value you are trying to add to peoples' lives, the satisfaction you'll feel, or the cause that you'll further. The path to a finished book is not a smooth or a straight line, but the end result will make you forget the pain. I've never given birth, but I've heard that finishing a book is a similar process, so keep pushing. And sorry, but there are no epidurals or Cesarean sections in writing.

- **Ask for help.** During the writing process, you'll need help to fill in the gaps in your manuscript. In our case, I needed help finding real-world examples for *APE*. Asking followers on Google+, Facebook, and Twitter worked well—it's like having an army of research librarians. For example, I needed an example of an author who wrote a book for the intellectual challenge so I shared a post on Google+.[†††] That's how I found out about *Gadsby*, the novel with no words containing the letter "E."

  Google+ enables you to create communities or join existing ones. In fact, we maintain a community for authors, writers, editors, and publishers called APE (what else do you think we'd call it?).[†††]

There are also organizations that can provide help. Here are three examples. First, the Romance Writers of America[†††] provides conferences, workshops, and networking events for some ten thousand members around the world. Second, *Writer's Digest* provides a Community Forum and a collection of resources.[†††] Third, there are hundreds of local writers' clubs around the world. Search on Google for "writers' club" to find them.[†††]

- **Don't hide under a bushel.** Tell the world you're writing a book—not that you're *thinking* of writing a book. People will start asking how it's progressing and when it will hit shelves and websites. If you don't finish it, you'll have to admit defeat in a public manner. Peer accountability is a powerful tool when you feel like giving up—and believe me, there will be days you'll feel this way.

- **Write every day.** The habit of writing every day controls doubt and prevents quitting. Maybe it's only writing a paragraph, massaging your outline, or refining your vomit. But if you wait for the perfect day when you're financially set; the kids are clothed, fed, and making straight A's; your house is in perfect order; and global warming has stopped, you'll never write. Come hell or high water, write every day, even if it's only for five minutes.

- **Embrace the pain.** Sportswriter Red Smith described writing by saying, "You simply sit down at the typewriter, open your veins, and bleed." Paul Gallico, author of *The Poseidon Adventure*, opined,

"It is only when you open your veins and bleed onto
the page a little that you establish contact with your
reader." Writing is painful. If writing were easy, there
would be more successful authors, so suck it up.

- **Don't let successful writers awe you.** Speaking of
  successful authors, it's OK for you to admire them
  for the quality of their writing or their success.
  However, don't let other authors awe you, because
  this is the first step to envy and self-doubt.

  I know many successful authors (and entrepreneurs), and the only thing that distinguishes
  them from most people is luck. Question: How do
  you get lucky? Answer: You keep writing, grinding
  away, and putting yourself out there. As the Chinese
  saying goes, "Man who waits for roast duck to fly
  into mouth must wait very, very long time."

One word describes the sum total of these concepts: focus. Try
to maintain a straight path from outline to manuscript with only a
few deviations. Kristen Eckstein, publishing coach and author of
How to Write a Non-Fiction Book in 3 ½ Days, tells her clients to jot
down new ideas for other books, articles, projects, and opportunities
and then file them away, out of sight.[†††]

Eckstein's suggestion provides the peace of mind that you won't
lose your great new ideas, but they aren't distracting you either.
Evernote, by the way, is a perfect application for this process.

How to Finish

Many people believe that writing is mystical: while overlooking a
windswept beach, your thoughts flow from your brain through your
perfectly manicured hands and out the gold nib of your Mont Blanc
fountain pen.

Dream on. I wrote much of *APE* in a closet in a dorm on the University of California–Santa Barbara campus. It was five feet by five feet. Shawn wrote his portions in various airport terminals, hotel rooms, and coffee shops. The key to writing is the willingness to grind, polish, and perfect your manuscript under lousy circumstances. Here's what works for me in the finishing stage:

- **Edit on paper.** Print your book in a format that approximates the final appearance. Printing it like a book makes errors more obvious—I don't know why this is true, but it is.

  Grab a red pen and go to a coffee shop. Do not bring your laptop. Sit in the back and slowly read your book. Mark mistakes as you go and correct them later when you get back to your laptop. You'll notice mistakes you don't see on a computer. Also, read with a ruler because it will force you to look at only one line at a time.

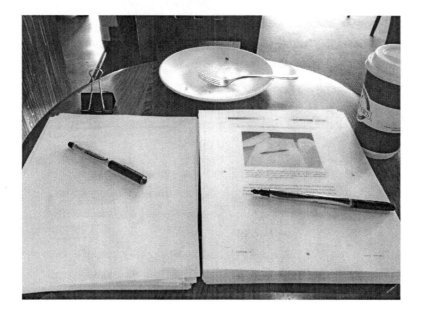

Figure 06.01. Shawn editing a 260-page printout of *APE*. Notice the printout is formatted with a six-by-nine-inch page margin to mimic a printed book.

- **Edit on a tablet.** Read your book on an iPad, Android tablet, or Kindle device sitting at the same coffee shop. You can bookmark problem areas or you can use an app like Adobe Reader[†††] to mark up your ebook. You'll notice mistakes that you don't see on a computer or on paper. The easiest way to get your book onto a tablet is to save your manuscript as a PDF, put it in a Dropbox folder, and then open it on your tablet with Adobe Reader.

- **Read it out loud.** Read your book to yourself or, even better, read it to someone who cares about your writing career. If you find a passage is hard to speak, people will find it hard to read.

- **Repeat.** Each time you change your book, repeat the process of reading it on paper and as an ebook. Over the course of completing a book, I do this about ten times on paper and ten times as an ebook.

As Zadie Smith, author of *White Teeth*, said, "Try to read your own work as a stranger would read it, or even better, as an enemy would." This editing process is my favorite stage of a book because it's like a sculptor removing excess stone to bring out the art. You'll learn that the key to a great book is editing—grinding, buffing, and polishing—not writing.

Summary

There are three stages of writing a book: starting, continuing, and finishing. They all require a combination of determination, desperation, and denial that all writers, at some stage, detest. Force yourself to make a little progress every day and, after a year or so, you'll have a book and you'll say, "That wasn't so bad after all."

CHAPTER 7

How to Finance Your Book

...and you may know how little God thinks of money by observing on what bad and contemptible characters he often bestows it.

Thomas Guthrie

Can You Sell 2,500 Copies?

This chapter explains how to finance your book and make money with it. One disadvantage of self-publishing is that you do not get an advance to pay the bills while you write. This is a big deal because many people cannot afford to write full-time.

Here are rough estimates for the major costs of publishing a 300-page, 60,000-word manuscript. They don't include any marketing costs—let's focus on getting a finished book first. Some people might argue that our costs are too high, but the big picture is that the process costs approximately $4,000:

Content editing	15 hours	$60 per hour	$900
Copyediting	30 hours	$35 per hour	$1,050
Layout and production	10 hours	$100 per hour	$1,000
Cover design			$1,000
ISBN (a unique tracking number for your book) purchases	10 numbers		$250
Total			**$4,200**

Try this simple model: Assume that most of your revenue will come from Kindle ebooks, and you'll make $2.00 per copy at a $2.99 price point. This means you need to sell approximately 2,500 ebooks to break even, not including your time and effort.

Time for a reality check: Can you sell approximately 2,500 ebooks? Think about this for a minute. If you self-publish a printed book, you could make $10 to $15 per copy, so could you sell five hundred copies? (See chapter 16: "How to Use Print-on-Demand Services" for an explanation of how we made this calculation.)

Reducing Costs

The minute is up. Let's say that $4,300 is out of the question. Then what? Then you emulate entrepreneurs all over the world and do what you have to do. You don't give up, that's for sure.

Instead you ask your friends, family, colleagues, fans, and acquaintances for help. (We explain techniques for doing this in chapter 8: "How to Edit Your Book.") You simplify your design expectations and learn how to use design tools yourself. You barter with editors and designers—surely you must have some skill that an editor and/or a designer needs.

These methods should enable you to reduce costs to $1,000 or so. But don't try to skip copyediting or to design the cover yourself. Now the question is "Can you sell five hundred ebooks?"

Independent Book Publishers Association

Another way to save some money is to join the Independent Book Publishers Association.††† Then you can take advantage of many discounts from publishing-industry vendors.††† Membership costs $129 per year for an author. Here are examples of a few of the many discounts available to members:

- 20 percent off all BookBaby services
- 33 percent off *Publishers Weekly* subscription
- Waiver of first-year PR Newswire membership fee
- 20 percent off FedEx Office services
- 50 percent off Lightning Source setup fee, plus increased volume discounts.

Recouping the $129 membership isn't hard, so you should consider joining the Independent Book Publishers Association.

Raising Money

Suppose you reduce costs as much as you can—you still need to eat while you're writing. You have two choices: First, you can tough it out. The path of most writers, artists, and entrepreneurs is to pursue their dream at night after their family is asleep. This is the reality of most authors' lifestyles. If achieving success were easy, more people would do it.

Second, you can "crowdfund" your book. Nelle Harper Lee, the author of *To Kill a Mockingbird*, is an early example of this. She worked as a reservationist for Eastern Airlines and wrote in her spare time. At one point she moved into a cheap apartment without hot water to reduce expenses so she could concentrate on writing. In 1956 her friends gave her enough money to devote her attention to writing,[†††] and she completed the first draft of *To Kill a Mockingbird* a year later.

Today crowdfunding is much more efficient. You can use a service such as Indiegogo, Unbound, Pubslush, or Kickstarter to generate sales revenue before you ship your book.[†††] This involves creating an online campaign for your book and then using social media to spread the word to your friends, family, and the public.

A campaign includes a description of your book, your background, and a video. You offer different benefits depending on the size of the commitment.[†††] These are the kinds of benefits that you could offer (each higher level includes the perks of the previous level):

- $10: public thank-you on Facebook
- $25: copy of the finished ebook
- $50: signed softcover version
- $100: Skype call with the author
- $500: your name in the acknowledgments section
- $1,000: character named after the contributor

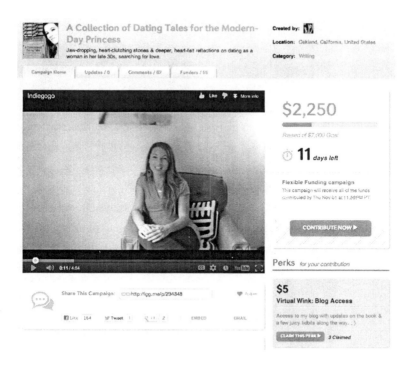

Figure 07.01. An Indiegogo book project.

Unbound and Pubslush provide crowdfunding for only books, whereas Indiegogo and Kickstarter offer a wide range of projects and products. On Unbound, authors pitch their ideas, and people pledge money to support it. If the pledges reach a minimum amount, the author writes the book. If not, Unbound refunds the money, or the pledger can switch it to another Unbound project. Pubslush operates in a similar manner, with an emphasis on books that support causes.

Crowdfunding can help you raise $5,000 to $25,000. This isn't enough for many people to write full-time, but it's a start. And the fact that people voted with their wallets is a harbinger of good sales and should provide encouragement.

Crowdfunding can help you raise hundreds of thousands of dollars if you're a celebrity like Seth Godin. He created an epic promotion on Kickstarter by positioning pre-selling as a way to demonstrate interest in his book to his publisher and bookstores.[†††] You might not raise $287,342 like he did, but people voting with their money by buying pre-sale copies is a good test of the viability of your book.

How to Make Money with Your Book

Maybe we should have placed this topic in the Publishing section of *APE*, but you'll need to know how you can make money with your book as you write it—or earlier!

First, the royalty deals in self-publishing are as good as or better than traditional publishing. In traditional publishing deals, authors get 15 percent of the suggested retail price of a book. For example, if your hardcover book has a suggested retail price of $25, you would make 15 percent of $25, or $3.75. You'd make 7.5 percent of the suggested retail price of a paperback book. Ebook royalties from traditional publishers are all over the map. A safe assumption is that they are 50 percent of the suggested retail price, so you'd get 50 percent of $12.50 for the ebook version of a $25 hardcover book, or $6.25.

As a self-publisher you can make $2 per book on a $3 Kindle ebook versus the $4 (rounded up) from a traditional publisher on a $25 suggested-retail-price book. So you need to sell two self-published ebooks at $2.99 each to make the same amount of money as selling one $25 suggested-retail-price hardcover from a traditional publisher. For ebooks, you need to sell three ebooks to make the same amount as a $12.50 ebook from a traditional publisher.

Second, you can sell the print version of your book to resellers and directly to readers. We'll get into the details of this in chapter 16: "How to Use Print-on-Demand Companies," but the high-level math is that when you sell to resellers, you make as much as the author and the publisher combined since there is no publisher. When you sell directly to readers, you make as much as the author, publisher, and reseller since there are no publisher and reseller.

Third, self-publishing enables you to monetize your book in ways that would give a traditional publisher an aneurysm:

- **Advertising and sponsorship.** Let's say you've written a guide to using iPhones. A case manufacturer who wants to reach your readership could sponsor your book.

    Samsung, for example, sponsored a giveaway of six thousand copies of the PDF version of *What the Plus!* to promote the Samsung line of tablets and smart phones. I used YouSendIt's ability to limit the number of downloads of a file to control this promotion. Sponsoring your book is also an attractive benefit for Indiegogo, Unbound, Pubslush, and Kickstarter supporters.

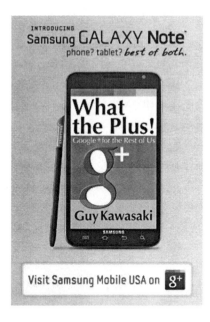

Figure 07.02. The Samsung ad in the free PDF version of *What the Plus!*

- **Affiliate links.** You can use an Amazon-affiliate link for books and products that you mention in your book. This means you'll get paid a few bucks when people buy them, and these links are also convenient for your readers because it makes purchasing easier. However, Amazon requires that these books and products are relevant to the substance of your book.
- **Freemium.** Ebooks make lousy gifts, but you could use them to seed the market and then sell the printed version of your book for people to give as gifts. Other than the opportunity cost of a lost sale, an ebook has zero cost, so a freemium model is viable.

- **Tchotchkes.** Maria Murnane, the author of *Perfect on Paper*, sells Honey Notes, Totes, and Tees printed with pithy quotes from the main character in her book.[†††] Perhaps there are complementary products to your books that you can sell too.

- **Speeches and consulting.** An informative book can generate speaking and consulting opportunities. Such opportunities are a natural outcome of a book that adds value to people's lives. Over the course of my career, I've made far more money on speeches than on book royalties.

Summary

We're not saying that you'll make barrels of money as a self-publisher, but the math works. Self-publishing is an inexpensive business, and the upside potential is there. You'll only achieve this potential if you write a good book and market it well, but at least self-publishing is an open and fair business.

[Publisher]

A person who publishes a book willfully appears before the
populace with his pants down....If it is a good book nothing
can harm her. If it is a bad book nothing can help her.

Edna St. Vincent Millay

This section explains how to take a manuscript and turn it into a
book. We assume that you have a rock-solid draft of your book, and
you're ready to begin editing, copyediting, laying it out, uploading,
and printing.

We'll examine multiple paths to getting your book ready for
distribution so you can pick the best one based on your target market,
level of technical expertise, and supply of patience.

This is the most complex section of *APE*. You might want to skim it just so you know what's here and return to it when you're making decisions about how to publish your book.

CHAPTER 8

How to Edit Your Book

I leave out the parts that people skip.

Elmore Leonard

No Shortcuts

This chapter explains how to transform your self-edited manuscript into a finished manuscript. A high-quality book requires extensive testing and copyediting. You can get these processes done without a traditional publisher, *but you cannot eliminate them.* Your goal is a book that looks and feels as good as any book from a big-time, traditional publisher.

Editing

Publishing a book, whether a traditional publisher does it or you do it yourself, requires two kinds of editing. First, content editing helps you make your book more appealing by changing the organization, structure, content, and style of your manuscript. Second, copyediting is what turns an amateurish book into a polished, professional one.

The self-edited author is as foolish as the self-medicated patient. In *Let's Get Digital,* David Gaughran provides an example of how *Esquire* editor Gordon Lish edited Raymond Carver's short story "What We Talk About When We Talk About Love."[†] Lish's editing marks on the original version shows how much value a content editor can add.[††]

If you think you're the first author in the history of mankind who doesn't need a copyeditor, keep two examples in mind: First, in 2010, Penguin Australia published a book called *The Pasta Bible.* The recipe for tagliatelle called for "salt and freshly ground black people." Penguin had to destroy seven thousand copies because of this gaffe although sales of the book quadrupled because of the publicity.

Second, every time I turn in the "final" copy of a book, I believe that it's perfect. In *APE's* case, upward of seventy-five people reviewed the manuscript, and Shawn and I read it until we were sick of it. Take a wild guess at how many errors our copyeditor found. The answer is 1,500. You read that right: one thousand five hundred, and you may still find some, because we went right to publishing after copyediting even though traditional publishers proofread a book twice after copyediting. If you see any errors, please send me an e-mail at Guy@Alltop.com.

You're going to read this again and again in *APE*: you cannot eliminate the need for a copyeditor. There are four methods to obtain both kinds of editing: enlisting friends, family, and coworkers; tapping niche communities; crowdsourcing; and hiring professionals. I do all four for every book! You can never get too much editing and feedback.

Method 1: Friends, Family, and Coworkers

I send the first complete draft of my manuscripts to an inner sanctum of five to ten people. I've known them for years and trust their judgment. I want them to act like "book murderers," a term Michael Alvear coined in his book *Make a Killing on Kindle.*[†††]

If you're starting your writing career, you may not have a cadre of friends, family, and coworkers to murder your book, but you must respect some people. Now is the time to tap these relationships.

Shawn is decades younger than me, and he's on his fourth book. His family and friends are not interested in reading an iOS development book, so he asks for volunteer readers when speaking at conferences. Each volunteer receives a "beta version" of chapters as well as the final book as a PDF a few weeks before its public release.

Shawn's method illustrates an important concept: If you don't ask, you don't get. I push this concept to the edge. For example, I noticed that Kristen Eckstein left insightful and helpful comments on my Google+ posts about publishing, so I contacted her to see if she'd like to read the manuscript of *APE*.

She agreed, and she returned the manuscript with 254 insertions, 165 deletions, 30 format changes, and 275 comments. I used 90 percent of them. From now on, she's on the friends and family list for my future books.

Method 2: Niche Communities

On the Internet, there's a community for everything, and this includes authors seeking feedback and readers willing to give it. If you don't have a large social-media following, you can join these communities and ask for feedback.

First, search for keywords on Google+ and Facebook that describe your genre and join these circles and groups. Then ask the people who seem to share your sensibilities to read your manuscript.

For example, if you were writing a book about self-publishing, and you were looking for people interested in this topic, search for "self-publishing" on Google+. (Note: do this search inside Google+, not a regular Google search of the entire Internet.)[†††]

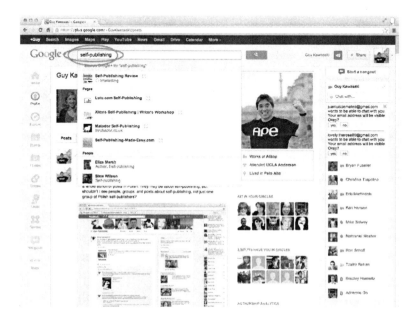

Figure 08.01. Searching for "self-publishing" on Google+.

You can do the same search on Facebook to find people, pages, and groups that are relevant to self-publishing.

Figure 08.02. Searching for "self-publishing" on Facebook.

After you find people who share your passions, start commenting on their posts and mentioning them in your posts. When you see a way to help them, seize the opportunity to create a relationship. You cannot expect strangers to jump at the opportunity to help you, but you can expect people to reciprocate because of what you've done for them.

While we're on the topic of reciprocation, allow me to digress and provide two power tips I learned from Robert Cialdini, the author of *Influence: Science and Practice*. First, when you've done something for someone, and the person thanks you, the optimal response is "I know you would do the same for me."

In other words, let them know that they owe you. Second, when people owe you, give them a way to pay you back so that they can clear their debt. The constant exchange of favor and reciprocation builds very strong relationships.

Back to niche communities...there are also standalone writing communities that focus on feedback and collaboration. For example, **Wattpad**††† helps writers and readers build relationships and exchange feedback. It emphasizes novels and poetry. Writers add 500,000 stories and poems to the site per month.

Figment††† also enables writers to share their works with readers. By facilitating this sharing, it helps readers to discover new writers and helps writers to obtain feedback. Figment's emphasis is on teen fiction.

LinkedIn††† hosts many special-interest groups, including ones for people interested in self-publishing. My favorite is Book Writing, Self Publishing, and Marketing for Business People.††† Discussions in this group focus on advice from writers to other writers about the entire process of authoring, publishing, and entrepreneuring.

Other sites to check out include Review Fuse, WritersCafé.org, Critters Workshop, and Critique Circle.†††

Method 3: Crowdsource

I ask my followers on Google+, Facebook, and Twitter to provide feedback from the beginning to end of the publishing process. For example, I shared a post on Google+††† to find testers for *What the Plus!* All people had to do was provide some information via an online form as well as to agree not to send the manuscript to others.†††

To my amazement, 241 people completed the form in twenty-four hours. I sent them the Word file of the manuscript after turning on "Highlight Changes" so that it was easy to find their comments. (Again, to do this, use this sequence: Tools menu, "Track Changes," "Highlight Changes," "Track changes while editing.")

Over the next ten days, more than a hundred people returned the file with comments. These were the results:

- Sixty-seven suggestions for how to make the book better (not counting duplicates of the same suggestions). These suggestions were closer to content editing than copyediting, which is why I crowdsource copyediting before using a professional.

- Twenty-seven factual errors (not counting duplicate reports of the same issues). These errors are also closer to content editing than copyediting. However, most editors from traditional publishers would not have caught these errors because detecting them required extensive expertise in Google+.

- One hundred and forty-seven grammatical and spelling errors (not counting duplicate reports of the same issues).

To make this kind of crowdsourcing work, you need at least five hundred followers. We explain how to gain followers in Section 3: "Entrepreneur." You might not be able to make crowdsourcing work with your first book, but you have to start somewhere.

Method 4: Professionals

For all the goodness of crowdsourcing, you still need someone to review your manuscript with a magnifying glass and a professional eye to optimize your content and to kill virtually every typographical, grammatical, and factual error.

You might not need a content editor if you have enough smart, hardcore voluntary readers, but the probability that you will find every spelling and grammatical mistake is zero. Word and other word processors may even *introduce* typos and grammatical mistakes:

I have a spelling checker,
It came with my PC.
It plane lee marks four my revue
Miss steaks aye can knot sea.

Eye ran this poem threw it,
Your sure reel glad two no.
Its vary polished in it's weigh.
My checker tolled me sew.

A checker is a bless sing,
It freeze yew lodes of thyme.
It helps me right awl stiles two reed,
And aides me when eye rime.

("Candidate for a Pullet Surprise" by Mark Eckman and Jerold H. Zar. Hat-tip to Bob Soltys for this pointer.)[†††]

The going rate for copyediting is $35 per hour, and copyeditors can work their magic at the rate of roughly ten pages per hour (although this can vary depending on the complexity of the material), so you'll pay approximately $1,000–$1,500 for a three-hundred-page manuscript. This is one of the dumbest places to try to save money, because poor copyediting destroys the quality of your book.

One of the challenges of hiring a copyeditor is figuring out if he or she is any good—particularly for your first book. Here are five ways to find a good one:

- **MCAT.** Rachelle Mandik was the copyeditor for *What the Plus!* and *APE*, and she put together a test called the Mandik Copyediting Aptitude Test (MCAT). It's an early version of the preface of *APE* with Rachelle's corrections. Give copyeditor candidates the document and compare their corrections to Rachelle's to determine how good they are. It's not a foolproof instrument, she cautions, but it's definitely a good place to start, especially for nonfiction. The document is at APETheBook.com.

- **Authors.** Ask authors for their recommendations. This pitch would work on me: "Dear Guy, I loved your book. May I ask who your editor and copyeditor were? I'd like to hire them to help me with my book."

- **Moonlighters.** Many content editors moonlight as independent consultants, so you may be able to hire the kind of editor you would have gotten at a traditional publisher anyway.

- **Social-media referrals.** Ask for referrals on Google+, Facebook, Twitter, and LinkedIn. I've found many good contractors and vendors using social media.

- **Websites.** Use a website like Guru or Elance to find independent contractors.[†††] Edit911 has an interesting model: it helps you hire PhDs.[†††] These sites enable customers to rate independent contractors just as eBay and Amazon enable customers to rate vendors. Serious independent contractors care a lot about their ratings.

  Another kind of website to use, though not strictly for finding editors, is Task Rabbit or Amazon Mechanical Turk.[†††] You post a task on these sites, and people submit bids to complete them. For example, as mentioned earlier, *APE* contains approximately four hundred hyperlinks. In order to check them all, we posted a project to Task Rabbit[†††] and in twelve hours there were forty-one bids. We accepted one bid for $36, and we had a complete test of all the links less than twenty-four hours after the original post. We were very happy with the result.

Chapter 20, "Self-Publishing Issues," provides information about the legalities of hiring independent contractors.

Guest Topic: Developmental Editing for Artisanal Publishing, by Alan Rinzler

After Alan Rinzler read *APE*, he sent me an e-mail to tell me that my coverage of developmental editing was not good enough. Being the "relentless pursuit of perfection" guy that I am, I was intrigued and asked him to write this guest piece about developmental editing.

Alan edited and published Toni Morrison, Hunter S. Thompson, Tom Robbins, Robert Ludlum, Clive Cussler, Shirley MacLaine, Jerzy Kosiński, Andy Warhol, and Bob Dylan. In his 50+ years in the business, he worked at Simon & Schuster, Bantam Books, Grove Press and John Wiley & Sons, and he founded Straight Arrow Books, the book division at *Rolling Stone*. He now works with authors as a private consulting editor. His blog is The Book Deal—An Inside View of Publishing.[†††]

Alan Rinzler: Before the digital revolution and advent of independent publishing, authors would usually have a literary agent who sold their books to a traditional book company, and they could expect rigorous developmental editing. This type of developmental editing isn't at all the same as copyediting, which focuses on correcting spelling, punctuation, grammar, and sometimes includes fact-checking.

Developmental editing is the process of identifying and revising weaknesses in the story, characterization, and literary style of the manuscript, whether the work is fiction, narrative nonfiction, history, biography, memoir, how-to, or any other form of writing. Specifically, a good developmental editor suggests significant, if not critical, changes such as:

- Adding or eliminating a character.
- Reorganizing the chapters so they communicate content with a purpose, such as education or social change, more logically and effectively.
- Changing the narrative voice from third-person to first-person, or first-person to third-person.
- Increasing or decreasing the amount of dialogue or visual and sensory description.
- Polishing the language, line-by-line, consistent with the author's voice.

These days, artisanal publishers can benefit from the same level of creative collaboration as traditionally published authors since freelance developmental editors are readily available. It's not necessary to live in close proximity, moreover, now that manuscripts are sent across the globe as e-mail attachments and the "track changes" feature in word processors such as Microsoft Word makes it possible for authors to accept or reject editing changes. Also, authors and editors can conduct Skype sessions at no cost, regardless of the distance.

Here are some tips for selecting and utilizing a good developmental editor:

1. **Accessibility.** The best developmental editor in the world is of no use unless he or she responds immediately to your inquiry and subsequent interactions. Traditional publishers used to allocate several months to developmental editing. This isn't realistic for artisanal publishing. A reasonable turn-around is two to three weeks in the brave new world of artisanal publishing.

2. **Track record.** The best indication of the quality of developmental editors is their record: Have they produced great books? Ask candidates for a list of books that they have edited. Even better, ask for an intro-duction to an author of a book they've edited to check their references.

3. **Clear financial terms.** Developmental editing is not inexpensive. A good developmental editor will evaluate your work at whatever stage you suggest—formative, in-progress, rough draft—and provide an estimate and time frame for completion. Watch out for prices in the $25/hour range, since they are more in line with copyediting, not developmental editing. Nor should you consider anyone who charges by the word or page, since that also indicates a kind of editing that isn't developmental.

4. **Compatibility.** If you live nearby, meet your prospective developmental editor. If that's not feasible, then have a good phone or Skype conversation. You don't have to be best friends with your editor, but you must trust and respect them. Humor and compassion go a long way in forging a productive relationship.

5. **Control.** Remember, it's your book. You are the final word on all suggested edits and revisions. Good developmental editors subsume their own egos and enter the world of the writer's consciousness. They never try to take over a book, conform or contort it to their ideas, or make any changes unilaterally, without your approval.

> Without a developmental editor, your book may not be as good as it could or should be, and it may disappear among the tsunami of titles that are available every day in the marketplace. No matter how well designed or marketed, your book has to deliver. It's the content that counts.

The Kirkus Solution

While writing *APE*, I learned that Kirkus Book Reviews, the book-review magazine and website, offers three editorial services:[†††]

- **Collaborative Editing.** This service focuses on content editing and examines tone, organization, voice, characterization, dialogue, and clarity.
- **Copyediting.** Kirkus copyeditors go through your manuscript line by line to fix typical copyediting issues such as grammar, spelling, and punctuation.
- **Professional Editing.** This package includes a consulting session and three rounds of editing that includes both collaborative editing and copyediting. At the end of the process your manuscript should be ready to publish.

We have not used these services, but Kirkus is worth looking into if you're on a tight budget. You can check its prices at the Kirkus website.

Summary

I enjoy the editing stage of writing a book the most. My goal is to produce the best book ever about a topic, so when people point out content or copyediting issues, I rejoice. There are five ways to obtain editing input, and I suggest that you use them all to produce something that you'll be proud of.

CHAPTER 9

How to Avoid the Self-Published Look

Don't self-publish. That's as good as admitting
you're too lazy to do the hard work.

Sue Grafton, LouisvilleKY.com, August 7, 2012[†††]

Appearance Is Everything

This chapter helps you avoid publishing a book that looks cheesy, vain, and amateurish. Steve Jobs taught me that little details separate the mediocre from the excellent. The way to avoid the "self-published" look is simple, and it increases the attractiveness, professionalism, and marketability of your book.

The first *outward* sign that your book is self-published is a crappy cover design. This topic merits a long discussion, so we'll address it in the next chapter.

The first *internal* sign that your book is self-published is crappy writing, but our writing and editing tips will help you avoid this. Sue Grafton notwithstanding (she did retract her statement[†††] in the epigraph above, but *S for Self-Publishing* is out of the question). The stigma of self-publishing has diminished, but it still exists. There's no reason why you can't make your book look like it's professionally published; remember, the goal is *artisanal* books.

Front Matter

Beyond the cover, the first sign of a self-published printed book is the lack of traditional front matter on the first few pages of your book. We recommend referring to *The Chicago Manual of Style*[†††] to ensure that your front matter is correct. This thousand-page tome also covers what you need to know about grammar, punctuation, and the mechanics of publishing.

Power tip: You should buy a copy of *The Chicago Manual of Style* because having one around makes you feel like a real writer, and it impresses people when they see it on your shelf. And you should not hire a copyeditor who doesn't own one. Here is a summary of the front matter of a (nonfiction) book according to *The Chicago Manual of Style*:

Name	Page	Description
Book half title	i	Main title, no subtitle.
Series title, frontispiece, or blank	ii	Title, volume, name of general editor, and titles of previous works in the series. Blank if not part of a series.
Title page	iii	Full title, name of author, name and location of publisher.
Copyright page	iv	Bio of author, publisher's address, copyright notice, "All Rights Reserved" clause, publication date and history, country of printing (unless POD printed in multiple countries), number and year of current printing, ISBN, ISSN (if applicable), Library of Congress (LCCN) data, permissions, and other credits.
Dedication	v	
Epigraph	v or vi (v if no dedication)	"Quotation that is pertinent but not integral to the text."
Table of contents	v or vii (v if no dedication or epigraph)	
Foreword	Keeping left-hand page blank, next right-hand page	Prefatory words by someone other than the author.
Preface	Keeping left-hand page blank, next right-hand page	Author's statement about the book.
Acknowledgments	Keeping left-hand page blank, next right-hand page	Extensive list of people to thank.

Ebook Front Matter

When it comes to ebooks, there is a tradeoff between the credibility of traditional front matter and the marketing benefits of facilitating people's ability to "look inside" books on Amazon.

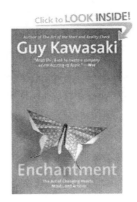

Figure 09.01. How Amazon displays a book that people can "look inside."

People can see approximately 10 percent of a book this way. Let's say your book is two hundred pages long; people will be able to read the first twenty pages. Do you want to use up your twenty pages on typical front matter? Even if you don't care about the wasted pages, there is no reason to force customers to click five to ten times to get to the good stuff.

This is like a pharmaceutical company running pages of FDA-required warnings and disclaimers ("In the event of an erection lasting more than four hours, seek immediate medical help to avoid long-term injury") before advertising the drug itself. For marketing purposes, a better order for ebook front matter, tradition be damned, is:

- Cover
- Blurbs (more on blurbs below)
- Table of contents
- Foreword or preface (but not both, and neither for fiction)
- Chapter 1…

You can stick everything else in the back because most of it doesn't matter to most people. This structure means that prospective readers can garner more information in less time to make a buying decision—which is the goal, after all. Remember: with a physical book, people can skip ahead pages at a time, so you can stick with *The Chicago Manual of Style*'s recommendations. On a website, too many clicks spoil the preview.

(Hat-tip: I got this idea from Michael Alvear in his book *Make a Killing on Kindle*.)

Organization Name

The second sign of self-publishing is that you've named the publishing company after yourself. One hundred years after their start—long after the founders died—names like Alfred A. Knopf, John Wiley, and G. P. Putnam sound prestigious and cool, but the name of your organization needs to sound prestigious and cool before you die.

For example, *The Schmoe Way* by Joe Schmoe from Schmoe Press doesn't cut it. Using your last name as the publisher's name screams "self-published" and, even worse, "I lack imagination." Pick a street name, a pet's name, a geographical landmark, or your favorite Pokémon character. Then Google your idea to ensure that no one else already uses it. Anything is better than your last name for your company's name. Nononina Press, the publisher of *APE*, is the first two letters of my four kids' names.

Blurb Overload

The third sign of self-publishing is an excessive number of testimonial quotes (known as blurbs in the publishing business). Good blurbs are short, sweet, and limited to six. They answer the question "Why should I buy this book?"

A book with more than six blurbs means that the author doth promote too much. This is like PowerPoint slides that try to overwhelm you with text. A better goal is to establish a reputation that is so well known and a topic that is so timely that no blurbs are necessary at all.

We recommend including blurbs in the front matter of your book for two reasons: first, they reinforce the wisdom of purchasing your book. You can never reduce cognitive dissonance too much—even for a $0.99 purchase.

Second, bloggers will often grab blurbs and use them in their review. We recommend putting blurbs on page i or ii to ensure that people see them. This requires pushing everything else back a page, but page count in ebooks is irrelevant, so it isn't a problem.

Blurbs on the thumbnail of the cover are too small to read, and there is no back cover. However, if you publish your book with Kindle Direct Publishing, you can include your blurbs in the online listing of your book.

Gaffes

The fourth sign of self-publishing is gaffes—unintentional mistakes that cause embarrassment. It's easy for self-publishers to make these gaffes because editing, particularly copyediting, is a different skill from writing. Here are the most common gaffes:

- **Improperly capitalizing the title and subtitle.** Use headline-style capitalization for titles and subtitles. This means capitalizing the first word, last word, and every noun, pronoun, verb, adjective, and adverb. Start articles, prepositions shorter than five letters, and conjunctions with lowercase letters. Contrary to popular belief, headline style does *not* mean lower-casing all "small" words. Some small words are verbs ("Is," "Are," and "Be" are prime examples) or other parts of speech aside from prepositions.

Follow these rules for your title page, book listing, and cover. During the production of *What the Plus!—Google+ for the Rest of Us*, we didn't realize that the cover said "Google+ for the rest of us" (sentence caps, not title caps). We had to change this and re-export all of our ebook files with a new cover image.

- **Omitting the serial comma.** A serial comma (or Oxford comma, as they say across the pond) prevents confusion when you are listing several items. For example, the probably apocryphal book dedication "To my parents, Ayn Rand and God" implies that the person's parents *were* Ayn Rand and God (that's quite the couple!).

  Then there is the TV listing of *The Times*: "...highlights of his [Peter Ustinov's] global tour include encounters with Nelson Mandela, an 800-year-old demigod and a dildo collector." (There must be more than one Nelson Mandela!)[†††]

  The addition of a serial comma makes the meaning of the phrases clear. The dedication is to three parties: parents, Ayn Rand, and God. Peter Ustinov met with three people in the episode of his television show. I search for every instance of "and" and "or" to ensure that I have not left out any serial commas.

- **Improper hyphenation.** Hyphenation and compounding words is constantly changing, but violating some rules marks you as a self-publisher. Here are the three main ones: hyphenate two or more words used as an adjective—"social-media sites"; hyphenate compound numbers—"forty-seven"; and hyphenate only between syllables as specified in the dictionary for end-of-line breaks—"enchant-ment."
- **Using two spaces between sentences.** In the old days of typewriters, characters were the same width, so two spaces were necessary to separate sentences for visual effect. With computers, characters are proportional, so they fit closer to each other, and one space is sufficient. Before you submit your manuscript, search for all double spaces and replace them with single spaces.

You can customize the grammar checker in Word to help you avoid simple issues such as two spaces between sentences. Select "Preferences" from the Word menu and click on the "Spelling and Grammar" icon.

Spelling and Grammar

◀ ▶   W
Back/Forward Show All   Q
                                            Search Word Preferences

Spelling

☑ Check spelling as you type   ☑ Ignore words in UPPERCASE
☐ Hide spelling errors in this document ☑ Ignore words with numbers
☑ Always suggest corrections   ☑ Ignore Internet and file addresses
☐ Suggest from main dictionary only   ☑ Flag repeated words

☑ Use German post-reform rules
☐ Enforce accented uppercase in French
☐ Russian: Enforce strict é

French Modes: Traditional and new spellings   ⇅
Spanish Modes: Tuteo verb forms only   ⇅
Portuguese Modes: Post-reform   ⇅
Brazilian Modes: Post-reform   ⇅

Custom dictionary: Custom Dictionary   ⇅   Dictionaries...

Grammar

☑ Check grammar as you type
☑ Show grammatical errors in Notebook Layout View
☐ Hide grammatical errors in this document
☑ Check grammar with spelling
☑ Show readability statistics
Writing style: Standard ⇅   Settings...

Recheck Document

Description of preference

Spelling and Grammar
Set options for the spelling and grammar checkers.

                                            Cancel   OK

Figure 09.02. Customizing how Word checks grammar.

- **Dumb apostrophes and quotation marks.** There's a world of difference between dumb apostrophes and quotation marks and their "smart" versions.

  There are two ways to ensure the correct usage of smart quotes and apostrophes. First, you can turn on a preference in Word to add them automatically. Second, you can type them in:

	Macintosh	Windows
Left apostrophe	Option-right bracket key (the key that's two over from the "p")	Alt key, then type "0145" on the numeric keypad
Right apostrophe	Option-Shift-right bracket key (the key that's two over from the "p")	Alt key, then type "0146" on the numeric keypad
Left quotation	Option-left bracket key (the one next to the "p")	Alt key, then type "0147" on the numeric keypad
Right quotation	Shift-Option-left bracket key	Alt key, then type "0148" on the numeric keypad

- **Dumb dashes.** Here's a guide to the proper use of hyphens and dashes.

	Usage	Macintosh	Windows
Hyphen	Break words into parts or join two separate words	Hyphen key	Hyphen key
En dash	Usually indicates a closed range of values such as dates, times, and numbers. Also used to join a word to an open compound (pre–Civil War).	Option-hyphen key	Alt key, then type "0150" on the numeric keypad

	Quotation Mark	Apostrophe	Dash
Smart	" "	' '	—
Dumb	" "	' '	--

Figure 09.03. The difference between smart and dumb quotation marks, apostrophes, and dashes.

- **Using quotation marks for emphasis.** There are three correct ways to use quotation marks. First, they indicate a direct quotation, such as "This is one small step for [a] man, one giant leap for mankind." Second, they act as "scare quotes" to alert readers that a term is used in a nonstandard sense, usually irony or sarcasm. Third, they replace the words "so-called."

    One of the most common misuses of quotation marks is to add emphasis. For example, does it make sense for a sign to say *All employees must "wash hands" before returning to work*?

- **Lack of indentation.** The first paragraph of a style should be flush left. However, you should indent every subsequent paragraph. For example, note how we indented the paragraph above this one.

- **Underlining.** There's **bold** text and there's *italic* text, but there's never <u>underline,</u> except as a hyperlink. If you format text with an underline that's not a hyperlink, readers will think your book has a broken or missing link.

- **Widows.** Three main types of widows exist. (1) Widowed text is when the last line of a paragraph appears on the following page or in the next column. (2) A widowed heading occurs when a heading is on one page and the following text is on the next page or in the next column. (3) A widowed bullet occurs when one bullet is on a page and the subsequent bullets are on the next page or in the next column.

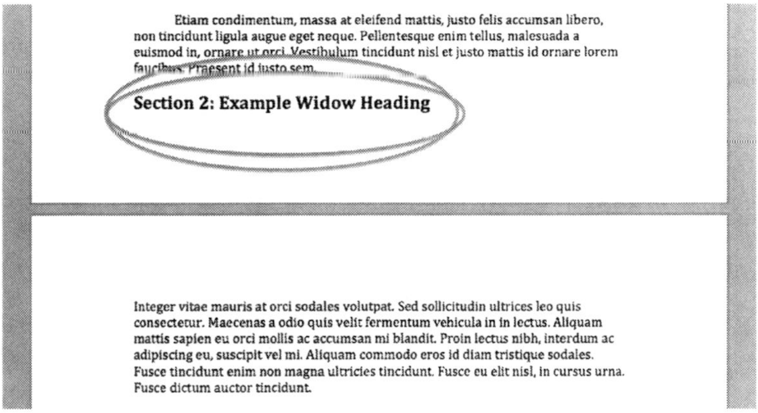

Etiam condimentum, massa at eleifend mattis, justo felis accumsan libero, non tincidunt ligula augue eget neque. Pellentesque enim tellus, malesuada a euismod in, ornare ut orci. Vestibulum tincidunt nisl et justo mattis id ornare lorem faucibus. Praesent id justo sem.

Section 2: Example Widow Heading

Integer vitae mauris at orci sodales volutpat. Sed sollicitudin ultrices leo quis consectetur. Maecenas a odio quis velit fermentum vehicula in in lectus. Aliquam mattis sapien eu orci mollis ac accumsan mi blandit. Proin lectus nibh, interdum ac adipiscing eu, suscipit vel mi. Aliquam commodo eros id diam tristique sodales. Fusce tincidunt enim non magna ultricies tincidunt. Fusce eu elit nisl, in cursus urna. Fusce dictum auctor tincidunt.

Figure 09.04. An example of a widow.

- **Orphans.** There are three kinds of orphans: (1) The first line of text in a paragraph is separated from the rest of the paragraph on the following page or next column; (2) A word or part of a word that is not long enough to clear the indent of the following paragraph is by itself on the last line of a paragraph (usually any word less than four characters); (3) Your book after your traditional publisher has given up on it, but I digress.

Widows and orphans are unavoidable in ebooks because people can adjust the font size and this changes the page layout. Don't focus on these issues for your ebooks, but if you print your book on paper or a static PDF, you must pay attention to them.

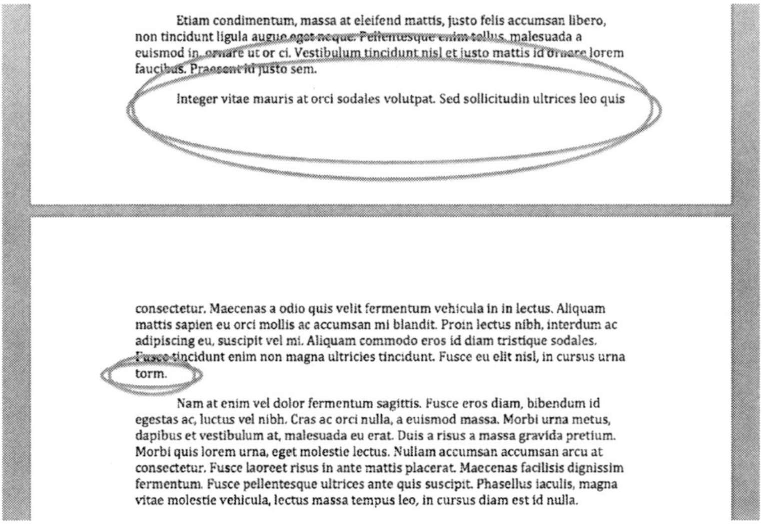

Etiam condimentum, massa at eleifend mattis, justo felis accumsan libero, non tincidunt ligula augue eget neque. Pellentesque enim tellus, malesuada a euismod in, ornare ut or ci. Vestibulum tincidunt nisl et justo mattis id ornare lorem faucibus. Praesent id justo sem.

Integer vitae mauris at orci sodales volutpat. Sed sollicitudin ultrices leo quis

consectetur. Maecenas a odio quis velit fermentum vehicula in in lectus. Aliquam mattis sapien eu orci mollis ac accumsan mi blandit. Proin lectus nibh, interdum ac adipiscing eu, suscipit vel mi. Aliquam commodo eros id diam tristique sodales. Fusce tincidunt enim non magna ultricies tincidunt. Fusce eu elit nisl, in cursus urna torm.

Nam at enim vel dolor fermentum sagittis. Fusce eros diam, bibendum id egestas ac, luctus vel nibh. Cras ac orci nulla, a euismod massa. Morbi urna metus, dapibus et vestibulum at, malesuada eu erat. Duis a risus a massa gravida pretium. Morbi quis lorem urna, eget molestie lectus. Nullam accumsan accumsan arcu at consectetur. Fusce laoreet risus in ante mattis placerat. Maecenas facilisis dignissim fermentum. Fusce pellentesque ultrices ante quis suscipit. Phasellus iaculis, magna vitae molestie vehicula, lectus massa tempus leo, in cursus diam est id nulla.

Figure 09.05. Example of an orphaned line and an orphaned word.

- **Passive voice.** The passive voice is weak, vague, and wordy. "New York publishers are being attacked by self-publishers" is not as powerful as "Self-publishers are attacking New York publishers." I search for every instance of "be" and "being" to eliminate as many instances of the passive voice as I can. Word's grammar checker can also help you spot the use of passive voice.

- **Lack of consistency.** Ensure that the voice and design elements of your book are consistent. Here are three examples. First, as we mentioned earlier, in this book "I" always refers to me, Guy. Shawn is always mentioned in the third person. "We" refers to our combined opinion and expertise.

  Second, bulleted lists should maintain a parallel structure. If one starts with a noun, they should all start with a noun. If one starts with a verb, they should all start with a verb.

  Third, consistency also applies to design. For example, in the print version of *APE*, when a new section starts, the section title is *always* on the next right-hand page, even if this creates a blank page to the left. Similarly, the first chapter after a new section *always* starts on the next right-hand page, *always* leaving the page on the back of the section title blank.

- **Excessive adjectives and adverbs.** These forms of speech are often overrated, overused, and vague. How *dark* was the night? So dark that you couldn't see your hand in front of your face? How *slowly* did he walk? Perhaps a toddler could move faster? How much did you *really miss* your mother? Maybe enough to make you cry at night? Find more concrete ways to describe things.

Metaphors and similes beat the crap out of adjectives and adverbs, so use them when you can. For example, rather than saying, "Hockey is very violent," you could say, "Hockey is war on ice."

- **Lack of guideposts.** This recommendation and the next one are for nonfiction writers. Use subheads to help your readers navigate sections of a chapter. The name of the chapter is not enough in nonfiction books because so much material is in each chapter. Real authors use subheads.

- **Long passages of text.** A bulleted list (like this one) is a sign of an organized mind. Rather than making your reader dig through long passages of text, use bulleted lists to highlight what is most important. Lists also make great back cover copy for your printed versions.

A great book that explains these kinds of gaffes and more is *The Mac Is Not a Typewriter* by my lovely friend Robin Williams. Also, you can't go wrong with *The Chicago Manual of Style*, and the Purdue Online Writing Lab works well as an online resource.[†††]

Crappy Interior Design

The fifth sign of self-publishing is a crude and simplistic interior design. This primarily applies to the print version of your book because readers can override the interior design of ebooks. Here's how to avoid interior-design signs of self-publishing:

- **Fonts.** Use a font besides Times New Roman, Arial, or Helvetica. Don't go crazy with a fancy font, but show a little style. For *APE* we used a font called Warnock Pro.
- **Blank pages.** Remove headings and page numbers on blank pages.
- **Line breaks.** Ensure that line breaks do not cause hyphenated words in headings and chapter titles.
- **Chapter-title pages.** Provide ample space on all chapter-title pages. Reserve the top half of a page for the title and start the first paragraph about halfway down the first page. Page numbers are either omitted or in a different location on these special pages.
- **Page numbers.** List page numbers in the top 0.25 inch of your page layout (between 0.5 inches and 0.75 inches from the edge of the page), aligned away from the spine, plus the correct running head (see below).
- **Running heads.** Show the book title in the left-hand page header and the current chapter title in the right-hand page header. For fiction writers, it's customary to show your name in the left-hand page header and the book title in the right-hand page header.

Summary

If you've come this far, you've invested many hours in your book. Don't blow it now. The whole point of self-publishing is to produce a book faster, better, and cheaper than a traditional publisher. These ways of avoiding the "self-published" look are simple and easy, and they increase the attractiveness, professionalism, and marketability of your book.

CHAPTER 10

How to Get an Effective Book Cover

Boys think girls are like books; if the cover doesn't catch their
eye, they won't bother to read what's inside.

Marilyn Monroe

Cover Design

This chapter helps you obtain an attractive and effective cover for your book. People look at faces and make instant judgments about likeability, trustworthiness, and credibility. Think of your book's cover as its face. People make the same decisions based on it.

Traditional publishers usually create a handful of designs and then ram them down the throat of authors. There's good news and bad news for self-publishers. The good news is that you have total control over your cover; the bad news is you have total responsibility for your cover.

Covers 101

Your cover must stand out in a sea of postage-stamp-size covers on websites. A cover that looks great in a six-by-nine-inch printed format won't necessarily work on the Amazon, Apple, Barnes & Noble, and Kobo website.

Kindle Publishing (The Easy Step by Step Guide ...
Jon Roetman
★★★★☆ (2)
Kindle Edition
$0.99

How to Create Nonfiction Book Ideas That Sell
James Thomson
★★★★★ (24)
Kindle Edition
$0.99

The Self Publishing Toolkit: Your All-in-One ...
› Daphne Dangerlove
★★★★★ (10)
Kindle Edition
$3.99

Figure 10.01. Your cover must stand out in this kind of context. How many of these titles can you read?

Here are guidelines for a cover that will make people want to click on it:

- **Simple, big, and bright.** Standing out on a web page full of covers requires using big type (60 points or more), simple graphics, and bright, high-contrast colors.
- **Arresting.** People are flipping through web pages, scrolling through lists, and making split-second decisions. Your cover has to stop them and make them click on it.

- **Logical.** Your cover should match your book's genre. For example, a young-adult fantasy book's cover should not look like a management tome. Look at the covers of other books in your genre for ideas.
- **Focused.** A good cover provides a focal point for people's attention. A dominant graphic or clip of text should leave no doubt about what the most important design element is.
- **Informative.** A good cover answers two basic questions: What is the name of the book? Who wrote the book? The graphic design should attract attention, and your text should satisfy the need for this basic information.

You could produce two versions of your cover: one for your ebook that is simplified to work in the postage-size context and one for your print version that is more complex. (Hat-tip to Paul Richard for this idea.)

Paths to Coverdom

Now you know the goals for your cover, and the question is how to achieve them. There are three paths:

- **Design it yourself.** The odds of being a good writer, copyeditor, and cover designer are zero. However, if you are a good designer, you can do it yourself. If you're not, you'll be OK as long as you can identify what is a good cover.

- **Use crowdsourcing.** I used a site called Crowdspring to design the cover of *Enchantment*, and I was overjoyed with the result.[†††] In the end, I used the idea from the winning entry and another designer executed the design.

  However, the design community will give you crap because some members consider crowdsourcing as a form of exploitation. Their objection is that many designers will create designs and only one will get paid. My response is, "Then don't submit a design."

  Think about this: Have you gotten paid for every word you've written? I haven't. And I give many speeches for free in order to develop business. Some designers believe they should never do anything for free. More power to 'em.

- **Find a designer.** The third path is to find a designer. Ask for referrals to designers on Google+, Facebook, Twitter, and LinkedIn. Ask the authors of books with covers that you like for referrals too. Most authors are happy to provide referrals because the designer will work harder on the next project for the author. In my case, Ana Frazao[†††] designed the *What the Plus!* cover, and Holly Thomson[†††] designed the *APE* cover, so tell them that I sent you.

Cover Power Tip

Power tip: leave enough space on the cover of your printed book for autographing. I stumbled upon this idea with *Enchantment*. The reasons to do this are:

- **Speed.** It's faster to sign a cover than an inside page. When there's a line of people waiting for your autograph, every second counts.
- **Visibility.** One reason people want an autographed book is to show that you met the author. A book that's autographed on the outside is more effective for this purpose.
- **Logistics.** You can send autographed covers to readers for approximately $2 each. These fans can replace their existing cover with the autographed one, and they are more likely to show off their covers to friends and relatives.

  People who wanted an autographed cover for *Enchantment* completed an online form[†††] and posted their picture with the book (or their tablet showing the cover) on Google+ or Facebook. My calculation was that it was worth $2 for people to provide social proof that they bought my book. Since my royalty was a little more than $2 on each copy, I broke even on each book.

I wish I could tell you that the cover was designed with this in mind, but it's not true. The cover was in place, and then I saw a way to autograph books faster and to engage with my readers.

Figure 10.02. The cover of *Enchantment* with an autograph.

One more power tip about covers and autographing: bring a pad of Post-it notes with you and ask people to write the name they'd like you to use on the cover. This will also make autographing go faster—especially in a noisy environment.

Covers in Context

Take a look at the Book Cover Archive; it's a collection of more than 1,200 book covers.[†††] Seeing row upon row of covers is a good exercise. When you double-click on a cover to see it in a larger size, it probably looks good. However, in the real-world context of multiple postage-stamp-size covers on a website, many do not work. If nothing else, you can pick out covers that you like to show to your designer.

Figure 10.03. Examples from the Book Cover Archive.

Summary

Not to get too metaphysical, but a cover is a window into the soul of your book. In one quick glance, it needs to tell the story of your book and attract people to want to read it. Unless you're a professional, hire a professional to create a great cover because, in spite of how the old saying goes, you *can* judge a book by its cover. Or at very least, people *will* judge a book by its cover.

CHAPTER 11

Understanding Book Distribution

If you only read the books that everyone else is reading,
you can only think what everyone else is thinking.

Haruki Murakami, *Norwegian Wood*

Channels of Distribution

This chapter provides an overview of the four main digital and print distribution channels. They are online ebook resellers (digital), direct sales (digital), author-services companies (digital and print), and print-on-demand (print). The chapters after this overview explain each channel in detail.

The self-publishing ecosystem is idiosyncratic, illogical, and fragmented. Apple, Amazon, Google, Adobe, Microsoft, and other self-publishing vendors try to optimize products and processes for themselves—creating a cross between a junkyard and a swap meet for authors.

The following decision matrix will help you clarify your options. It begins with two fundamental questions:

- What kind of book do you want to publish?
- Do you need help getting professional editing, cover design, layout design, and production?

The answers to these questions will help you decide on which channels of distribution to use. (You may use more than one, so you could be in multiple boxes in the matrix.)

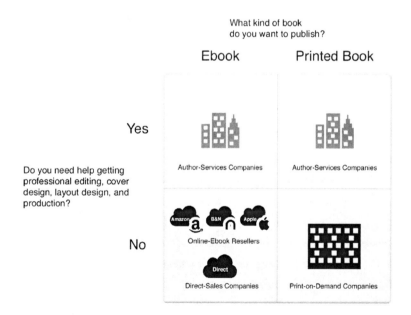

Figure 11.01. Distribution-channel decision matrix.

Online Ebook Resellers

Amanda Hocking is the heroine of self-publishing. She spent years pitching her vampire-romance novels to traditional publishers with no success. In April 2010 she learned that an exhibition about Jim Henson, the creator of the Muppets, was coming to Chicago. But Amanda, a Muppets fan, had no money to make the trip.

Undaunted, Hocking decided to self-publish her novels with Kindle Direct Publishing to pay for the $300 trip.††† She started with *My Blood Approves*, and by October 2010, she made over $20,000.††† Over the next twenty months, she made $2.5 million. The rest, as the saying goes, is history.

Hocking is not the norm for self-published authors. Many stories about self-publishing cite her because her experience is unusual, not typical. Still, people need heroes for inspiration and for proof that success is possible. Not every entrepreneur is going to start the next Apple, either, but it's great to know that two guys in a garage started the most valuable company in the world.

Amazon (Kindle Direct Publishing), Apple (iBookstore), Barnes & Noble (Nook), Google (Google Play), and Kobo are the major online ebook resellers. For most self-published authors, they represent the easiest and most lucrative way to sell books. You may never need any distribution channel other than online ebook resellers.

| Author | Author manages online-resellers | Readers buy ebook |

Figure 11.02. Distribution through online ebook resellers.

Pros:

- **Inexpensive.** All you need to self-publish an ebook is a computer, word processor, and Internet access. If you start distribution through other channels, you may need more professional tools, but you can worry about this later.
- **Easy.** Fiction writers can click on an "Upload" button, find their Word file, transmit it, wait for the reseller to process the file, and start selling in a few days. This isn't true for complicated nonfiction books because of file-conversion issues, but it is possible for most fiction authors.
- **Quick.** You can convert your book from manuscript to market in less than a week. The best case, Kindle Direct Publishing, prides itself on a forty-eight-hour turnaround. Amazon and Apple also enable you to launch your non-translated book in dozens of countries at the same time.
- **Lucrative.** You can make up to 70 percent of the selling price of an ebook from online resellers. Making $2 on a $3 book is a sweet deal if you can achieve a large volume.

Cons:

- **Limited reach.** You will miss people who prefer printed books. This is especially true for nonfiction books. For example, many engineers still prefer buying a printed book for technical topics such as iOS development, and many photography fans would rather own a printed book than an ebook.
- **Less "real."** We're not Luddites or book snobs, but we still think that hefting, smelling, and autographing a printed book is special. Later we'll explain ways to distribute both ebook and printed versions of your book, but if you only publish ebooks, you will miss this feeling.

Direct Sales of Ebooks

Authors such as Ryan Estrada, Andrew Hyde (*This Book Is About Travel*), and Nathan Barry (*App Design Book*) sell their ebooks via Gumroad.[†††] They placed their files on the service and added the link to their websites. People can click on the link, pay for the file, and then download it. The authors pay a transaction and hosting fee to Gumroad.

Author

Author manages online-sales
(Gumroad, E-junkie, or ClickBank)

Readers buy
ebook

Figure 11.03. Distribution through direct sales.

This method is the simplest, most direct, and possibly offers the highest profit per book. However, it requires the ability to drive people to a website, compared to online resellers who already have traffic. You'll also need hosting, payment, and customer-service functionality. Other companies that provide this type of service are E-Junkie and ClickBank.[†††] Ganxy is a company that provides an ebook-focused product.[†††]

Pros:

- **Direct and immediate control.** These companies are big hard disks in the sky with order processing. You make your decisions about pricing and revisions, and they execute.
- **High profits per book.** These companies don't do more than host your file and handle transactions. Therefore, their costs are lower, and you can make the most money per copy through them.

Cons:

- **Marketing burden.** There's always a catch! You have total control and can make the most profit per book, but the onus is upon you to get people to your website or to click to buy your ebook.
- **Reduced synergy.** These websites don't have anything like sales rankings and the "Customers Who Bought This Item Also Bought" synergistic promotion.
- **Reduced opportunities for affiliate fees.** The Amazon Affiliate program enables authors to earn fees from traffic generated by their marketing efforts. For example, after you send someone to your book's page on Amazon, if that person buys a Samsung TV from Amazon, you can make an affiliate fee. Gumroad and E-Junkie don't pay affiliate fees, though ClickBank does.
- **Best suited for selling only the PDF version.** These sites can sell any file format that you upload, but this doesn't mean that your readers will know what format to buy for their reader app and how to install your book. Do you want to help a person trying to read a MOBI file (more on formats later) in iBooks?

Before you go nuts selling books directly, check on sales-tax issues. This applies to US authors who sell to people in the same state of residence—authors outside the United States should check with a tax specialist in their country. Resellers such as Amazon or Apple automatically handle state sales-tax issues for you. When you sell printed books directly to people in your state, it's your responsibility to report and record taxes.

In most states, the sale of digital goods such as ebooks *is not* subject to sales tax as long as there is no physical product involved and the transaction/experience is purely digital (online marketing, online distribution). In some states, engaging in physical marketing of a digital product (for example, flyers and meet-the-author events) creates a condition where digital sales may be subject to sales tax.

This issue is a hot and fluid topic in many states because states are looking for alternative sources of revenue. Before you start selling digital copies of your book directly to individuals, you should contact your state's department of revenue or a tax attorney and ask whether digital sales are subject to sales tax.

Author-Services Companies

Ray Sabini is a fourth-grade teacher in New York. After reading a letter from Benjamin Franklin extolling the virtue of curing the smell of human gas, he wrote a book called *Sweet Farts* about a student who tries to find the cure for farting.[†††]

Sabini used the pen name Raymond Bean so that a book about farting did not harm his reputation as a teacher. He pitched the book to traditional publishers for eighteen months with no success. Then his wife told him about a company called BookSurge that helped authors self-publish their books.

Sabini used the company to release *Sweet Farts* in November 2008. By March 2009 it was an Amazon children's bestseller. It did so well that Amazon Publishing contacted him to write two more books to make a three-part fart series.

BookSurge is now part of CreateSpace, the author-services company of Amazon.[†††] Sabini completed his fart series with Amazon Publishing, but he still used CreateSpace for his twelve-part series *School Is a Nightmare*, because he wanted to publish a new title every ninety days.[†††]

Author   Author-services companies   Readers buy
              (Manage online-resellers and POD)   ebook or
                                              printed book

Figure 11.04. Distribution through author-services companies.

Firms such as CreateSpace, Lulu, Blurb, and the imprints (an imprint is a brand name within a parent company) of Author Solutions (Dellarte, AuthorHouse, Wordclay, Trafford, Xlibris, Palibro, Inkubook, and iUniverse) act as intermediaries between authors and online and brick-and-mortar resellers.[†††] These companies provide services such as copyediting, conversion, layout, cover design, printing, and then send your book to resellers.

Pros:

- **Fewer reseller programs to join, learn, maintain, and track.** It's time consuming to create an account, pick your price, upload your Word file and cover, provide banking information, and monitor sales and payments for one reseller. Try doing this for three or four. Author-services companies can alleviate much of this pain.
- **One-stop shopping.** If you're new to publishing, you may not have all the contacts and vendors that you need for editing and cover design. Author-services companies may provide what you need to publish your book.

Cons:

- **Reduced revenue.** The services these companies provide come at a price. You can buy them on an à la carte basis for some services, but you usually pay a percentage of your royalty off the top.
- **Overdependence.** The good news is that you have to deal with fewer organizations. The bad news is that if your author-services vendor experiences an outage when you're in the publishing process, you're in deep trouble. Worse, if your vendor experiences financial issues, you may never collect your royalty.
- **Poor quality.** Author-services companies often use independent contractors and offshore labor to provide editing services. These people may not be native speakers of your language, and true fluency is necessary for good editing. You won't have much choice in selecting them, so you might be able to find better ones yourself. That said, you might not want the burden of finding them yourself.
- **Extensive "fine print."** You'll learn more about this in chapter 15: "How to Use Author Services." For now, suffice it to say that some of the options that look easy and inexpensive might come back to haunt you later if you're successful. If you're not successful, it won't matter.

Print-on-Demand

Walkerville Publishing[†††] is in Walkerville, Ontario, right across the border from the home of the second best baseball team in 2012 (Detroit). (If you visit Walkerville Publishing's website, I'm warning you in advance that you're going to get Al Stewart's "Time Passages" stuck in your head.) Walkerville Publishing is two people: Chris Edwards and his wife, Elaine Weeks. He writes books, and she copy-edits them.

Years ago he got a Groupon coupon from CreateSpace to publish a book, so he took his collection of photos of Windsor and printed a local-history book called *Windsor Then*. A local paper ran a story about the book, and he ended up selling 3,000 copies. He still uses CreateSpace as his print-on-demand supplier—as opposed to an author-services company—and orders 300 copies at a time.

You can use an author-services company as a print-on-demand supplier or a pure-play printer such as Lightning Source[†††] so that you don't end up with boxes of books sitting around unsold if you overestimate demand. Both these types of companies work on short lead times so that you can order books "on demand"—that is, when you need them.

Author   Print-on-Demand   Author   Readers
            Companies

                                 Bookstores
                                 (Amazon.com, B&N, Brick-and-Mortar)

Figure 11.05. Distribution through brick-and-mortar bookstores.

Many bookstores will not sell self-published books. Author-services companies may tell you that they can get you brick-and-mortar distribution, but they are shading the truth. Bookstores can order your book from them if someone requests it, but this doesn't mean they will buy your book for inventory.

Pros:

- **Reaches people who prefer printed books.** Despite the oversimplifications and misinterpretations, remember that ebooks are still only 10 percent of total book sales in the United States. The only way you can try to reach the other 90 percent is to offer your book in a printed format.
- **Psychic satisfaction.** One of the pleasures of writing a book is seeing it for sale on a bookstore shelf—preferably face-out in the "new and noteworthy" section. Offering your book in a printed format is the only way to achieve this.
- **Control of final form.** Working directly with a printer provides you with more design and format options. It also gives you the freedom to do special editions for appearances and signings.
- **Higher margins.** Selling a printed book directly to customers has some of the highest margins in the publishing business. The flip side of selling direct, though, is that there are the costs of order processing, fulfillment, and inventory.

Cons:

- **Complexity.** This path involves more work than using author-services companies. Printers only take print-ready PDFs of your cover and manuscript. They also do not provide any handholding, assuming that an experienced production person is managing the process.
- **Commitment to accept returns.** You don't have to order thousands of copies of inventory, but customers and bookstores can return printed books for refunds. We've never heard of having to accept an ebook return.
- **Sales-tax reporting.** You will probably have to collect and pay state sales tax for books sold directly to readers in your state of residence, although you won't be responsible for books sold at a wholesale price to resellers.

Summary

This is the big picture of the distribution channels that are available to self-publishers. The simplest path is to write your book in Microsoft Word and upload it to Kindle Direct Publishing. If you need some help, or don't trust uploading a Word document, author-services companies can help. If you know what you're doing, print-on-demand can offer the best profit per book. Don't obsess about making the wrong choice, however, because most distribution decisions are changeable.

CHAPTER 12

How to Sell Your Ebook Through Amazon, Apple, Barnes & Noble, Google, and Kobo

As far as we can discern, the sole purpose of human existence is to kindle a light in the darkness of mere being.

C. G. Jung, *Memories, Dreams, Reflections*

This chapter provides in-depth information about Amazon, Apple, Barnes & Noble, Google, and Kobo. They represent most of the potential online sales of your book. There are two methods to get to them: set up an account at each one or use an author-services company to manage the relationships for you. This chapter explains the first method. Chapter 15: "How to Use Author-Services Companies" explains the second method.

Amazon

Description: Kindle Direct Publishing (KDP) is the Amazon self-publishing service for ebooks. It is the gorilla in the market and can account for most of your sales. Amazon owns this market. Let's face it, Amazon equals online books the way Volvo equals safety and Starbucks equals coffee.

There's a wide selection of Kindle devices from Amazon as well as a Kindle app for Macintosh, Windows, BlackBerry, Android, and iOS devices. People can also read their Kindle books using web browsers. Kindle Direct Publishing is the path of least complexity, most sales, and greatest visibility for most self-published authors.

Getting started: If you have written a novel or a nonfiction book with no tables, graphics, and bulleted or numbered lists, you're in good shape with Kindle Direct Publishing. Write your book in Word, use Word's styles, design a cover (or have one designed), upload it at Kindle Direct Publishing, and one to two days later, you're in business.[†††]

We want to ensure that you completely understand Kindle Direct Publishing's royalty deals. There are two rates: 70 percent and 35 percent. The 70 percent rate has these caveats:

- You must price your book between $2.99 and $9.99 in the United States. The price range requirements vary for other countries.
- Kindle Direct Publishing deducts a delivery charge from your royalty based on the file size of your book. In the United States, for example, the charge is $0.15 per megabyte. This is not a big deal if you're publishing a pure-text novel (approximately one megabyte or $0.15, unless you're a descendant of Tolstoy).

- Delivery charges in other countries are: United Kingdom: £0.10 per megabyte; Germany, France, Spain, and Italy: €0.12 per megabyte; India: $0.12 (US) per megabyte.
- Kindle Direct Publishing automatically matches prices from other resellers, and your royalty is calculated on the lower price.

The 35 percent rate, while obviously lower, has some advantages:

- There is no delivery charge.
- Kindle Direct Publishing matches prices of other resellers but continues to pay royalty based on the "digital list price" not what customers paid unless the ebook was free.

However, the size of your file determines the price range that you can use under the 35 percent plan:

- Less than or equal to three megabytes: $0.99–$200
- Greater than three megabytes but less than ten megabytes: $1–$200
- Ten megabytes or more: $2.99–$200

The 70 percent choice is not a no-brainer. You need to consider the size of your file and the delivery charge it will incur, as well as the likelihood that other resellers will heavily discount it. Kindle Direct Publishing provides an up-to-date explanation on its website.[†††]

Fine print:

- Kindle Direct Publishing compresses your file. For example, *What the Plus!* is a fifty-four-megabyte Word file with more than one hundred pictures. Adobe InDesign turned it into a twenty-two-megabyte MOBI file. Kindle Direct Publishing compressed this file to 3.85 megabytes, so it cost approximately $0.58 to deliver each copy under the 70 percent royalty deal. (The website will tell you the delivery file size and cost estimate when you set the list price).

- Lossless Word conversion for complex books is challenging. To achieve the best possible conversion, you should upload books to Kindle Direct Publishing in the MOBI file format. Conversion to the MOBI file format from Word is covered in chapter 13: "How to Convert Your File."

- Kindle Direct Publishing monitors the price of your book on other reseller sites and matches the price automatically. You have no choice in the matter, so if one of your other resellers is running a special, Kindle Direct Publishing will immediately match the price, and you will earn your normal royalty percentage of the lower price.

Apple

Description: iBookstore is Apple's platform for selling ebooks, and it is the second biggest player. There are two types of ebooks in the iBookstore: First, the traditional ebook that we know and love; second, Multi-Touch ebooks that only work on iPads. Multi-Touch ebooks allow you to implement rich media and interactive elements far beyond the traditional ebook.

Getting started: The first step is to register for an account on the iBookstore website.[†††] You must upload your book to iBookstore in either the EPUB or Multi-Touch format.

Fine print:

- The iBookstore requires that you set up an account as an iTunes Content Provider, which is managed through a service called iTunes Connect.[†††] iTunes Connect is a portal for information such as sales tracking, banking information, contracts, and support.
- You manage and upload books with a desktop app called iTunes Producer; it is available as a free download to registered iBookstore content providers on iTunes.[†††] iTunes Producer is Macintosh-only software and currently requires that you are running at least OSX 10.6.
- You can only create Multi-Touch ebooks using iBooks Author, an Apple program available as a free download from the Apple App Store.[†††] This program is also Macintosh-only.

- *You must sell Multi-Touch ebooks through the iBookstore.* However, you can give away your book, or sample chapters, outside of iBookstore. You also can sell a PDF exported from iBooks Author outside of iBookstore.
- Royalty is calculated at 70 percent for all sales, and worldwide distribution is available.

Barnes & Noble

Description: Nook is the name of the Barnes & Noble tablets and eReader apps. Tablets range in price from $99 to $179. This market is the third largest after Amazon and Apple. Nook offers an app for Macintosh, Windows, iOS, Android, and online reading. Nook's advantage, compared to online resellers, is that it sells tablets through Barnes & Noble's brick-and-mortar stores.

Getting started: To make your book available to Nook owners, you use a service called PubIt.[†††] Nook offers a simplified path that lets you upload a Word document with Word styles and a cover. After a few days, you're in business.

Fine print:

- Like Kindle Direct Publishing, PubIt allows authors to upload a Word document. However, to achieve the most accurate conversion of your manuscript to a book on Nook readers you should upload an EPUB file.

- When you upload an EPUB file, remove any encryption that may have been added by your application (for example, Adobe InDesign and Pages). Encryption sometimes occurs automatically by these programs when embedding fonts and other assets. (Chapter 13: "How to Convert Your File" covers the EPUB format and these tools in more detail.)
- Royalties are calculated automatically based on the price of your book:

  - » $0.01–$2.98 pays 40 percent royalty
  - » $2.99–$9.99 pays 65 percent royalty
  - » $10–$199.99 pays 40 percent royalty

Google Play

Description: Google Play[†††] is Google's content business that sells music, books, magazines, video, games, and applications. It is a worthwhile bet because of the success of Android smart phones and tablets as well as Google's ability to direct the river of web traffic. Google Play's basic deal is that you set a suggested retail price, and there's a 52 percent/48 percent split between you and Google Play, respectively.

Getting started: The look and feel of Google Play's web pages for authors and publishers is rapidly evolving. To stay up to date with changes, go to Books.Google.com and click on "Information for publishers" at the bottom of the page.[†††]

There are two ways to provide your book to Google Play. The first is similar to other ebook resellers: upload your EPUB file (if you want to offer the ability for people to change fonts and sizes) or your PDF file (if you don't care whether people can change fonts and sizes). The second way is unlike other ebook resellers: you can send Google a physical copy, and Google will scan it.

Fine print:

- You can control how much of your book people can browse for free on Google Books, with a minimum of 20 percent.[†††]
- You can upload books that are less than ten megabytes via the standard HTML website. If your EPUB or PDF is larger than ten megabytes, you need to use the Google Uploader Java application.[†††]
- You can either manually set a price for each territory, or you can configure Google Play to automatically set the price based on a percentage (which you define) of the lowest list price found in other channels.

Kobo

Description: Kobo[†††] sells tablets and ebooks and gives away reading apps for computers and tablets. Its philosophy is that people should "have the freedom to read any book, anytime, anyplace—and on any device." Rakuten is the owner of Kobo; it's a $6 billion Japanese ecommerce company.[†††] Kobo offers more than 2.5 million books and sells its tablets through stores such as Walmart, Best Buy, WHSmith, Libris, and Mondadori.

Getting started: There is a program for authors called Kobo Writing Life and a program for publishers called Kobo Publisher Operations.[†††] You sign up for an account if you're an author, and you fill out a questionnaire if you're a publisher.[†††]

Fine print:

- Kobo accepts Word and MOBI files and converts them. You may also submit your own EPUB file.
- Kobo lets you sell the Kobo EPUB file through other retail channels.
- The Kobo royalty rate is 70 percent for the author. You must price your book between $1.99 and $12.99, otherwise Kobo uses a 45 percent royalty.

Complexities Along the Paths of Least Complexity

These services offer the path of least complexity, but none of them deliver your book exactly like your Word document. They all involve a conversion, whether these services do it after you upload your file (Kindle Direct Publishing and Nook) or you convert it prior to uploading (iBookstore and Google Play). Kobo lets you do this either way.

If you're a novelist who focuses on ebooks, you can skim most of the rest of this section and never look back. For everyone else, the process can get complex when you want to do any of the following:

- Include graphics and pictures plus their captions.
- Include tables, footnotes, and bulleted lists.
- Make a whizzy Multi-Touch book containing, to quote the original Apple press release, "interactive animations, diagrams, photos, videos, unrivaled navigation, and much more."

In a perfect world, you'd write your book in Word, upload it to the four online reseller sites and one print-on-demand printer, and out would pop books, completely identical to your Word document, for each site and printed on paper. Then, for kicks, you could make a cool Multi-Touch book in your spare time.

However, this isn't a perfect world. Anytime anything converts a file, something *wonky* can happen to your formatting. For example, chapter headers get misaligned, numbered lists restart in the wrong place, formatting changes, hyperlinks evaporate, and other issues appear that you won't know about until reviewers or readers start to complain.

Kindle Direct Publishing, Nook, and Kobo let you upload a Word document that removes some complexity, but when you do this, they automatically convert your book to formats optimized for their devices. Apple and Google require you to convert your book from Word before even uploading, which creates more chances for formatting to change. The next chapter explains the conversion process in detail.

Comparing the Options

This table summarizes the four online ebook resellers. For a neat tool to help you estimate royalty payments across multiple platforms, visit APETheBook.com:

	Kindle Direct Publishing	iBookstore
Royalty	35 percent, or 70 percent: $2.99–$9.99 less delivery charges	70 percent
Time until available for sales	One day	One week
Price limits	35 percent: Less than 3MB, $0.99–$200 3MB–10MB , $1.99–$200 Greater than10MB, $2.99–$200 70 percent: $2.99–$9.99	EPUB: $39.99 Textbooks: $14.99
File size limits	50 MB, additional restrictions EPUB: 200 MB depending on price	Multi-Touch: 2GB (1GB Max 20 MB recommended
Input formats	DOC, HTML, MOBI, EPUB, TXT, RTF, PDF	EPUB, IBOOKS (Multi-Touch)
Output format	MOBI	EPUB
Conversion difficulty	Low (DOC); Medium (MOBI)	Medium (EPUB); high (Multi-Touch)
Cover design size and format	JPEG or TIFF Minimum 1000px on longest side Ideal height/width ratio is 1.6 For best quality, recommended 2500px on longest side	JPEG or PNG Minimum of 1400px on short side
Multiple admin	No	Yes
Countries	246 countries and territories	32 countries and territories
Pricing for individual countries	All countries "pegged" to US pricing, but you can override a country's price.	Set one country at a time.
Attitude	"We want to dominate the world, and we'll do whatever it takes to make you happy so we can achieve this goal."	"We are Apple, and we have the bestselling tablet and the coolest technology, so love it or leave it."

Nook	Google Play	Kobo
40 percent: $0.01–$2.98, 65 percent: $2.99–$9.99, 40 percent: $9.99+	52 percent	70 percent
One to three days	Two days	One to three days
$199.99	No limits	$1.99–$12.99
20 MB	10 MB via website, 1.2 GB via Google Uploader	10 MB
DOC, HTML, EPUB, TXT, RTF	EPUB and PDF	EPUB, DOC, DOCX, MOBI, and ODT
EPUB	EPUB	EPUB
Low (DOC); Medium (EPUB)	Medium (EPUB)	Medium (EPUB)
JPEG Less than 2MB Sides must be between 750px and 2000px	JPEG, PDF, TIFF No specific requirements on size mentioned, but assume at least 1000px on longest size	JPEG or PNG • Less than 2MB
No	No	No
"Worldwide"	229 countries and territories	200 countries
Percentage of list price	US and UK only, so not an issue	Set one region at a time
"We have the largest brick-and-mortar footprint but we recognize readers are starting to go digital"	"We are Google. Our users are already using us as a cloud for everything else, now we're adding books, movies, and music through Google Play.	We'll do whatever it takes to beat Amazon.

The Espresso Book Machine

Throughout most of *APE* we assume that you want to sell your book. However, this may not describe your situation. Perhaps you wrote a memoir or you traced your family's genealogy, and the order of magnitude of your readership is your family and friends.

Your situation may be that you "always wanted to write a book." You are not interested in reselling a large quantity—you may simply want to hold your book in your hand. Or perhaps you're an author and want to proofread your book in a printed format.

We respect these desires, and we have a solution for you: print your book using an Espresso Book Machine.[†††]

This is a self-contained gizmo about the size of the kind of photocopy machines you see in FedEx Office stores. It prints and binds a softcover book in ten minutes. The submission requirements are easy: a PDF of the cover and a PDF of the text.[†††] The cost to print a book is $10 to $15. YouTube has a video of it in action—search for "The Espresso Book Machine."[†††] Johannes Gutenberg would be proud.

Figure 12.01. Espresso Book Machine in action.

Figure 12.02. An early draft of *APE* printed with the Espresso Book Machine.

Espresso Book Machines are located around the world, and someday big-box retailers, drugstores, and supermarkets may have them.[†††] Right now many of the Espresso Book Machines are installed in independent bookstores, so you can print your masterpiece and help a bookstore, too! You can also e-mail your PDF files and have your book sent to you. Check out the Bookshop Santa Cruz website to learn more.[†††]

Figure 12.03. Locations of the Espresso Book Machine.

The ramifications of the Espresso Book Machine go beyond personal self-publishing. An advantage of ebooks is that their storage costs are trivial. The same is not true for printed books, because there are physical-storage and cost limitations. The Espresso Book Machine can provide the best of both worlds: an infinite selection of books that you can print in a local store. As of the end of 2012, the Espresso Book Machine collection, a selection of books provided by authors and publishers, contains seven million books, but this selection will grow larger. Then, perhaps, "out of print" will become even more of an oxymoron.

Summary

Many self-publishers only need to use the online reseller channel. There are five great choices: Amazon, Apple, Barnes & Noble, Google, and Kobo. They operate in similar ways, and they are an easy way to break into self-publishing.

CHAPTER 13

How to Convert Your File

I am so clever that sometimes I don't understand
a single word of what I am saying.

Oscar Wilde, *The Remarkable Rocket*

Conversion or Subversion?

This chapter explains the process of converting your Word document to the formats of ebook resellers. This is the hairiest chapter in *APE*. Shawn could write a book and teach a daylong course about this topic alone, but don't worry because we'll cover everything crucial without tying you up for hours.

If you're a novelist or a nonfiction writer with a simple book, you may not need to use any of these tools. If you're not, you may need to learn at least one of them—or find someone who has. If I can take up hockey at age forty-eight never having skated before, you can learn how to convert your file.

As I mentioned, B.S. (Before Shawn), I asked five experts about the best way to self-publish *What the Plus!* and got eight different answers. The responses included: "Just upload the Word file to each service." "Use Calibre." "Remove your bulleted and numbered lists."

"Use InDesign." "Use an author-services company." "Write it in Scrivener." "Upload it to Smashwords and be done with it." So that you don't face the same confusion and frustration, we will provide a definitive answer to the simple question, "How do I make an ebook?"

File Formats

Let's start with the "simple" topic of file formats. You might think that all the resellers accept a Word file and then sell a common file, and you'd be wrong. This is a chart from the Wikipedia entry that explains ebook formats.[†††] It might make your head explode.

Reader	Plain text	PDF	ePub	HTML	Mobi-Pocket	Fiction-Book (Fb2)	DjVu	Broadband eBook (BBeB)	eReader	Kindle	WOLF	Tome Raider	Open eBook
Amazon Kindle 1	Yes	No	No	No	Yes	No	No	No	No	Yes	No	No	No
Amazon Kindle 2, DX	Yes	Yes	No	Yes	Yes	No	No	No	No	Yes	No	No	No
Amazon Kindle 3	Yes	Yes	No	Yes	Yes	No	No	No	No	Yes	No	No	No
Amazon Kindle Fire	Yes	Yes	No	Yes	Yes	No	No	No	No	Yes	No	No	No
Android Devices	Yes	Yes	Yes	Yes	Yes	Yes	Yes	No	Yes	Yes	No	Yes	Yes
Apple iOS Devices	Yes	Yes	Yes	Yes	Yes	Yes	Yes	No	Yes	Yes	No	Yes	Yes
Azbooka WISEreader	Yes	No	Yes	Yes	Yes	Yes	No	No	No	No	No	No	No
Barnes & Noble Nook	Yes	Yes	Yes	Yes	No	No	No	No	Yes	No	No	No	No
Barnes & Noble Nook Color	Yes	Yes	Yes	Yes	No	No	No	No	No	No	No	No	No
Bookeen Cybook Gen3, Opus	Yes	Yes	Yes	Yes	Yes	Yes	No	No	No	No	No	No	Yes
GNU/Linux Operating System	Yes	Yes	Yes	Yes	?	Yes	?	?	?	?	?	?	?
Foxit eslick	Yes	Yes	Yes	No	No	No	No	No	Yes	No	No	No	No
Hanlin eReader V3	Yes	Yes	Yes	Yes	Yes	Yes	Yes	No	No	No	Yes	No	No
Hanvon WISEreader	Yes	Yes	Yes	Yes	No	No	No	No	No	No	No	No	No
iRex iLiad	Yes	Yes	Yes	No	Yes	No	Yes	No	No	No	No	No	No
iRiver Story	Yes	Yes	Yes	No	No	Yes	Yes	No	No	No	No	No	No
Kobo eReader	Yes	Yes	Yes	No	No	No	No	No	No	No	No	No	No
Nokia N900	Yes	Yes	Yes	Yes	No	Yes	Yes	No	No	No	No	No	Yes
NUUTbook 2	Yes	Yes	Yes	Yes	No	No	No	No	No	No	No	No	No
OLPC XO, Sugar	Yes	Yes	Yes	Yes	No	No	Yes	No	No	No	No	No	No
Onyx Boox 60	Yes	Yes	Yes	Yes	Yes	Yes	Yes	No	No	No	No	No	No
Mac OS X	Yes	Yes	Yes	Yes	?	Yes	?	Yes	Yes	?	?	?	Yes
Windows	Yes	Yes	Yes	Yes	Yes	Yes	Yes	?	Yes	Yes	?	?	Yes
Pocketbook 301 Plus, 302, 360	Yes	Yes	Yes	Yes	Yes	Yes	Yes	No	No	No	No	No	No
Sony Reader	Yes	Yes	Yes	No	No	No	No	Yes	No	No	No	No	No
Viewsonic VEB612	Yes	Yes	Yes	Yes	No	No	No	No	No	No	No	No	No
Windows Phone 7	Yes	Yes	Yes	Yes	No	No	No	No	No	Yes	No	No	No

Figure 13.01. Wikipedia explanation of file formats.

To cover all the major ebook resellers and brick-and-mortar stores, you'd need three basic file types: EPUB, MOBI, and PDF. Most online resellers sell your book in the EPUB format. The problem is that Kindle Direct Publishing does not. Kindle Direct Publishing sells ebooks as MOBI files, which means even though more eReader *models* use EPUB your largest *market of readers* uses MOBI. Until that changes, you need to worry about MOBI.

Notice that the file type associated with Kindle in the Wikipedia table is actually ".azw." The .azw file type is identical to the modern-day MOBI file type. The only difference is the DRM (digital rights management) Amazon adds to the file to protect it on Kindle devices. So to achieve the best Kindle version adaptation, you should upload MOBI files.

Tool by Tool

There are many tools you can use to create ebooks, and more are available every week. The rest of this chapter will explain the tools you will most likely encounter when converting your manuscript to an ebook.

Adobe InDesign

Description: If you worked for a traditional publisher, you'd probably use Adobe InDesign to lay out books. It is a professional-grade publishing tool. Shawn and I believe that Adobe InDesign is the best way for you to convert your Word document to the formats ebook resellers require.

Getting started: Adobe InDesign costs approximately $700 as a standalone product. You can also purchase InDesign as a bundle with other Adobe products such as Photoshop and Acrobat Pro; however, those bundles start at $1,299 and peak at approximately $3,000.

Fortunately, you can subscribe to InDesign for $19.99 per month with a one-year minimum or $29.99 per month with no minimum.[†††] If you need more than InDesign, Adobe offers a service called Adobe Creative Cloud for the Adobe Creative Suite programs (InDesign, Photoshop, Illustrator, Acrobat Pro, Bridge CS6, and Media Encoder).[†††] It costs $49.99 per month with a one-year commitment or $74.99 per month with no commitment. It costs $29.99 per month for students and teachers.

This means that instead of spending $700 to buy InDesign, you can subscribe to InDesign, use it to create your book, and then cancel your subscription at the end of the month. Even starting with zero knowledge, you should be able to convert your book in a month. If you need the other Adobe products such as Photoshop, you can subscribe for $50 per month and then cancel your subscription at the end of the month.

Out of the box, Adobe InDesign will export both EPUB and PDF formats. Using the free plugin from Amazon, you can export MOBI as well.[†††] However, InDesign's ability to export all three file types doesn't mean you should have one master InDesign document (.indd) that you export from.

In reality, you should create an InDesign document that is customized for each export format. This is because each format will handle a few things differently, such as the optimal image size, bullet styles, covers, metadata, and table of contents.

The MOBI plugin will automatically generate and insert the necessary pages for a Kindle-compatible table of contents based on styles (for example, Chapter Header). An EPUB will require you to manually create a hyperlinked table of contents or manually define a separate table of contents document in the export. Finally, PDF documents will also need a manually created table of contents as well as additional front matter like a cover (which will be part of the EPUB and MOBI metadata).

We recommend creating your PDF layout, duplicating the document, and deleting necessary pages for EPUB, and then duplicating and deleting the table of contents for MOBI. Trust us, this will make sense when you get into it.

How We Used InDesign

To save you a lot of time figuring things out, here's the procedure that we used to create *What the Plus!* and *APE* with InDesign:

- Create a new Adobe InDesign document with the page dimensions of your print book (or PDF). The traditional book size is 6 ⅛ by 9 ¼ inches. If you don't plan on having a print or PDF book, you can use the default document size of 8 ½ inches by 11 inches. For *What the Plus!* and *APE*, Shawn used 6 inches by 9 inches.

- Load your manuscript by selecting, "Place" from the File menu. This will enable you to place your Word document directly into your InDesign document. Click in the top-left corner of the page margins *while holding the Shift key.* This will place the Word document and automatically insert as many pages as needed. (If you click on the page, InDesign will fill your Word document to the current page.)

  There are other ways to place your document so it flows within a page template, allowing you to automatically add things like page numbers, but for this example we'll take the easy route and just place the document.

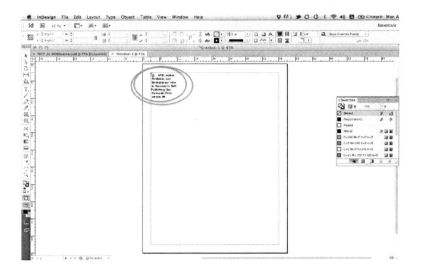

Figure 13.02. Loading your manuscript into InDesign.

- After you place your Word document, you'll notice the InDesign document's paragraph styles panel. (If the panel isn't open, go to the Window menu.) Confirm that it contains all of the styles you used in Word. Some of the styles might not look exactly the same, but that's OK because you can fix that the same way you make changes to styles in Word.

  As you can see in the following image, the NormalFirst style has a first-line indentation even though the first-line indent was set to zero in Word. By double clicking the style in InDesign and removing the indentation, it will fix all of the NormalFirst paragraphs in the InDesign document.

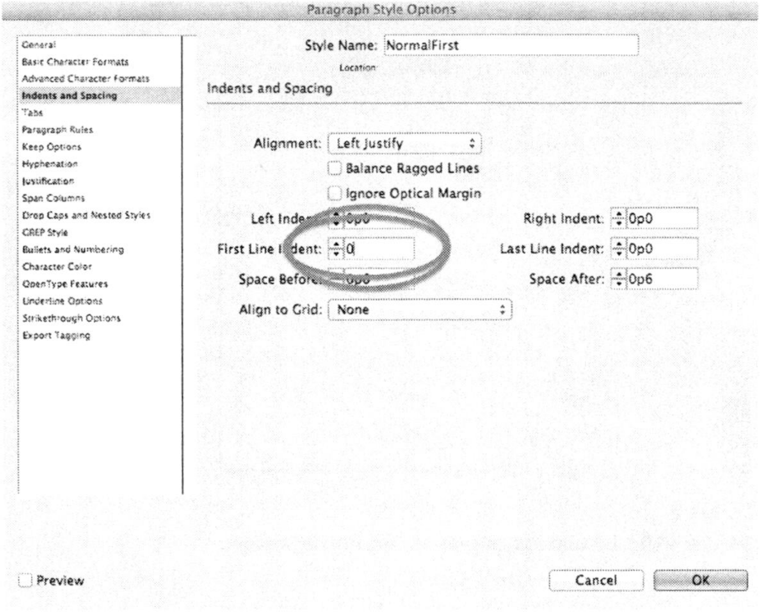

Figure 13.03. Fixing the InDesign NormalFirst style.

- Define which paragraph styles are used to generate the table of contents by selecting Layout > Table of Contents Styles. You must define the table-of-contents styles before exporting the MOBI version of your ebook.

  The paragraph styles of your document are used to create the metadata needed for the table of contents (for example, Section Title, Chapter Title). You then indicate which level in the outline those paragraph styles represent. Section title is level one, and chapter title is level two. If you don't have sections, your chapter titles will be level one.

InDesign reads your document, start to finish, finding those paragraph styles and uses the text of the paragraph to automatically generate each table-of-contents entry.

This means before you start setting up your table of contents, you must have a document formatted with paragraph styles (this is one reason why we recommend you use them from day one instead of formatting your document after the fact).

If you formatted your Word document with paragraph styles and imported it into InDesign, InDesign imports the styles along with the text. Therefore, when you use Word's styles and then import to InDesign, you will be able to use those same styles to define your table of contents. If you don't write with styles from day one, *you must create them* and format your document before setting up a table of contents.

The nice thing about InDesign—and what makes all this effort worthwhile—is that you have to do this style stuff only once! In the InDesign paragraph-style fly-out menu, you have the option of selecting "Load Paragraph Styles." Here you can select an InDesign document that has your entire style sheet pre-prepared.

When you load the styles from that document, it will automatically apply them in the new document. For example, the styles in *What the Plus!* were similar to the styles for *APE*, so loading the styles from *What the Plus!* eliminated hours of work.

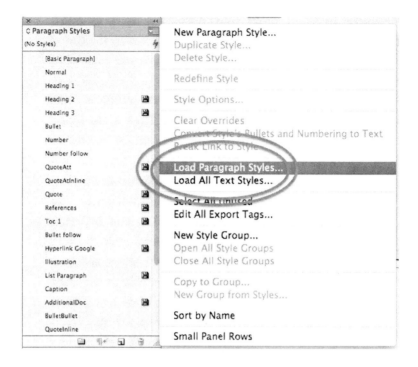

Figure 13.04. Loading InDesign paragraph styles.

Fine print:

- Accept all changes in Word and turn off track changes *before* placing the document in InDesign. Failing to do so may result in wonky behavior.
- One of the gotchas of working with Word and InDesign is that bullets and numbering from Word often do not import well into InDesign. Most of the time, you'll get something that looks like the following figure:

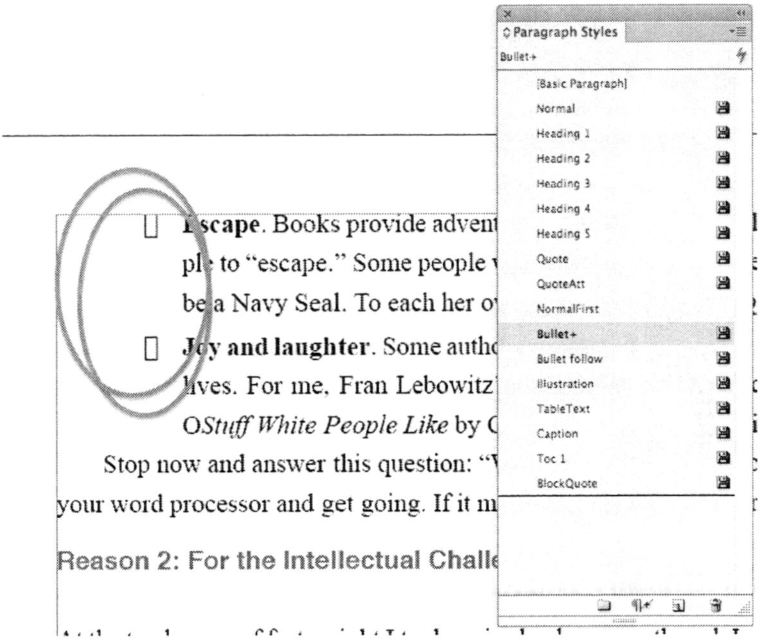

Figure 13.05. Missing bullets after placing a Word document into InDesign.

The bullets in the text are missing characters, and the paragraph style is actually Bullet+. To fix this, you'll have to go into the Bullet+ style, format it properly, and then click on it to apply it to the paragraph in the document. Once you get the style formatted properly, you can fix any remaining missing bullets by reapplying the Bullet+ style to that paragraph.

- Don't trust tables to work on any free-flow text reader. If you have tables in your book and plan to have readers on Kindle, iBooks, Nook, Google Play, or Kobo, we recommend that you convert them to images. We have yet to find anyone who can make a table with more than two rows and columns look good in a format where people can change fonts and sizes.

- Placing Word documents with URLs that contain the "#" symbol causes errors. (If you work for Adobe, please fix this!) You should convert them to bit.ly URLs or another link-shortening service before importing them into InDesign. If you don't, InDesign will create bad hyperlinks. We spent days going through about 310 URLs to figure out which ones were bad and why in *What the Plus!*

  As an alternative, you can set up redirect links that point to the target URLs. This way, if a website changes or you find a better source, you can change the redirect link instead of having to release a revision of your book. This is what we did for *APE* at APETheBook.com. (Hat-tip to Kristen Eckstein for this suggestion.)

- When InDesign imports a Word file, you'll find that file doesn't contain the best version of your photos. Instead, after you import into InDesign, you should replace each image placed by Word with one that's linked to the export format (use the "Place" command in InDesign's File menu). Amazon recommends JPEG image files be at least 600 by 800 pixels. Standard resolution for JPEGs, especially if you plan to print your books, is 300 dpi.

- It's a good idea to increase the frame of the object so it's slightly larger than the image object itself. This will prevent Kindle from cutting off any borders you might have (Kindle usually crops images by one or two pixels when rendering on-screen).

Think of InDesign as a hub, not a destination. Your Word file goes into InDesign and then you send out various formats of it to resellers and your printer. Admittedly, though, InDesign is a beast like Word. To help you get started with InDesign, we've uploaded a book-design template at APETheBook.com.

There are also YouTube tutorials for learning InDesign and online training sites like KelbyTraining.com and Lynda.com.[†††] (Disclosure: Shawn has worked with Scott Kelby and the fine folks at KelbyTraining for three years.) Finally, TheInDesigner is a useful website to learn how to create book-length documents with InDesign.[†††]

Apple iBooks Author Tool

Description: iBooks Author is a standalone Macintosh app from Apple that produces Multi-Touch iBooks. Multi-Touch books are only available through the iBookstore and only work on iPads. If you've used other iWork applications (such as Pages and Numbers), you'll feel familiar with the interface of iBooks Author.

Getting started: The iBooks Author tool is available from the Apple App Store as a free download.[†††] You can export Multi-Touch ebooks as either a PDF or iBOOKS file for free distribution. You can also choose "Publish" from the File menu to publish the book to the iBookstore. When you do this, iBooks Author automatically launches iTunes Producer with a new submission pre-populated with your ebook.

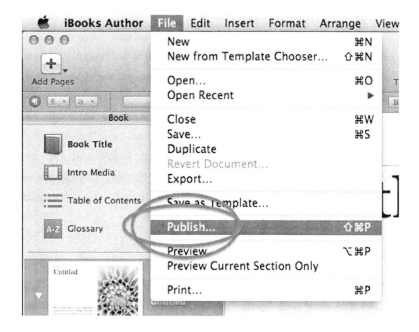

Figure 13.06. Publishing from iBooks Author.

Fine print:

- When working with iBooks Author, you have to
  create both a landscape and portrait layout for your
  book. When you work in landscape orientation, you
  use a static layout. When you work in portrait orientation, you use a layout where font and size changes
  the flow of text. To switch between these orientations, use the "Orientation" toggle in the iBooks
  Author toolbar.

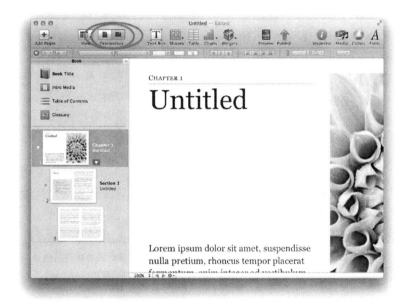

Figure 13.07. Toggling between orientations in iBooks Author.

- Instead of laying out your book and then defining your table of contents, iBooks Author builds your book in parallel with the table of contents. The left sidebar of iBooks Author shows the current outline of your book. This outline is used to generate table-of-contents pages and section headers automatically throughout iBooks Author.
- iBooks Author lets you import Word and Pages documents. When you import documents from Word, you have the option to preserve Word styles or override them with local styles. The import is not

great, so do not expect to import and map styles as easily as with InDesign. After import you will need to go through and construct your table of contents because this is one style that will not carry over.

- iBooks Author lets you place rich-media assets such as audio, video, HTML, and more. These media assets will appear in line with the text in landscape orientation. This will appear in the left sidebar in the portrait orientation. For more information on rich-media widgets, check out iBook Lesson: BookWidgets by Erica Sadun.[†††]

- If you have a rich-media book (like a photography book) where the free-flow text in portrait orientation wouldn't add any benefit to the reader, you can lock your book to the landscape orientation. To lock the orientation, click the blue "Inspector" button in the top-right corner of iBooks Author, select "Document Inspector," and check the box "Disable Portrait Orientation."

Figure 13.08. Locking the orientation in iBooks Author.

Erica Sadun and Steve Sande over at the Unofficial Apple Weblog (TUAW.com) have put together a great series on using iBooks Author.[†††] Some highlights to start with are:

- iBook Lessons: The Absolute Beginner
- iBook Lessons: Book Samples and Rookie Mistakes
- iBook Lessons: Style Sheets
- iBook Lessons: Take Control of iBooks Author

Pages

Description: Pages is part of Apple's iWork software, and it competes with Microsoft Word. As mentioned earlier, we consider Word the best option for writing your manuscript because it is the most mature and most used word processor.

Pages, however, is useful when working with EPUB conversion. If you don't want to dive head-first into a professional tool like Adobe InDesign, Pages is a Plan B—especially if you plan on working primarily with iBooks Author and iBookstore.

Getting started: Pages is available through the Apple App Store for $19.99.[†††] You can also write your book in Microsoft Word and use Pages only for conversion.

You export to the EPUB format by choosing File > Export and then selecting the EPUB option in the toolbar. Pages does a decent job of exporting the EPUB format. The only drawback is that it cannot export MOBI files. Kindle Direct Publishing will let you upload an EPUB file, but it converts EPUB to MOBI before your ebook goes on sale, which introduces chances for something to go wrong.

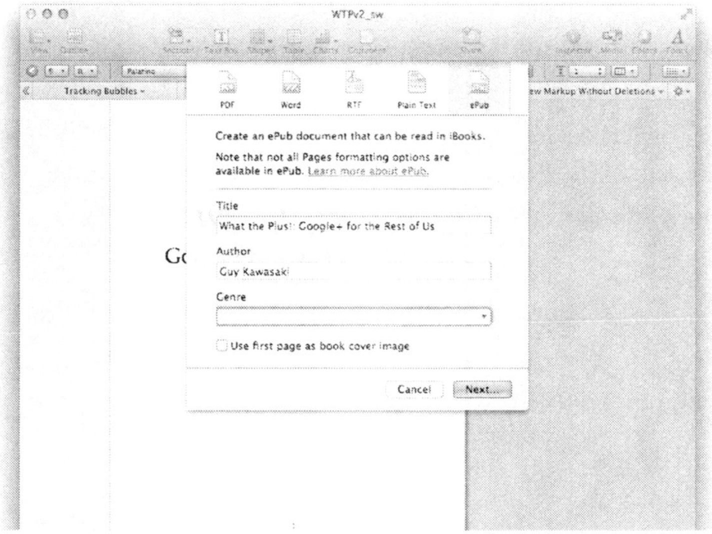

Figure 13.09. Exporting to EPUB from Pages.

Fine print:

- If you open a Word document in Pages, it will do a fair, but not perfect, job of conversion. You may have to go through and adjust some styles so that they look as you originally intended.

- An easy way to get started with Pages is to download Apple's "ePub Best Practices" sample document.[†††] Read the document and then use it as a template for your book.

- When going between Pages and Word documents, the two areas that are most likely to cause conversion issues are tables and bullets. For some reason, these two layouts never look the same going between formats (indents are always wrong, table styles are always different).

- Pages lets you define the outline of your document similar to the way iBooks Author lets you define the outline of your book. iBooks Author will import Pages documents with nearly lossless conversion (iBooks Author was built by the same engineers that worked on iWork). When you import a Pages document to iBooks Author for a Multi-Touch book, it will automatically bring in the styles and outline from Pages.

- Pages has a "track changes" feature that shows changes made and tracked in the Word format. However, we do not recommend bouncing back and forth between Pages and Word. Try to stay in one format as long as possible and then make the transition once to avoid weird results such as the loss of text and formatting.

Calibre

Description: Calibre is a free, open-source application that is available for Macintosh, Windows, and Linux. It is an ebook-management tool that can import and export a multitude of formats.

Calibre's real power is the ability to manage multiple ebooks. You can drag them into Calibre and then manage their metadata (author, ISBN, and cover) for various formats. You can also create a single EPUB file, load it into Calibre, and export MOBI and PDF formats. (However, Calibre may change the appearance of your document while converting it.)

Getting started: Calibre offers downloads for Macintosh, Windows, and Linux. For support, visit Calibre's FAQ page.[†††] Once you've downloaded the application, adding books is as easy as dragging them into Calibre.

Fine print:

- You cannot convert a Word document with Calibre. It only supports these input formats: CBZ, CBR, CBC, CHM, DJVU, EPUB, FB2, HTML, HTMLZ, LIT, LRF, MOBI, ODT, PDF, PRC, PDB, PML, RB, RTF, SNB, TCR, TXT, TXTZ. Of these, you should probably export a PDF file from Word. You can export a Word file to HTML and then import it into Calibre, but this process can introduce some wonkiness.

  Once you have your book in Calibre, you can export it to the following file types: AZW3, EPUB, FB2, OEB, LIT, LRF, MOBI, HTMLZ, PDB, PML, RB, PDF, RTF, SNB, TCR, TXT, TXTZ.

- Going from EPUB to MOBI with Calibre (or any other tool) is like creating a compressed image from another compressed image. Both formats simplify the book's structure and layout, and each time you go between these simplified layouts you are making your book a little worse and increasing the chance for problems to arise.

  This illustrates one of the reasons why InDesign has so much value. It acts as a high-level document structure that contains as much information about the layout as possible. This allows it to retain that information when you export it to EPUB and MOBI.

- Calibre offers an in-app testing environment for various formats, but if a reseller offers a separate testing app (Kindle Direct Publishing and IBookstore both do), it's a good idea to test in those applications too.

EPUB Converter Sites

Description: If you Google "epub conversion," you'll get more than 6.3 million results.[†††] Instead of going through each of these results, we'll examine one in particular and discuss why you might use it.

When you upload a Word document to Kindle Direct Publishing or Nook, you trust everything to these services. You'll be able to see a preview in a web browser after you upload your book, but you won't see your book on a real device until it's available for sale.

By using a conversion site like 2Epub, you can preview your book on an actual Kindle or Nook before uploading it.[†††] Based on our experience, 2Epub provides an accurate conversion to EPUB from Word. So, while we do not recommend using an EPUB conversion site as the best option, you can use these sites to check your manuscript.

Getting started: Go to 2Epub and upload your document. It accepts DOC, DOCX, EPUB, FB2, HTML, LIT, LRF, MOBI, ODT, PDB, PDF, PRC, RTF, and TXT, and it exports EPUB, FB2, LIT, LRF, and MOBI.

Fine print:

- 2Epub does not accept files larger than twenty-five megabytes.
- It's a good idea to double-check the privacy policies and terms of use of converter sites. We couldn't find any red flags in 2Epub, but we didn't check any other converter site, so uploader beware.
- Sometimes Word-to-EPUB conversion works better if you use HTML as an interim step. In the File menu of Word you can save as HTM (instead of DOCX). This gives you the option to edit the HTML and clean up the junk that Word sometimes exports. Then instead of uploading the DOCX file, you upload the cleaner HTML files. The cleaner your files are before EPUB conversion, the better.

Comparing the Options

	Adobe InDesign	iBooks Author tool	Calibre	EPUB converter sites
Word styles	Yes	Yes and no, have to redefine styles for the table of contents	No, only converts EPUB	OK for preview, but will have problems
Graphics	Yes	Yes	Yes	Yes
Captions	Yes	Yes	Yes	Yes
Word Tables	No, use images instead	Yes (static layout)	N/A, Calibre does not accept Word files	No
Links	Yes	Yes	Yes	Yes
Footnotes	Yes	Yes for static layouts	Yes	Yes

Testing Your Ebook

In the traditional publishing process, authors receive "page proofs" twice. (A page proof is a mockup of the final, typeset version of your book.) The first time is when your book is laid out after copyediting, at which point proofs also get sent to a professional proofreader to hunt for any mistakes the copyeditor may have missed or that the typesetter introduced. The second time is after the typesetter makes all the corrections you and the proofreader found in first proofs. You know with great certainty how your book will look after the second page proofs.

Only a foolish or first-time author would make the same assumption about an ebook. Many things can go wrong. As Shawn mentioned, we learned this the hard way with *What the Plus!* when the hyperlinks in the PDF version did not work.

You need to check the final version of your file under real-world conditions on a host of devices, such as computers, Android tablets and phones, iOS tablets and phones, Kindles, Nooks, and Kobo tablets. Don't assume that the final version is identical to your Word version or that your book will look the same on a Kindle device as it does on the Kindle reader app on an iPad.

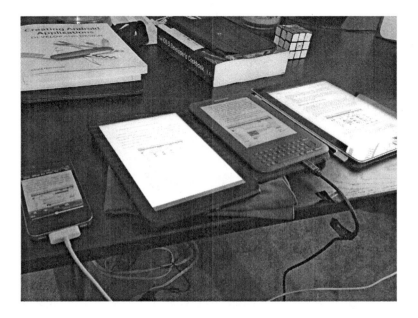

Figure 13.10. Shawn checking the Kindle version (MOBI) of *What the Plus!* as it appears across Kindle Apps on multiple platforms.

Ebooks 101[†††] by the Rockley Group provides a good checklist for testing your book. Here's a summary:

- **Hyperlinks.** Click on every link in the ebook in every format.
- **Images.** Ensure that all the images appear in the ebook and that they are properly scaled.
- **Spacing.** Look for spacing gone awry, which then makes the formatting wrong.
- **Weird characters.** Look at every page to see if fonts got substituted and if nonsense characters appeared like gremlins in the night.
- **Simulate customer use.** Change the font, font size, and portrait/landscape views to see what happens when customers do the same thing.

Ebooks 101 provides a list of tools you can use to automate the process too:

- **EPUBCheck.** This free tool enables you to check EPUB files. You can use it online or download it.[†††] Its website includes a handy explanation of the common error codes that you may encounter.[†††]
- **Kindle Previewer.** Amazon provides this free tool to help you ensure that your ebook looks good on Kindle devices and in Kindle apps. It does not support the Kindle Keyboard tablet, however.[†††]
- **iBook Proofer.** Apple provides this as a proofer for EPUB books. It runs as a simulator on Macintoshes but does not work with Multi-Touch books. It is available as a free download in the "Deliver Your Content" section of iTunes Connect.

- **iBooks Author.** This tool enables you to launch your Multi-Touch ebook on an iPad by connecting your iPad to your computer using the iPad cable. Chose the "Preview" option in the iBooks Author toolbar to see what your book will look like.
- **Adobe Digital Editions.** Our friends at Adobe provide this software to read and manage EPUB and PDF books. You can also use it to test your book in these formats.[†††]

If you want peace of mind, buy a copy of your book from every reseller and check it. This is the best way to see what your customers are getting. The other way is that customers will contact you to tell you that something is wrong. The former is preferable to the latter.

Things Nobody Tells You

To quote Steve Jobs, "There is one more thing." When working with ebook conversions, you may discover errors and inconsistencies that nobody ever mentions. This is geeky stuff, but this list may prevent you from ripping your hair out trying to find answers on Google:

- **EPUB is zipped HTML.** EPUB files are HTML files compressed into a special ZIP file. This means that you can change the extension of an EPUB file to .zip, unzip the file, and then edit the HTML. When you're done, you can simply repackage your EPUB using ePub Zip.[†††] You'll see why this is useful in the next few tips.

- **Restarting numbered lists.** Nonfiction books often contain numbered lists that are interrupted by a figure or caption. In Word, you can right-click a number and select "Continue Numbering" or "Restart Numbering." But when this style is translated into HTML, numbering almost always restarts after each change in the paragraph style.

  To fix this, unzip your EPUB file and manually edit the HTML so that the <ol> HTML tags don't restart. Once you fix the numbering, you can repackage the EPUB with ePub Zip.

  Another option is to convert your numbered lists to text when you export. This will prevent your lists from restarting. However, when the list is on actual devices, the tabs will be misaligned because the number indicating the list item is part of the paragraph text. So depending on how long the paragraphs are in your list, you might not want to convert the styles to text.

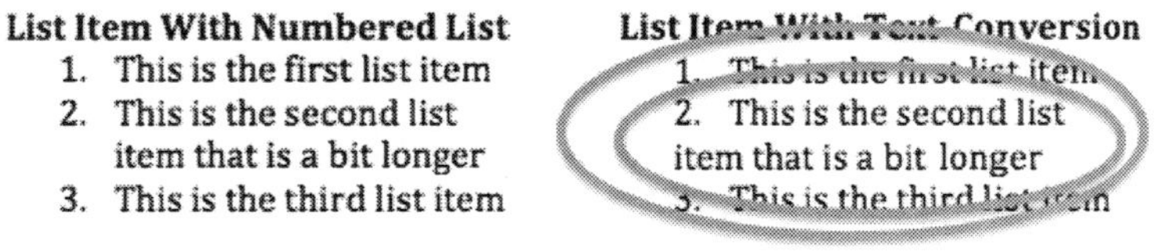

List Item With Numbered List
1. This is the first list item
2. This is the second list item that is a bit longer
3. This is the third list item

List Item With Text Conversion
1. This is the first list item
2. This is the second list item that is a bit longer
3. This is the third list item

Figure 13.11. Misaligned bullets after converting the number style to text.

- **Nook encryption.** Adobe InDesign and Pages often embed fonts in the EPUB file during export. When fonts are embedded, an encryption file accompanies them. If you try to upload an EPUB file to PubIt (Nook's reseller system) that contains an encryption, the uploader will complain and reject your EPUB (iBookstore, Google Play, and Kobo don't care).

  The fix is to unzip your EPUB like you did with the numbered lists and delete the encryption.xml file. After deleting this file, rezip your EPUB with ePub Zip.

- **Use the optimal image sizes.** The recommended images for Kindle are JPEGs at least 600 by 800 pixels in size. iPad and Android tablets have bigger screens, many of which are high-density. We recommend images that are 768 by 768 pixels, at a resolution of at least 300 dpi. This will ensure images fit the minimum width of the iPad screen and that the images will be sharp. (The iPad represents 70 percent of the tablet market share as of August 2012.)

- **Create a print-ready PDF and an interactive PDF.** In the print-ready PDF, you should format the character style of all your hyperlinks so they are the normal font color and not underlined. In your interactive PDF, you should format your hyperlinks so they look like links in blue and are underlined so that people know they can click on them.

- **Avoid special characters in the file names of images.** Images with characters such as !, @, #, &, %, and $ in their file names will embed properly in InDesign and will export to the EPUB format without issue. However, if you try to upload the EPUB to a service like Google Play, it will fail because of the image names. Make sure you always validate your EPUB files using the EPUB tools mentioned in the previous section. (This goes for all EPUB-based services: iBookstore, Nook, Google Play, and Kobo).

- **Use a 10-point font with a 1.5 (or 15-point) line spacing.** When creating a print layout, these are the sizes to use for readability. Always use a serif font with justified text in your "Normal" paragraph.

- **Printed books require at least a 0.5-inch page margin.** Depending on the number of pages and the type of binding, you might want a slightly larger page margin on the spine. For example, this book has a 5.5-inch by 8.5-inch trim size and has the following page margins: Top 0.5 inches; Outer-Edge 0.5625 inches; Bottom 0.6875; and Spine 1 inch. The slightly larger margin in the spine allows for pages to bend and fold without any text getting too close to the gutter, making it hard to read. The more pages in your book, the more room you'll need on the spine edge of the page.

- **Printed books should always have an even-numbered total of pages.** This might seem like a duh-ism, but remember that odd pages are on the right, and even pages are on the left. Unless you want to leave the back of your last page blank, you need an even number of pages.

- **Use special alignments.** Most people are familiar with align left, align right, center, and justify. With print books, you have two more options: align toward spine, and align away from spine. These are useful for page numbers, which should be aligned away from the spine if not centered at the bottom of the page (though we prefer align away from spine).

- **Make all the components of a cover.** Remember that the cover of a printed book includes the front cover, spine, and back cover. If you are doing a hardcover book, you'll need a dust jacket that adds a front flap and a back flap. The spine width is dependent on the number of pages in your book (see your printer or author-services company for calculation formulas), so you won't know how wide to make your spine until you know the length of your book.

Summary

Was that so bad? Actually, for a novice, it is daunting, but there's nothing wrong with finding a Shawn or InDesigner to help you. You don't need to memorize all this information, you can always return to *APE* for information in the future. So for now you can relax, the hardcore tech aspect of *APE* is over.

CHAPTER 14

How to Sell Ebooks Directly to Readers

We are inclined to believe those whom we do not know,
because they have never deceived us.

Samuel Johnson, *The Idler*

What and Why

This chapter explains how to sell your ebook directly to readers without using an online reseller such as Amazon, Apple, Barnes & Noble, Google Play, or Kobo. (We cover selling your printed book directly to readers in chapter 16: "How to Use Print-on-Demand Services.") Readers can get your book and revisions immediately, and you can make as much money as possible on each sale.

However, this is too perfect a picture, so keep two factors in mind. First, somehow you need to get the ebook to your customers and their money to you. This can entail website hosting, fulfillment, payment processing, shipping, and customer service.

Second, this method only works if you have the ability to expose your readers to your offering. While people might stumble upon your book on Amazon, iBookstore, Nook, Google Play, and Kobo because of internal recommendation engines and large amounts of traffic, this isn't going to happen with this type of sale.

Gumroad

Gumroad[†††] charges $0.25 per download plus 5 percent of the sale for hosting and selling your file. For example, if you sell a PDF for $3, Gumroad keeps $0.40 ($0.25 + 5 percent of $3) and you'd get $2.60. This is more than you'd get from Kindle Direct Publishing for the same transaction. Gumroad also offers a "$0+" option. This means that people can pay whatever they want to—including nothing.

I used Gumroad to distribute a PDF of *What the Plus!* Unfortunately, I didn't track results when I varied the price from $2.99 to as low as "pay what you want." Over the course of a month, 26,717 people clicked on the link, and 1,632 people downloaded it.

Most people paid $0, but the donations amounted to $803.23, so the average amount paid was approximately $0.50 per copy. This was four months after the introduction of the book. By that time, I had given away approximately 15,000 copies and sold 15,000 copies.

People cannot pay with PayPal because Gumroad only accepts credit cards. Also, Gumroad asks for a minimal amount of personal information, so it cannot provide information about where your customers live. Someday you may need this information to charge sales tax or value-added tax for digital content.

Gumroad requires a preexisting and loyal audience that will click on a link that you provide. As a first-time author, this may be difficult, but you'll learn how to build your "platform" in the next section of the book, "Entrepreneur." If you can make this work, there are two big benefits: retention of more of the selling price and access to the e-mail addresses of everyone who has bought the file.

E-Junkie

E-Junkie[ttt] is another way to sell your book directly. Unlike Gumroad's per-copy flat fee and percentage, E-Junkie charges according to the number of files and storage space that you use. The number of downloads is unlimited.

A collection of ten files totaling less than fifty megabytes costs $5 per month. Therefore, if you had one book that is less than fifty megabytes (which is a huge size for a book), you'd only pay $5 per month, and you could sell an unlimited number of copies.

Unlike Gumroad, customers can use PayPal, Google Checkout, TrialPay, Authorize.net, and credit cards (through the PayPal system). Finally, also unlike Gumroad, E-Junkie can calculate sales tax and VAT charges because it knows where your customers reside.

ClickBank

ClickBank[ttt] is a third way to sell ebooks directly. You create an account, upload your file, price it, and sell it. There is a $49.95 activation fee to get started. Customers can use credit cards or PayPal.

A key difference between ClickBank and the other two services is ClickBank's affiliate program. The scenario ClickBank paints is that people discover great books in the ClickBank marketplace.[ttt] Then they join the ClickBank affiliate program, get an affiliate link to their favorite books, and promote the link on their blog and through social media.

The company says that it has 100,000 affiliates in 200 countries. It claims to have paid more than $1.8 billion to affiliates and vendors (the people who upload files) and to process 30,000 transactions every day.

The revenue split with ClickBank is different from the other direct-sales sites. ClickBank operates on a wholesale price/retail price model, which means you set a wholesale price (the price at which ClickBank and other affiliates buy the book from you) and a retail price (the price customers see and pay). Your revenue is the wholesale price, since you are selling to ClickBank, and they are the seller of record to customers.

Ganxy

Ganxy[†††] is an interesting start-up in this segment. It enables you create a "showcase" for your ebook and sell it in EPUB, MOBI, and PDF format. Ganxy provides payment functionality, file hosting, and customer service.

Ganxy charges 10 percent of net sales, where net sales is the selling price of the ebook less a payment-processing fee. Think of it as a website like Gumroad, E-Junkie, and ClickBank that is dedicated to selling ebooks.

Figure 14.01. Selling an ebook with Ganxy.

Caveats

If you can convince people to buy your book from these services, you can make more money per book. Nathan Barry's *App Design Handbook* is an example. Barry has a concentrated market of app programmers, and these programmers are willing to pay his book's price of $39.

For these programmers, the book isn't a $2.99 Gothic-romance whim. Designing apps is their livelihood, so a $39 price point for a book that can help them succeed isn't a problem. Barry makes approximately $38.20 per book, so if he sold 2,000 copies, he could buy a Porsche.

On the other hand, online ebook resellers such as Amazon and Apple pay less per copy, but they may sell more copies. Also, direct sales do not count toward sales rankings for bestseller lists, and books on these lists tend to sell more because they are visible.

If your customers are not price sensitive and you have a way to reach them, then selling direct can work. If these conditions do not exist, then it may be better to make less money per copy but sell more copies using online resellers and bookstores.

PayPal

If you're wondering about using PayPal to sell ebooks, it's not applicable to most self-publishers because this would require creating a website where your readers have an account, and you control access to your ebook's file. Essentially, you'd have to become your own E-Junkie and manage an ecommerce site.

PayPal provides payment collection, and when someone pays, it tells your website to grant access—for example, if someone buys more weapons in an online game. Credit cards such as MasterCard and Visa work in similar ways. However, these companies do not act as your store by hosting your ebook and selling it.

So your customers can pay with PayPal and credit cards, but on Gumroad, E-Junkie, and ClickBank, not directly to you.

Get Physical

Here's one more idea: **Enthrill Books** enables you to provide a physical manifestation of ebooks in the form of gift cards. Authors can buy preactivated cards to sell or give away. Recipients then download the ebook in EPUB or MOBI format for their devices. The cards cost authors approximately $1 to $1.50 in quantities of five hundred or more.

Let's suppose that you sell your ebook through Amazon for $2.99, and you decide to match Amazon's price for the card. You'll make $1 to $1.50 by selling Enthrill gift cards, which is approximately one-half of Kindle royalties. However, having a physical card may enable you to close twice as many sales.

I anticipate using Enthrill cards at appearances so that I have something to autograph. Believe someone who's done it, taking five hundred books to an event is a pain. And Enthrill gift cards would have solved the challenge of selling five hundred ebooks that pushed me down the path of self-publishing.

Finally, publishers can buy Enthrill gift cards that are not preactivated and take part in Enthrill's retail distribution network that provides ebook gift cards to retailers such as supermarkets, and these retailers activate the gift cards at the time of purchase.

Summary

Selling your ebook directly to customers is one of the most profitable channels of distribution for a self-publisher. You won't benefit from the ongoing traffic of a reseller such as Amazon, but if you can drive people to your website, direct selling can work.

CHAPTER 15

How to Use Author-Services Companies

Service is often the art of making good
on somebody else's mistake.

Cavett Robert

What and Why

This chapter explains how author-services companies work. These firms provide services such as copyediting, cover design, and interior design, as well as distribution to resellers. They are designed to alleviate the tasks of publishing books and getting them into resellers. We examine a few of these companies to help you understand this channel.

Lulu

Lulu[†††] is a self-publisher's publisher. You can find almost all of the services provided by a traditional publisher, from cover design and copyediting to worldwide printing and distribution. If you don't want to manage your book on iBookstore and PubIt (Nook's reseller system), you can upload your manuscript as a Word file, and Lulu will handle conversion, placement, and distribution to these services.

Or you can use Lulu for only printing your book. This allows you to maintain direct control of your ebook while still offering the option of print. Lulu makes your printed book available on sites like Amazon and Barnes & Noble as well as listing your book in the databases used by brick-and-mortar bookstores for ordering inventory. This doesn't mean brick-and-mortar bookstores will stock your book, but they can buy your book for customers.

Getting started: The first step is to create a new account at Lulu's website. Your books in Lulu are managed from a dashboard. From the "My Lulu" tab, you can create and manage your books. Lulu also operates like an ecommerce website, so you can purchase author services such as cover designs.

Fine print:

- Lulu manages the relationship with multiple ebook resellers (CreateSpace, on the other hand, only works with Kindle Direct Publishing). This means any revenue from these resellers will go to Lulu, which in turn pays you.
- Lulu receives a 10 percent cut of revenues. For example, if you sell your book through the iBookstore via Lulu for $9.99, Apple takes 30 percent. From the remaining $7, Lulu takes 10 percent, which leaves you with $6.30.

- Lulu said good-bye to DRM in a blog post on January 8, 2013.[†††] It stopped offering DRM as an option when publishing EPUB or PDF through Adobe Digital Editions. External partners (such as Kindle) may still add DRM, but in cases that Lulu controls, books will be DRM-free.
- For print books, Lulu accepts PDF, Microsoft Word DOC, Microsoft Word DOCX, RTF, TXT, JPG, PNG, and GIF.
- Print books (both color and black-and-white) must be between 68 and 740 pages long.

Better Business Bureau rating: A+, 148 complaints in the last three years.[†††]

Smashwords

Description: Smashwords is an ebook distributor working on a 15 percent commission. It does not offer design and editing services. Smashwords focuses on ebook resellers such as Apple, Barnes & Noble, Kobo, and Sony—but not Amazon. People can also buy books directly from its website.

Smashwords accepts Word files or EPUB files, and automatically converts Word files to EPUB, Sony Reader, MOBI, Palm, PDF, RTF, and plain text. To combat the conversion problems we've highlighted before, Smashwords suggests that you format your document using its style guide before uploading it.

This style guide explains how to set up Word styles so Smashwords can convert the book as accurately as possible. Conveniently, the style guide is available as a free book on Smashwords.com in every ebook format it supports. Not conveniently, the style guide is more than 24,000 words long, so you need to read a book to format a book.[†††]

Getting started: Registration at Smashwords takes about thirty seconds: Visit the sign-up page and after confirming your e-mail address, you're set.[†††] A summary of your books, royalties, ISBNs, and sales reports can be accessed from your Smashwords dashboard. To create your first book, select the "Publish" tab in the main navigation.

Fine print:

- Book prices can either be free or any price above $0.99.
- Smashwords takes a 15 percent cut of revenue generated by your book, and a 29.5 percent cut if the revenue was generated through an affiliate link.
- Smashwords does not offer any DRM (digital rights management), but we don't recommend that you add DRM to your book anyway. (We'll discuss DRM further in chapter 20: "Self-Publishing Issues.")
- Books usually appear for sale within minutes after you upload them. Unlike Kindle Direct Publishing, iBookstore, and Kobo, Smashwords does not review your file. This speed isn't necessarily a good thing, because you might need one last chance to review your ebook before it goes on sale.
- You use the Channel Manager in the Smashwords dashboard to control which entities sell your book. Channel options include: Apple (iBookstore), Barnes & Noble (Nook), Diesel eBook Store, Kobo, Sony Reader Store, and Bilo.com.
- Smashwords will not automatically publish to Kindle Direct Publishing, but you can make a MOBI version available on your listing at Smashwords.

Better Business Bureau rating: D+, five complaints in the last three years.[†††]

BookBaby

Description: BookBaby manages Amazon, Apple, and Barnes & Noble accounts. BookBaby charges a one-time fee based on the service level you want and then pays out 100 percent royalties. It also offers design and editing services.

Getting started: To get started, first create an account at BookBaby.[†††] When you're ready to publish your book, you pick which package (service level) you want to use. There are three options:

- **Basic.** $99. You supply an EPUB file, and BookBaby distributes it to online resellers. (For Amazon, BookBaby converts the EPUB file to MOBI but doesn't offer additional quality checks.)[†††]
- **Standard.** $149. BookBaby converts your file to EPUB and MOBI and helps you check it with the popular eReaders. You can include up to ten graphic elements at no charge.[†††]
- **Premium.** $249. BookBaby provides all the services of the standard package plus more review and checking services, as well as up to 50 graphic elements.[†††]

Fine print:

- BookBaby distributes to all of the major ebook resellers except Google Play. For a full list of distributors, visit BookBaby's FAQ page.[†††]

- When you sign up for BookBaby, you set the threshold that triggers BookBaby to pay you. When your account reaches that amount, BookBaby will pay what it owes you on the following Monday (minimum $20).

- BookBaby charges you when you want to make corrections and fixes to your book once you've submitted it. The costs are $50 for 1 to 10 changes, $75 for 11 to 25 changes, and $100 for 26 to 50 changes. For the Basic level of service, you have to upload a new file and pay $99 to make any changes.

- BookBaby pays via paper check, ACH deposit, or PayPal. If you elect to receive payment via a paper check, BookBaby charges a $1.50 processing fee.

Better Business Bureau rating: not rated.

Author Solutions

Description: Author Solutions is a company that operates eight imprints: Dellarte, AuthorHouse, Wordclay, Trafford, Xlibris, Palibro, Inkubook, and iUniverse. Traditional publishers such as Harlequin, Hay House, and Thomas Nelson also "embed" Author Solutions into their selection of imprints. For example, Author Solutions operates the WestBow Press imprint of Thomas Nelson.

All permutations of Author Solutions sell services to help you write, edit, design, produce, and market your book. Penguin—yes the same Penguin that published *Enchantment* but couldn't sell five hundred ebooks—recently bought Author Solutions for over $100 million.

A single word to describe Author Solutions is "aggressive." This company, through all its own imprints and embedded imprints, tries its best to sell you ancillary services—probably because there's not enough money in printing alone. For example, the AuthorHouse imprint offers an $899 Social Media Marketing Setup Service[†††] that will help you set up social-media accounts, send you the login information, and provide "easy-to-follow instructions on how to update your accounts."

(Ironically, Author Solutions could definitely use help with its social-media efforts. It created a fake account on Google+, Facebook, and Twitter for "Awesome Publishing Consultant" Jared Silverstone. Writer Emily Suess figured out that Jared was a stock photo from iStockphoto and not a real person.)[†††]

Here's another example of a high-price package: You can buy the Newsmaker Publicity Campaign[†††] for $5,999 and receive a publicist who will work "on your behalf for six weeks," a press release that will go to 1,000 media outlets, six weeks of news tracking, a ten-to-fifteen-minute radio interview on the AuthorHouse Internet radio show, and a copy of the radio interview.

Something tells us that the publicist won't be working for forty hours a week on your book, and maybe it's "Jared" in his spare time when he's not posing for stock photos.

Author House claims to have helped 150,000 writers, who published 200,000 books, so it's bound to have upset some of its customers. However, I also communicated with several authors who were happy with its services.

A person who's familiar with social media may consider $899 to open three accounts a ridiculous amount—but a complete neophyte might not. Maybe its fees are reasonable for people who have no clue about how to do things. Value is in the eye of the beholder.

Getting started: The first step to working with any Author Solutions imprint is to register at its website. You can then select various package deals depending on your genre. There are a plethora of other services that you can also buy.

Fine print:

- We'll use AuthorHouse as an example of how Author Solutions imprints work. AuthorHouse sells its services as "self-publishing packages." It has two ebook packages, black-and-white ($349, with 50 images) and full-color ($449, with 80 images). It even has "Hollywood" packages that offer to put your manuscript in front of its Hollywood entertainment partner (for $4,099).
- For print books, AuthorHouse has five different packages priced at $749, $949, $1,299, $1,799, and $2,999. The value of the expensive packages is open for interpretation. If you think you need a book-signing kit, AuthorHouse sells one for $325 (Amazon.com sells a pack of Sharpie markers for $5).[†††]
- AuthorHouse retains ownership of your formatted file, cover, and ISBN. If you want to switch publishers, you may have to re-create your files or buy them from Author House for $250 each, even though you already paid once for creating them. However, Author Solutions told me that few people ever try to get their file back to switch platforms.

Better Business Bureau rating: A, 347 complaints in the last three years.[†††] As a relative data point, the Better Business Bureau rated Apple a B+, with 2,413 complaints in the last three years.[†††]

Blurb

Description: Up to this point, we've covered the publishing of novels and other text-heavy formats. Blurb is an author-services company that specializes in photo-heavy books like portfolios, photography books, and cookbooks.

Blurb primarily enables people to get personal copies of their books. There is an option to sell your book through the Blurb Bookstore, but this isn't the primary goal.[†††]

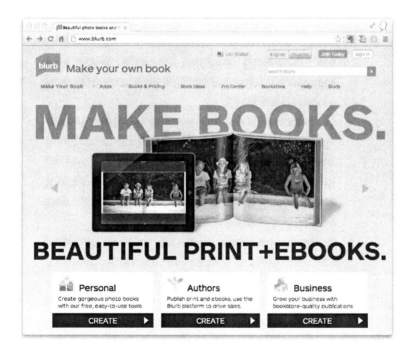

Figure 15.01. The Blurb website shows their emphasis on books with pictures.

Getting started: After you register for an account, you use a downloadable application to create and upload books. The application is called BookSmart, and it is free after registration.

Fine print:

- Pricing depends on the size of paper, type of paper stock, cover style (softcover or hardcover), number of pages (your book must be at least twenty pages long), and speed of delivery. Blurb provides a free pricing tool on its website.[†††]
- Blurb Premium Paper is available for books of 240 pages or fewer.
- Blurb doesn't charge you anything up front for its services, but if you want Blurb to keep your book online and sell it for you, you must buy at least one copy.
- Blurb ebooks are limited to the iPad. You cannot read a Blurb ebook on an Android, Nook, or Kindle. Essentially, Blurb turns a print book into a fixed-format ebook for iOS devices.[†††]
- Blurb provides a free Adobe InDesign plug-in to help you create Blurb ebooks.[†††]

Better Business Bureau rating: A+, twenty-four complaints in the last three years.[†††]

CreateSpace

Description: CreateSpace[†††] is an Amazon company that helps you publish softcover books. It is a hybrid of the author-services and print-on-demand model. You can use its free tools to create a cover, review your interior design, and solicit feedback from readers or use your own vendors and consultants. Then CreateSpace will print your book on demand and make it available through Amazon in the United States, the UK, Germany, France, Italy, and Spain, as well as make your ebook version available for Kindle.

If you need more help, you can also purchase professional services from CreateSpace that include design, editing, copywriting, and marketing. You can also increase distribution by paying $25 for "expanded distribution" to bookstores, libraries, academic institutions, distributors, and other online resellers. Again, this doesn't mean that they will "stock" your book but if someone asks for your book, they can order it.

CreateSpace manages the inventory and shipping of printed books. If you go the free-services route (most authors do), CreateSpace only makes money when your book sells. Your royalty is based on the interior design of your book, trim size, and number of pages. For example, a black-and-white softcover book, six inches by nine inches that's two hundred pages long with a $20 list price yields a per-copy royalty of $8.75. CreateSpace also offers a free royalty calculator[†††] so you can get an idea of how to price your book.

Getting started: You can publish on CreateSpace for free or purchase services to help you complete your book. Once you have an account, you can create new titles from your dashboard by clicking the "Add New Title" button. When working with a title, you can either choose an advanced setup, which presents everything on one page, or you can use the creation wizard that walks you through each step. There are four stages in the CreateSpace process: Setup, Review, Distribute, and Sales & Marketing.

Fine print:

- CreateSpace can provide a free ISBN, but we recommend that you provide your own ISBN in order to control who is listed as the publisher of your book. (Chapter 17: "How to Upload Your Book" explains ISBNs in gory detail.)
- CreateSpace's prices for black-and-white books are similar to those of Lulu (see below) and other services. However, CreateSpace's color editions are much cheaper. For example, CreateSpace charges $37 for a three-hundred-page, full-color book with a page size of 7.5 by 9.5 inches. Lulu would charge $68 for the same book.
- For print books, CreateSpace accepts PDF, Microsoft Word DOC, Microsoft Word DOCX, RTF, and TXT.
- Based on our experience, CreateSpace is fast. We uploaded print pages to CreateSpace on Christmas Day, 2012, and had the first-proof copy of *APE* on Shawn's doorstep December 27—less than forty-eight hours later.
- Unlike Lightning Source (covered in chapter 16: "How to Use Print-on-Demand Companies"), CreateSpace does not charge you for changes unless you have enabled expanded distribution.

- If Amazon sets a street price on your print book from CreateSpace, and that street price is not the result of price-matching another online reseller, then your royalty is still calculated on the original list price, not the street price. This means cheaper books for readers, high royalty for authors, and more volume for Amazon.
- Black-and-white print books must be between 28 and 878 pages. Color print books must be between 28 and 480 pages.

Better Business Bureau rating: A+, nine complaints in the last three years.[†††]

Summary

There are hundreds of author-services companies that would love your business. It's impossible to review them all, but this chapter provided a framework. Our advice is that you do as much as you can yourself (with the exception of copyediting), and only buy the services that you absolutely can't or don't want to do.

CHAPTER 16

How to Use Print-on-Demand Companies

A literary academic can no more pass a bookstore
than an alcoholic can pass a bar.

Carolyn G. Heilbrun

What and Why

This chapter explains how to use print-on-demand services to sell printed books directly to people and through resellers. Maybe it's only us, but we think it's cool to see one's book in a bookstore. Although it's never happened to Shawn or me, seeing your book in Target, Costco, or Walmart is pretty special too. Finally, when you make a speech or appearance, people will want to buy your book to get it autographed. None of this can happen unless you print your book on paper.

As the Walkerville Publishing story from chapter 11 illustrated, author-services companies can print your books, and bookstores can order them from them. However, the print quality and the profit margins of books from these services aren't always well suited to large-scale selling by you or by resellers. When you get to the point of selling thousands of copies of books, you probably need a hardcore printer, not an author-services company.

There are thousands of printers around the world. The traditional procedure is that you send a printer the files for your cover and your text, and the printer makes your book and ships copies to you. What has changed is the lead times for production. In the old days, it took weeks to get more books printed. Now it takes days, so you can order books "on demand"—that is, when you need them. As people's expectations of printing schedules increase, all printers will soon be print-on-demand.

Lightning Source

Description: We'll use a printer called Lightning Source to illustrate how this method works. There are many other printers to choose from, but Lightning Source has an international reach, so it's accessible to many authors. If you decide to go down this path, ask a few authors that you know for their recommendations.

When you print your book with Lightning Source, it's available to thirty thousand wholesalers, retailers, and booksellers in one hundred countries through Ingram Book Company. It does not offer services such as editing, cover design, layout, and marketing assistance.

Lightning Source requires a serious commitment to printing a book. There are setup costs, and there is no handholding as there is with author-services companies. You must provide a print-ready PDF and your own ISBNs.

You are in full control of the discount offered to wholesalers, retailers, and booksellers. Because of the work involved, some people might find that working directly with printing companies like Lightning Source crosses the line from being a "self-published author" to being a "publishing start-up."

The advantage is that Lightning Source offers low printing costs, which enables you to provide affordable books to a large number of readers. Lightning Source will print your book as you define it, and that's it. You have the option of softcover or hardcover, color or black-and-white.

Lightning Source offers three distribution models:

- **Print-to-Publisher**[†††] means you order copies of your book, and Lightning Source will ship the books to you, wholesalers, retailers, and warehouses. These books appear to come from you, and you pay Lightning Source for printing, handling, and shipping. You bill and collect from the recipients of the books.

- **Print-to-Order**[†††] means that Lightning Source sells your book on your behalf and pays you the difference between the wholesale price and printing costs. This option is the most applicable to self-publishers. We provide a detailed example below.

- **Print-to-Warehouse**[†††] means that Lightning Source prints your book and ships it to your warehouse for inclusion with books from other sources—also known as "cross-docking." This service is applicable to only large publishers who place large orders.

Getting started: To get started, go to Lightning Source and click the "Create a New Account" button. Unlike author-services companies, Lightning Source uses an application-approval process to weed out writers and organizations that are not likely to generate significant orders.[†††] This process takes three or four days.

The initial application with Lightning Source requires a company name and an explanation of the applicant's role within that company. You can apply as a self-publisher, but Lightning Source expects to deal with people who know their way around publishing.

When Lightning Source invites you to complete your application, they will ask for additional information, such as a tax identification number, ACH deposit information, and a credit card for payment or authorization to run a credit check so they can extend a line of credit.

Fine Print:

- The setup fee is $75. (As mentioned before, Lightning Source offers significant discounts to members of the Independent Book Publishers Association.)[†††] Revisions to your book that are not the result of an error made by Lightning Source cost $40 per file.
- Lightning Source offers both black-and-white and color printing options in all standard sizes in hardcover and softcover formats.
- Printing costs are calculated based on a number of factors including size of paper, color versus black-and-white, and method of distribution. The basic formula is Number of Pages × Cost Per Page + Unit Cost for Book = Total Print Cost.

- Black-and-white cost per page is $0.015 or $0.020, depending on the trim size for Print-to-Publisher distribution and $0.013 or $0.018 for Print-to-Order distribution.
- The cost for color printing is $0.025 or $0.030 per page depending on the trim size, and there is no discount for channel distribution.
- Softcover unit costs are $0.90 or $1.30, depending on the trim size.
- Hardcover unit cost without a dust jacket is $6. Hardcover unit cost with a dust jacket is $7.55.
- When ordering copies of your book in bulk, Lightning Source offers discounts on total print cost based on the number of units. The discounts, as of August 2012, are as follows:

  » 50–99 books: 5 percent
  » 100–249 books: 10 percent
  » 250–499 books: 20 percent
  » 500–999 books: 25 percent
  » 1,000–1,499 books: 30 percent
  » 1,500+ books: 35 percent

- Lightning Source requires that you sign a separate contract for distribution in the United States, UK/Europe, and Australia. Additionally, you must set a separate wholesale and list price for each of these distribution channels.

- Despite the fact that using Lightning Source requires a high level of commitment, we found it odd that their system does *not* allow multiple admin users on the same account. If you want multiple people to have access to the Lightning Source backend, they have to share a single account.

For more information on calculating printing costs at Lightning Source, visit APETheBook.com.

Plan A: Selling Books Yourself

Selling printed books directly to people can be a lucrative business because you would capture all the margin between what a book costs to make and what a customer pays for it. Let's do the math using Lightning Source's Print-to-Publisher model.

Suppose that you want to print five hundred copies of a two-hundred-page, black-and-white softcover novel. Here's approximately what it would cost:

- 200 pages × $0.015 per page (an intermediate price in the Print-to-Order range) = $3.00 per book
- $3.00 per book + $0.90 per book softcover unit cost = $3.90 per book
- $3.90 per book × .75 (25 percent quantity discount for five hundred copies) = $2.93 per book

Let's set the retail price at $20. If you can sell your book at the full retail price, then you make $20.00 − $2.93 = $17.07 each. This may be the case when you are not using any other resellers, so you are the only source of the book.

Let's say resellers also sell your book, so you discount your selling price by 40 percent to match the usual street price: $20.00 less 40 percent = $12.00. Then you'll make $12.00 – $2.93 = $9.07 for the books that you sell to customers. You don't have to match prices, but it is odd if you're selling your book for more than your resellers.

You can also use Lightning Source's Print-to-Order model. In this case, it will sell your $20 suggested-retail book for $10 to resellers. You will make the difference between $10.00 and $2.93, or $7.07. Here's an interesting fact: you could use CreateSpace as a print-on-demand vendor much the same way as Lightning Source's Print-to-Order model. You will make $8.75 on sales to Amazon and $4.75 on sales to Ingram, the book distributor. So in the case of selling books to Amazon, it's better to use CreateSpace (without any paid author-services features).

When you sell directly to customers, you have to consider the costs of processing orders, shipping and handling (which you can pass along to the customer), returns, lost shipments, credit-card fraud, unsold or damaged inventory, and whatever problems a retailer experiences. You need to be sly about doing this. For example, the US Postal Service provides free flat-rate shipping boxes, and you can take payments through PayPal or accept credit cards using Intuit GoPayment or Square.[†††]

Plan B: Selling Books Through Resellers

Plan B is that you do sell your book through resellers. A printer like Lightning Source can handle this for you. Here's how the math works in this scenario. You set two prices for your book: (1) The suggested retail price for customers and (2) the wholesale price resellers such as Amazon and Barnes & Noble will pay. Lightning Source calculates your revenues by subtracting the printing costs from the wholesale price.

If you set the retail price of your book at $20.00, then your wholesale price should be approximately $10.00. (Lightning Source recommends offering a 50 to 55 percent discount to attract retailers.) This means that you would make $10.00 − $3.02 = $6.98 per book.

By using Lightning Source, you have the ability to set the street price of your book because you control the margin. However, don't let this fool you: resellers don't like small margins and may refuse to order your book for customers, much less stock it.

When all the dust settles, there are three ways you can sell your printed book.

- Full retail: $16.98 profit per copy
- Discounted: $8.98 profit per copy
- Through resellers: $6.98 profit per copy

You probably cannot do both full retail and discounted because when people come to your website, they need to see only one price. You must pick one or the other method. But you can do full retail or discounted and sell through resellers at the same time. In all cases, though, your profit can be a lot more than the $2 you'll make for the Kindle ebook version.

Summary

Don't forget that many people still prefer a printed book, and ebooks account for approximately 10 percent of the US publishing business. However, you don't want to end up with a garage full of unsold books, so find a printer that will print on demand like Lightning Source or CreateSpace (without the author services).

CHAPTER 17

How to Upload Your Book

No one can make you feel inferior without your consent.

Attributed, though disputed, to Eleanor Roosevelt

Details, Details

This chapter explains the process of uploading a book to resellers and services. We'll use the Kindle Direct Publishing process since most authors want to sell their books on Amazon. First, though, let's cover the issue of ISBNs.

ISBN

Somewhere in the publishing process, unless you're going to distribute your book only through Amazon, you'll encounter the need for an ISBN for your book. (Amazon assigns its own number called an Amazon Standard Identification Number if you're not using any other resellers.) ISBN stands for International Standard Book Number. The ISBN is a unique number that identifies books and audiobooks.

One agency manages ISBNs in each country. Each agency sets its own price. For example, a government agency in Canada issues the numbers for free. In the United States, a company called Bowker issues the numbers and charges for them.[†††]

Each format of your book (hardcover, softcover, ebook, and audiobook) requires a unique ISBN. However, an ebook that you sell via Amazon, Apple, Barnes & Noble, Google Play, and Kobo are considered the same entity and require only one ISBN.

The print version of your book requires a second ISBN. If you have a softcover and a hardcover version, each format needs a separate ISBN. If you have a color version and a black-and-white version, each variation requires its own ISBN as well.

Bestseller lists such as the *New York Times* and the *Wall Street Journal* may not combine the sales figures of your ebook and printed book. Sales of softcover and hardcover are counted in different lists too. Recent changes in some of these lists provide aggregate sales ranks, but for now, most of them are still separate. Amazon also calculates separate sales rankings for Kindle and non-Kindle books.

If you write a second edition, and people can continue to buy both the first and second edition, then each edition needs an ISBN for each format of the second edition. Bowker defines an "edition" as a new version where 20 percent or more of the content has changed.

This is why you need so many ISBNs. The cost of ISBNs in the United States is $125 for one, $250 for ten, $575 for one hundred, and $1,000 for one thousand. Author-services companies can provide an ISBN for your book. However, the author-services company thereby permanently becomes the publisher of record, and this will complicate your life if you want to move your book to a different author-services company.

Also, book reviewers and libraries may conclude that a book with an author-services company as the publisher of record is a vanity-press effort and underestimate the quality of the book.

For the cost of $250, there is little reason to take any risks with another entity as the publisher of record. To buy your ISBN, go to the MyIdentifiers site of Bowker.††† You'll be asked about buying barcodes when you check out. You only need barcodes for physical books which you can get later.

Step-by-Step Kindle Direct Publishing

To familiarize you with the process of uploading a book, we'll walk you through the procedure of Kindle Direct Publishing. Other resellers use a similar procedure, so you'll be able to reuse much of your efforts.

Getting started: Determine if you want to participate in the Kindle marketing program called KDP Select.††† This is a program that involves a ninety-day exclusive that enables people to borrow your book. In return, Amazon compensates you for loaning the book and enables you to give your book away for five days. (More about KDP Select in the next chapter.)

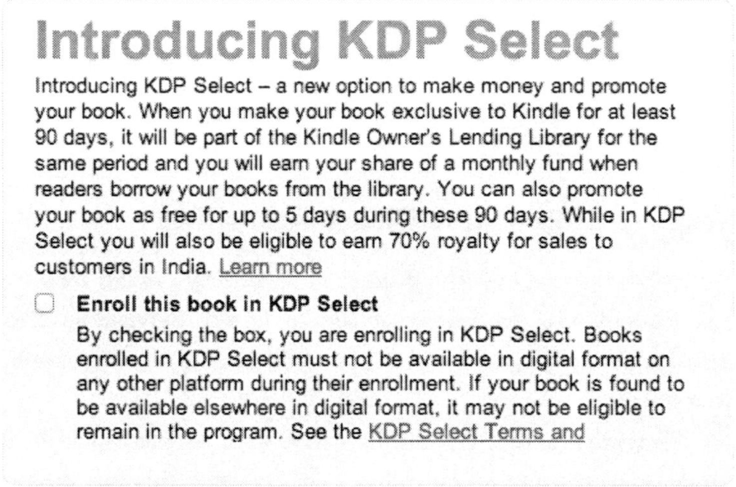

Introducing KDP Select

Introducing KDP Select – a new option to make money and promote your book. When you make your book exclusive to Kindle for at least 90 days, it will be part of the Kindle Owner's Lending Library for the same period and you will earn your share of a monthly fund when readers borrow your books from the library. You can also promote your book as free for up to 5 days during these 90 days. While in KDP Select you will also be eligible to earn 70% royalty for sales to customers in India. Learn more

☐ **Enroll this book in KDP Select**

By checking the box, you are enrolling in KDP Select. Books enrolled in KDP Select must not be available in digital format on any other platform during their enrollment. If your book is found to be available elsewhere in digital format, it may not be eligible to remain in the program. See the KDP Select Terms and

Figure 17.01. Make a KDP Select decision.

Step 1: Enter basic information such as your book's title, description, and ISBN. Many people refer to this information as the "metadata" of a book. The form says that an ISBN is optional because Amazon will assign a number ("Amazon Standard Identification Number") if you aren't selling your book through other resellers.

The book description is one of the most important pieces of writing you'll do for your book. Here are the three C's of optimal book descriptions:

- **Clear.** People are going to skim the description, not read it as if it's Holy Gospel. In a few seconds, people need to get the gist of your book.
- **Compelling.** Now that people understand your book and find the topic interesting, the next step is to compel them to read it. The way to do this is to explain how your book adds value to their lives.

- **Clever.** This is the place to utilize the commonly used keywords for your book's genre to aid discoverability when people search.

To show you what we mean, here's the description of *APE* that we used for our Kindle submission:

In 2011 the publisher of my *New York Times* bestseller, *Enchantment*, could not fill an order for 500 ebook copies of the book. Because of this experience, I self-published my next book, *What the Plus!* and learned firsthand that self-publishing is a complex, confusing, and idiosyncratic process. As Steve Jobs said, "There must be a better way."

With Shawn Welch, a tech wizard, I wrote *APE* to help people take control of their writing careers by publishing their books. The thesis of *APE* is simple but powerful: a successful self-publisher must fill three roles: Author, Publisher, and Entrepreneur.

We call this "artisanal publishing."

Artisanal publishing features writers who love their craft and who control every aspect of the process from beginning to end. In this new approach, writers are no longer at the mercy of large, traditional publishers, and readers will have more books to read.

APE is 300 pages of tactical and practical inspiration. People who want a hype-filled, get-rich-quick book should look elsewhere. On the other hand, if you want a comprehensive and realistic guide to self-publishing, *APE* is for you.

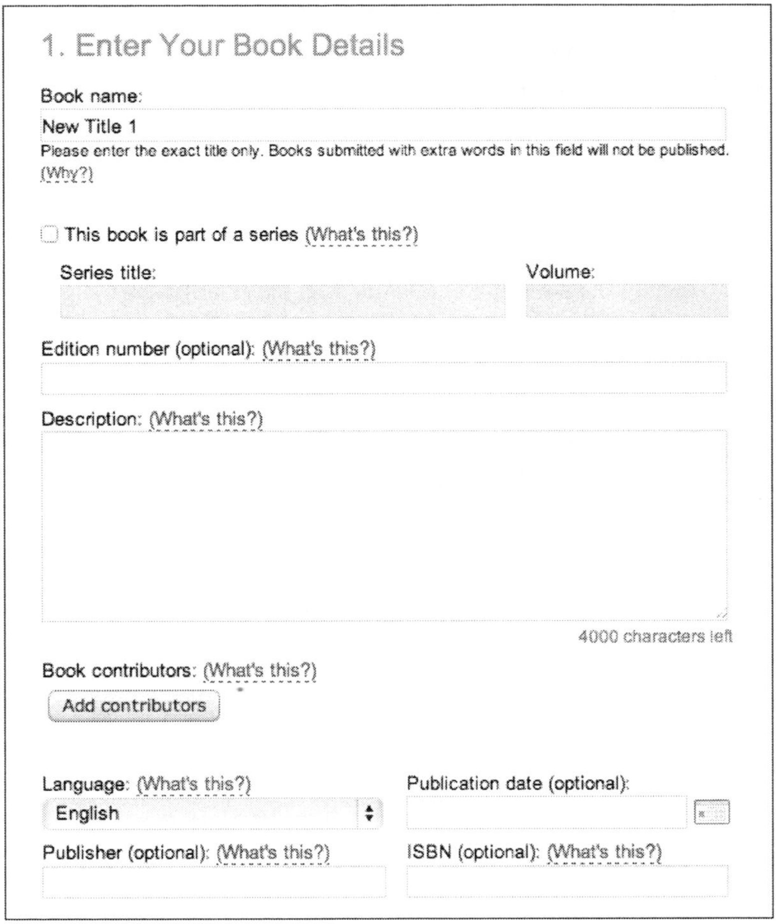

1. Enter Your Book Details

Book name:

New Title 1

Please enter the exact title only. Books submitted with extra words in this field will not be published. (Why?)

☐ This book is part of a series (What's this?)

Series title: Volume:

Edition number (optional): (What's this?)

Description: (What's this?)

4000 characters left

Book contributors: (What's this?)

Add contributors

Language: (What's this?)   Publication date (optional):

English   ⬍

Publisher (optional): (What's this?)   ISBN (optional): (What's this?)

Figure 17.02. Entering basic details.

Step 2: Confirm that you own the publishing rights.

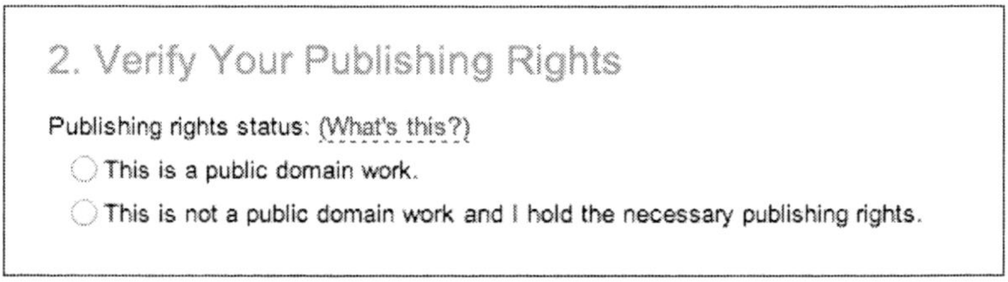

---

2. Verify Your Publishing Rights

Publishing rights status: (What's this?)

⭘ This is a public domain work.

⭘ This is not a public domain work and I hold the necessary publishing rights.

Figure 17.03. Verifying publishing rights.

Step 3: Choose up to two categories for your book. Think of a category as the online equivalent of the sections and shelves in a brick-and-mortar bookstore.

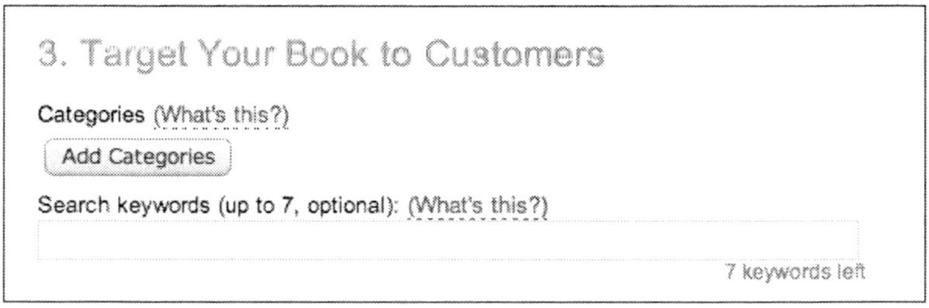

---

3. Target Your Book to Customers

Categories (What's this?)

[Add Categories]

Search keywords (up to 7, optional): (What's this?)

7 keywords left

Figure 17.04. Targeting customers by picking categories.

Step 4: Upload your book cover. The recommended size is 2,500 pixels by 1,563 pixels. Kindle Direct Publishing accepts JPEG and TIFF files.

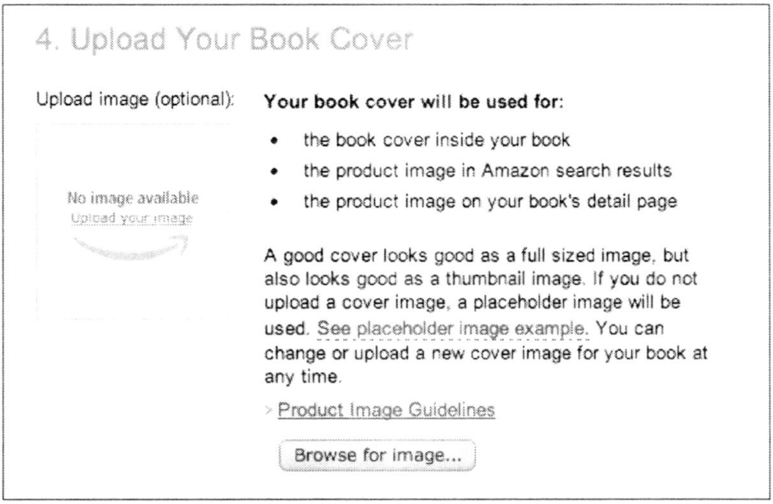

4. Upload Your Book Cover

Upload image (optional):

No image available
Upload your image

Your book cover will be used for:

- the book cover inside your book
- the product image in Amazon search results
- the product image on your book's detail page

A good cover looks good as a full sized image, but also looks good as a thumbnail image. If you do not upload a cover image, a placeholder image will be used. See placeholder image example. You can change or upload a new cover image for your book at any time.

> Product Image Guidelines

    Browse for image...

Figure 17.05. Uploading the cover of your book.

Step 5: Choose whether to add digital rights management (DRM) to your book. We recommend that you do not enable digital rights management because it inconveniences readers and doesn't stop pirates. There's more information about DRM in chapter 20: "Self-Publishing Issues."

Upload your file in Word, HTML, MOBI, EPUB, plain text, RTF, or PDF format. We recommend that you upload a MOBI file to minimize the chances of wonky conversion.

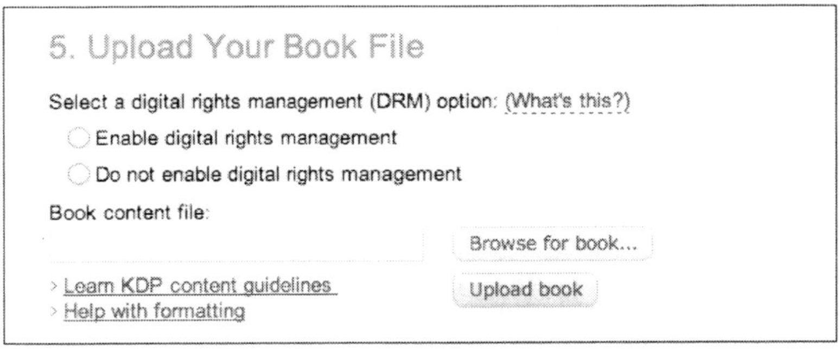

5. Upload Your Book File

Select a digital rights management (DRM) option: (What's this?)

◯ Enable digital rights management

◯ Do not enable digital rights management

Book content file:

Browse for book...

› Learn KDP content guidelines

› Help with formatting

Upload book

Figure 17.06. Uploading your book after selecting a digital rights management option.

Step 6: Preview your book to ensure that it looks the way you want.

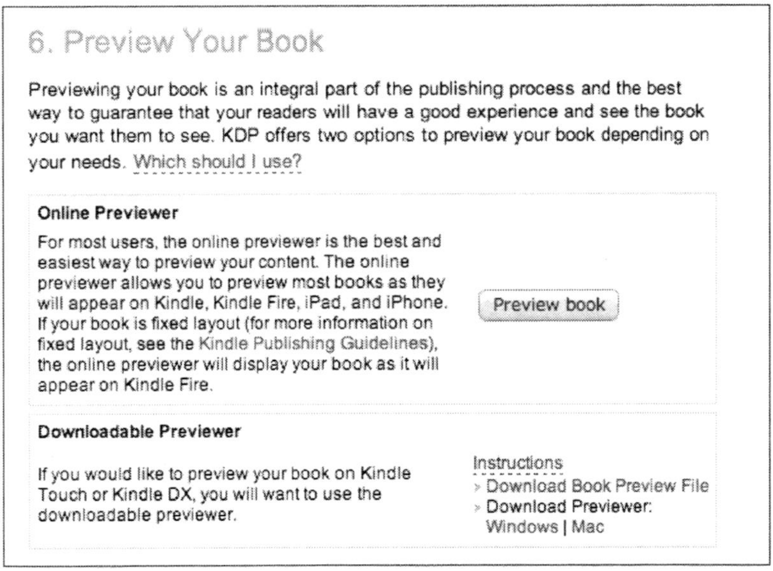

6. Preview Your Book

Previewing your book is an integral part of the publishing process and the best way to guarantee that your readers will have a good experience and see the book you want them to see. KDP offers two options to preview your book depending on your needs. Which should I use?

Online Previewer

For most users, the online previewer is the best and easiest way to preview your content. The online previewer allows you to preview most books as they will appear on Kindle, Kindle Fire, iPad, and iPhone. If your book is fixed layout (for more information on fixed layout, see the Kindle Publishing Guidelines), the online previewer will display your book as it will appear on Kindle Fire.

Preview book

Downloadable Previewer

If you would like to preview your book on Kindle Touch or Kindle DX, you will want to use the downloadable previewer.

Instructions

› Download Book Preview File

› Download Previewer: Windows | Mac

Figure 17.07. Previewing your book.

Step 7: Select the regions of the world where you own the rights to your book. Since you're self-publishing, you probably own world-wide rights.

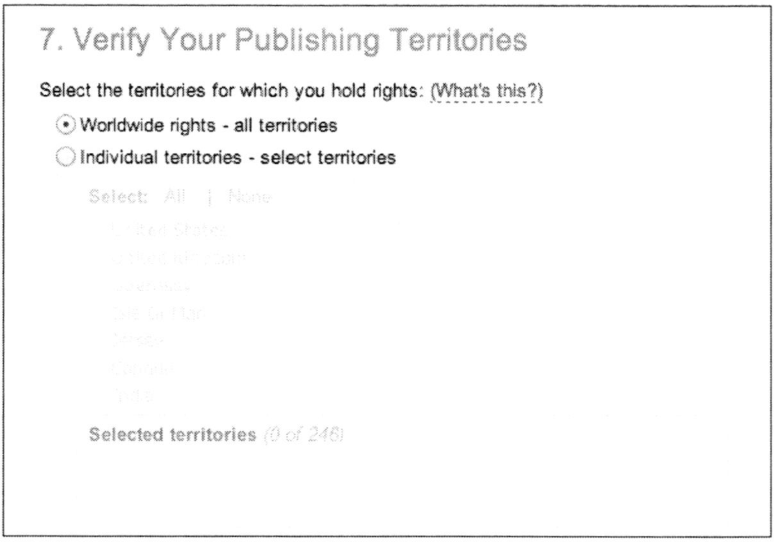

7. Verify Your Publishing Territories

Select the territories for which you hold rights: (What's this?)

- ⦿ Worldwide rights - all territories
- ◯ Individual territories - select territories

  Select: All | None

  United States
  Great Britain
  Germany
  South Africa
  Japan
  Canada
  India

  Selected territories (0 of 246)

Figure 17.08. Selecting your territories.

Step 8: Select your royalty rate and set prices. Don't forget that the 70 percent royalty rate incurs delivery charges and the 35 percent rate doesn't. You can set prices for each country or peg your price to the US price.

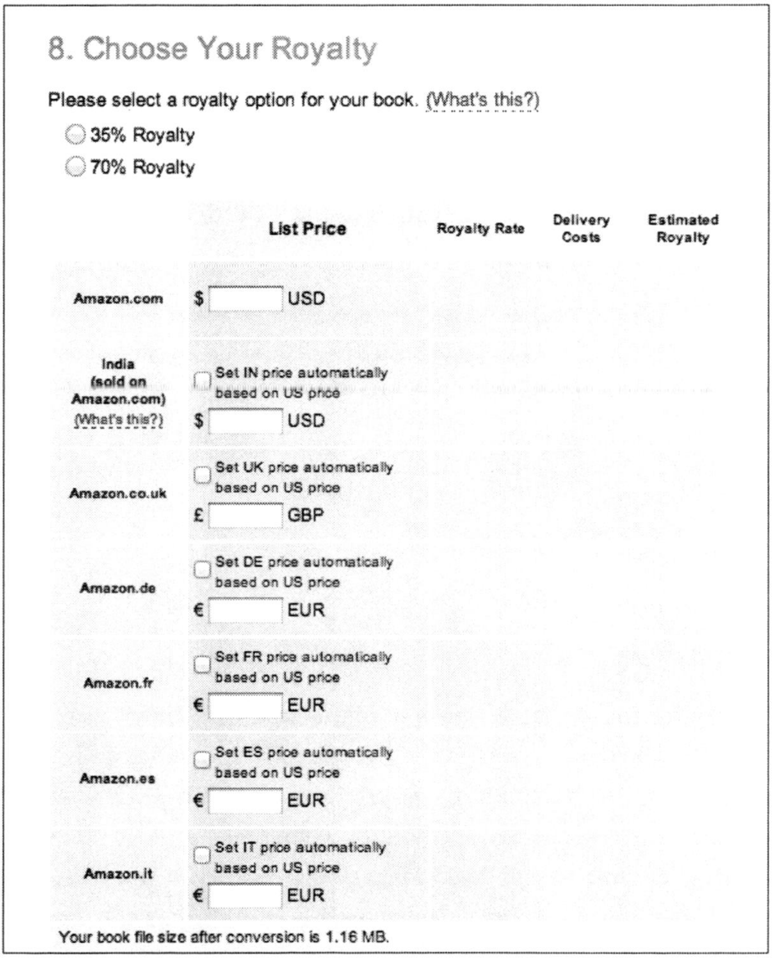

8. Choose Your Royalty

Please select a royalty option for your book. (What's this?)

35% Royalty

70% Royalty

	List Price	Royalty Rate	Delivery Costs	Estimated Royalty
Amazon.com	$ USD			
India (sold on Amazon.com) (What's this?)	Set IN price automatically based on US price $ USD			
Amazon.co.uk	Set UK price automatically based on US price £ GBP			
Amazon.de	Set DE price automatically based on US price € EUR			
Amazon.fr	Set FR price automatically based on US price € EUR			
Amazon.es	Set ES price automatically based on US price € EUR			
Amazon.it	Set IT price automatically based on US price € EUR			

Your book file size after conversion is 1.16 MB.

Figure 17.09. Selecting the royalty rate and setting prices.

Step 9: Determine whether people can lend their books. You can opt out of this if you selected the 35 percent royalty rate and have not participated in any other reseller's lending program.

9. Kindle Book Lending

☑ Allow lending for this book (Details)

Figure 17.10. Making your Kindle Book Lending decision.

Step 10: Confirm that you have the right to publish the book and agree to the terms.

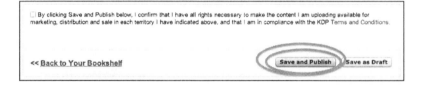

Figure 17.11. Publishing your book!

Summary

Every format of a book needs a unique ISBN; all ebook platforms (Kindle, iBookstore, Nook) count as one format and thus only needs one ISBN. The hundreds of self-publishing vendors work in pretty similar ways: provide information about your book, upload the cover, upload the manuscript, and in less than a week, you're in business. The most important step in this process is crafting the book description, so spend a few hours making it as compelling as you can.

CHAPTER 18

How to Price Your Book

Being rich is not about how much money you have or how many homes you own; it's the freedom to buy any book you want without looking at the price and wondering if you can afford it.

John Waters, *Role Models*

If Only It Were Simple

This chapter explains how to price your book. We wish pricing were a science so that we could tell you exactly what to do. Unfortunately, it's a complex dance between reducing sales by charging too much and failing to maximize revenue by charging too little.

All we can do is lay out the variables so that you can make an informed decision. Fortunately, as a self-publisher, you can test and change your decision if it's not working.

Pricing Variables

There are six major variables that affect the price of your book. Here is a discussion of each to help you decide on a strategy.

Costs. There are two kinds of costs: preparation and production. Preparation costs include such processes as design, editing, and layout. You might pay them only once, but nonetheless, you need to recoup them.

Production costs refer to how much it costs to make copies. If you're publishing only an ebook, the cost per unit is almost zero. If you're printing your book, you'll incur hard costs such as paper, printing, binding, and shipping.

Economic conditions. How is the job market for your target customers? While your book's price is probably one or two Starbucks cappuccinos, economic conditions matter to people and influence their buying decisions.

Brand. How strong is your brand? How many people know about you? Simplifying the issue, here are the most common conditions:

- First-time author without an established base of readers. Implication: charge less.
- First-time author with an established base of fans and high visibility. Implication: charge more.
- Repeat author with a proven record and established base of readers. Implication: charge even more.

Competition. How much does the competition charge for books in your genre? You cannot charge the same price as well-established authors such as J. K. Rowling. You should look at authors who are at the same stage as you.

Goals. What are your goals for your book? Here are the most common:

- Maximize short-term (six months to a year) revenue. Implication: charge more.
- Maximize long-term (a year or more) revenue. Implication: charge less.
- Establish yourself as a sector expert. Implication: charge less.
- Build a base of readers for future works. Implication: charge less.
- Spread your ideas. Implication: charge less.

Pricing philosophy. What's your pricing philosophy? First, let's dismiss "I worked hard on this book, so it's worth lots of money." It doesn't matter how hard you work. What matters is what people are willing to pay.

These are the common pricing philosophies:

- High price connotes high quality. Low price connotes low quality. Implication: charge more.
- High price connotes cluelessness. Low price connotes awareness. Implication: charge less.
- High price connotes greed. Low price connotes empathy. Implication: charge less.
- The relationship between price and quality is random. Implication: take your best shot and change the price if it's not working.

Pricing Strategies

Weighing all these variables is a challenge, but there's no right and wrong answer. There's only what works and what doesn't work. Here are some strategies to consider:

- Start at a low price—for example, $0.99 or even free—to achieve critical mass and bestseller status, and then raise the price to $2.99 or more.
- Give away one format of your book in the hopes that people will pay for another format to improve the reading experience. You could charge nothing for a PDF version and sell every other format.
- Charge a premium price—for example, $9.99 or more—because you have a small audience but it's one that cherishes your information. For example, you could probably charge $99 for an Asian American mother's guide to getting a kid into Stanford. Over time reduce the price.
- Charge a premium price, but run price promotions. The high price communicates high value, so getting a deal feels valuable.

KDP Select

Our friends at Kindle Direct Publishing offer another kind of pricing paradigm. It's a program we mentioned in the previous chapter called KDP Select.[†††] In exchange for a ninety-day Amazon exclusive, your book goes into the "Lending Library" and you can offer the book for free for up to five days.

People who own Kindle devices (not Kindle apps running on other devices) and who are Amazon Prime members can participate in this program. Participants can borrow books from a collection of 180,000 titles to read on their Kindle devices. Authors in the Lending Library program also receive a portion of the Kindle Owners' Lending Library fund based on how many times people borrowed their book.

David Kazzie, author of *The Jackpot,* provided an illustrative experience with KDP Select. *The Jackpot* was dead in the water—it sold twenty-one copies on Amazon and one copy on Barnes & Noble's website from December 1, 2011, to January 24, 2012. He pulled his book from all the other resellers and joined the KDP Select Program.

He decided to give the book away for two days, and people downloaded 25,000 copies of the book from January 25 to January 26. On January 27, the book was no longer free, but sales rocketed. It started the day ranked around #225,000 and ended up at #76 that night.

The Jackpot spent more than a week on the Top 100 Kindle Bestseller List, rising as high as #34, and attracted dozens of five-star reviews. Amazon featured *The Jackpot* in its "Big Deal" Kindle promotion in March, and seven months later, the book continues to sell at a rate far better than it did before Kazzie enrolled it in the KDP Select Program.

David attributes the success of this promotion to the follow-on effects of the free offer. For example, *The Jackpot* started to appear in people's "Customers Also Bought" list and on Amazon's "Most Popular" lists. In addition, websites covering Kindle news listed it as a free book.

Summary

Pricing is an art, not a science. There are many factors involved to consider and many theories to test. However, one of the advantages of self-publishing is that you can alter your pricing to see how it affects sales, so our recommendation is that you take your best guess and adjust from there. We think it's better to guess low and work up; at least this way more people will read your book as you find the right price.

CHAPTER 19

How to Create Audio and Foreign Language Versions of Your Book

If I am selling to you, I speak your language.
If I am buying, *dann müssen Sie Deutsch sprechen.*

Willy Brandt

Different Strokes

This chapter explains how to publish your book in different formats and languages. A traditional publisher handles these issues for authors. As a self-publisher, you have to manage both processes for yourself to maximize your revenue.

Audio for Customers

My friends love to listen to books while they exercise or drive. I never do this because I like to read a book, not hear it. However, customers should be able to access books in any way they want. Here are three organizations that produce audiobooks:

- **Audible** markets a collection of approximately 100,000 audio versions of books. When you buy an audiobook on Apple's iTunes store, it's usually from Audible. Amazon bought Audible in 2008.[†††]
- **Books on Tape** is part of Random House. It sells readings on CDs. A book can fill three or more CDs. Prices range from $25 to $100 per book.[†††]
- **OverDrive** is a digital content distributor of ebooks and audiobooks that focuses on the school and library market.[†††]

Audio for Authors

You can produce an audiobook version using a service from Audible called the Audiobook Creation Exchange.[†††] Here are the steps that you go through:

- Confirm that you own the audio rights to your book.
- Create a profile with a short description of your book, your thoughts on the best kind of narrator, and a short excerpt.
- Post your book. Producers and narrators will see your post and hopefully express interest. You can also listen to sample narrations and hold a "casting call."
- Audition producers and narrators and then pick one. Also, an audiobook publisher may see your post and contact you to buy audio rights.
- Cut a deal. The service provides the paperwork and mechanism. You can choose to pay on a per-hour basis or share royalties.

Amazon will link the audio version of your book to the details page of your Kindle or printed book so that customers are aware of your available formats.

Another method to create an audio version is to narrate the book yourself. Then you can sell the audiobook through Audible too. Reading your own book helps you form a close personal bond with your readers. However, this requires a good reading voice and as much as fifty hours of work.

Remember: an audio version of your book counts as another format, so you will need another ISBN for it.

Translation

Translation of your book involves weighing the risk and reward of each geographic market. It costs approximately $0.10 per word to translate a book from English to most languages. *APE* has 63,000 words, so it would cost $6,300 to translate it. Assuming we would make $2 per copy in each language, would we sell three thousand copies to break even in each language? I doubt it.

When it comes to foreign rights, traditional publishers offer advantages because they have established relationships with publishers around the world. By contrast, one strategy for self-publishers is to market the hell out of your book in your home country and then hope that foreign publishers contact *you* to buy foreign rights.

The typical deal with a foreign publisher is that they pay an advance of a few thousand dollars and then manage the translation process. All you do is cash checks. The challenge in this scenario, however, is coming to a legal agreement with strangers working at publishing companies thousands of miles away.

If you decide to translate your book yourself, these practices can help you do it in a quick and cost-effective way:

- **Avoid culture-specific metaphors and analogies.** You can make translation easier by avoiding troublesome phrases. For example, expecting people around the world to understand a "Hail Mary pass," "going top-shelf," or "bowling a chinaman" isn't going to work.
- **Use pictures and graphics.** These elements can communicate ideas and information without words.
- **Ask authors.** Authors in similar genres might know which languages merit translation. Also ask them how they got their books translated.
- **Ask your author-services company.** Your author-services company may offer translation as a service.
- **Don't scrimp.** A poor translation can do you more damage than not translating your book at all. Either do it right or don't do it at all.

Here is the ranking of the twenty-five most populous countries in the world according to the CIA website[†††] (as American taxpayers, Shawn and I thought we should get something from the CIA):

1. China 1,343,239,923 July 2012 est.
2. India 1,205,073,612 July 2012 est.
3. United States 313,847,465 July 2012 est.
4. Indonesia 248,645,008 July 2012 est.
5. Brazil 199,321,413 NA
6. Pakistan 190,291,129 July 2012 est.
7. Nigeria 170,123,740 NA
8. Bangladesh 161,083,804 July 2012 est.
9. Russia 142,517,670 July 2012 est.
10. Japan 127,368,088 July 2012 est.
11. Mexico 114,975,406 July 2012 est.

12. Philippines 103,775,002 July 2012 est.
13. Vietnam 91,519,289 July 2012 est.
14. Ethiopia 91,195,675 NA
15. Egypt 83,688,164 July 2012 est.
16. Germany 81,305,856 July 2012 est.
17. Turkey 79,749,461 July 2012 est.
18. Iran 78,868,711 July 2012 est.
19. Congo, Democratic Republic of the 73,599,190 NA
20. Thailand 67,091,089 NA
21. France 65,630,692 NA
22. United Kingdom 63,047,162 July 2012 est.
23. Italy 61,261,254 July 2012 est.
24. Burma 54,584,650 NA
25. Korea, South 48,860,500 July 2012 est.

Another way to look at this is in terms of the number of people who speak a language. Here's the ranking, according to Wikipedia:[†††]

1. Mandarin 935 million, 14.1%, China, Taiwan, Malaysia, Singapore (part of Chinese)
2. Spanish 387 million, 5.85%, Hispanic America, Spain, United States, Equatorial Guinea
3. English 365 million, 5.52%, Australia, Canada, Ireland, New Zealand, United Kingdom, United States, South Africa, Isle of Man, Jersey, Guernsey, Falkland Islands
4. Hindi 295 million, 4.46%, India (includes approx. 100 million speakers of other Hindi languages)
5. Arabic 280 million, 4.23%, Northern Africa, Middle East (a language family, not a language)
6. Portuguese 204 million, 3.08%, Angola, Brazil, Cape Verde, East Timor, Guinea-Bissau, Macao, Mozambique, Portugal, São Tomé and Príncipe

7. Bengali 202 million, 3.05%, Bangladesh, West Bengal (India), Tripura (India)

8. Russian 160 million, 2.42%, Russia, former Republics of the Soviet Union, Mongolia, Israel

9. Japanese 127 million, 1.92%, Japan

10. Punjabi 95.5 million, 1.44%, Punjab region (Pakistan, India)

11. German 92.1 million, 1.39%, Austria, Belgium (Eupen-Malmedy) Germany, Luxembourg, Liechtenstein, Switzerland, South Tirol (in Italy)

12. Javanese 82.4 million, 1.25%, Java (Indonesia)

13. Wu 79.5 million, 1.2%, Shanghai (China) Part of Chinese

14. Indonesian/Malay 76.9 million, 1.16%, Indonesia, Malaysia

15. Telugu 75.9 million, 1.15%, Andhra Pradesh (India)

16. Vietnamese 75.6 million, 1.14%, Vietnam

17. Korean 75.5 million, 1.14%, North Korea, South Korea

18. French 73.8 million, 1.12%, Belgium (Wallonia, Brussels), Canada (particularly Quebec, New Brunswick and Eastern parts of Ontario), France, Switzerland

19. Marathi 72.9 million, 1.1%, Maharashtra (India)

20. Tamil 70.0 million, 1.06%, Sri Lanka, Singapore, Tamil Nadu (India), Malaysia, Mauritius

21. Urdu 65.6 million, 0.99%, Pakistan, India (mutually intelligible with Hindi)

22. Turkish 62.6 million, 0.95%, Turkey, Greece, Bulgaria

23. Italian 59.4 million, 0.9%, Italy, Switzerland, San Marino

24. Cantonese 59.2 million, 0.89%, Hong Kong and Guangdong (part of Chinese)

25. Thai 56.2 million, 0.85%, Thailand

Population and number of speakers are only two factors. Other important factors include the level of literacy, relevance of your book, people's ability to pay, and intellectual property laws.

Summary

We hate leaving any money on the table, so translating a book and creating an audiobook version are interesting to us. However, both these processes are expensive and time consuming. In most cases, traditional publishers don't rush these versions to market either. This is one area where we recommend that you take a cue from their practices.

CHAPTER 20

Self-Publishing Issues

I love deadlines. I love the whooshing
noise they make as they go by.

Douglas Adams, *The Salmon of Doubt*

Details, Details

This chapter examines publishing issues such as rip-offs, copyright, digital rights management (DRM), libraries, work-for-hire documents, and revisions. These topics are often hidden from authors working with traditional publishers, but you'll have to encounter them head-on.

Rip-offs

The allure of publishing a book is so powerful that unsuspecting writers overpay for services or allow unscrupulous companies to rip them off.

We're not referring to situations where you paid a fair price only to find out that the editor, copyeditor, or cover designer was mediocre. That's your fault for making a poor choice. We are not referring to paying for services that you don't have the time or inclination to perform yourself. Value is in the eye of the beholder.

We're talking about rip-offs involving grotesque overpayment and purposeful deceit. Here are the warning signs of an impending rip-off:

- **Get-rich-quick.** Does the company's website and promotional material feel like they're promising ways to get rich quick? Self-publishing is not the way to get rich quick, and anyone who tells you that is either a liar, a crook, or an idiot. Turn on your bull-shiitake detector in this situation.

- **Payment up front.** A legitimate publisher will never ask you for money up front to publish your book. The whole concept of an advance is for the publisher to pay *you* up front, not vice versa.

  Avoid independent consultants and contractors who ask for 100 percent payment in advance for services. The most you should pay is 50 percent up front. Upon acceptance of the work, pay the final 50 percent. This is fair to both parties.

  You may have to pay companies in advance for services. Theoretically, they are more established so the likelihood of them botching the job or disappearing is minimal. Still, try to pay up front for as little as possible.

- **Total fees exceeding $4,000.** If you're about to pay any entity (especially author-services companies) more than $4,000, step back and evaluate your decision. You may pay a total of $4,000 for all services (content editing, copyediting, cover design, layout design, and production), but there are few individual services in self-publishing that should cost more than $4,000.

- **Guaranteed marketing and blog exposure.** No one can guarantee reviews in publications such as the *New York Times* or *Publishers Weekly.* No one can guarantee that bloggers who matter will review your book. If you want dozens of reviews in important blogs and publications, (a) write a good book, and (b) start developing relationships with reviewers and bloggers right now.
- **Minimum copies from a printer.** This is a buy-on-demand from a print-on-demand world. If you're a novice author, place your first order for twenty copies: one for you, one for your parents, and eighteen for friends. Sure, the per-copy price when you order five thousand copies is a lot cheaper, but you only need this many if you can sell them.

  Printers like Lightning Source work so fast these days that you should not fear going out of stock unless your book requires special binding or paper, and it's right before Christmas. And don't forget the Espresso Book Machine for a handful of copies.

Typically crooks and bozos do not advertise that they're crooks and bozos, so you need ways of checking out vendors:

- Search in Google for the "[name of the company] + complaints."
- Ask if anyone in your social-media circles has used or heard about the company.
- Search for the company on the Better Business Bureau website.[†††]
- Search for the company at Writer Beware and Preditors and Editors.[†††]

Finally, if you do get ripped off, you should let your fellow authors know so that they can avoid the same fate.

Copyright

We were going to summarize copyright law for you, but the United States Copyright Office has a great FAQ, so here it is verbatim. (How's that for irony?)

Q: What is copyright?

A: Copyright is a form of protection grounded in the U.S. Constitution and granted by law for original works of authorship fixed in a tangible medium of expression. Copyright covers both published and unpublished works.

Q: What does copyright protect?

A: Copyright, a form of intellectual property law, protects original works of authorship including literary, dramatic, musical, and artistic works, such as poetry, novels, movies, songs, computer software, and architecture. Copyright does not protect facts, ideas, systems, or methods of operation, although it may protect the way these things are expressed. See Circular 1, Copyright Basics, section "What Works Are Protected?".[†††]

Q: How is a copyright different from a patent or a trademark?

A: Copyright protects original works of authorship, while a patent protects inventions or discoveries. Ideas and discoveries are not protected by the copyright law, although the way in which they are expressed may be. A trademark protects words, phrases, symbols, or designs identifying the source of the goods or services of one party and distinguishing them from those of others.

Q: When is my work protected?

A: Your work is under copyright protection the moment it is created and fixed in a tangible form that it is perceptible either directly or with the aid of a machine or device.

Q: Do I have to register with your office to be protected?

A: No. In general, registration is voluntary. Copyright exists from the moment the work is created. You will have to register, however, if you wish to bring a lawsuit for infringement of a U.S. work. See Circular 1, Copyright Basics, section Copyright Registration."

Q: Why should I register my work if copyright protection is automatic?

A: Registration is recommended for a number of reasons. Many choose to register their works because they wish to have the facts of their copyright on the public record and have a certificate of registration. Registered works may be eligible for statutory damages and attorney's fees in successful litigation. Finally, if registration occurs within five years of publication, it is considered prima facie evidence in a court of law. See Circular 1, Copyright Basics, section "Copyright Registration" and Circular 38b, Highlights of Copyright Amendments contained in the Uruguay Round Agreements Act (URAA), on non-U.S. works.[†††]

Q: I've heard about a "poor man's copyright." What is it?

A: The practice of sending a copy of your own work to yourself is sometimes called a "poor man's copyright." There is no provision in the copyright law regarding any such type of protection, and it is not a substitute for registration.

Q: Is my copyright good in other countries?

A: The United States has copyright relations with most countries throughout the world, and as a result of these agreements, we honor each other's citizens' copyrights. However, the United States does not have such copyright relationships with every country. For a listing of countries and the nature of their copyright relations with the United States, see Circular 38a, International Copyright Relations of the United States.

Q: Does my work have to be published to be protected?

A: Publication is not necessary for copyright protection.

The bottom line is that your book is automatically copyrighted, but if you have nothing better to do, you can register it. It only costs $35.[III] However, we doubt that you'll have the time or resources to sue for statutory damages. And even if you win, we doubt that you'll collect the damages. The entities that have money can probably out-litigate you, and they are unlikely to purposely violate your copyright.

Shawn and I have never registered any of our past books. When we have encountered file-sharing sites distributing illegal copies of our books, we've told our publishers, and their response has been "There's nothing we can really do about it."

The flip side of copyright issues is when you violate the copyrights of others. It's easy to avoid hypocrisy:

- Cite the source.
- Observe the Creative Commons rules.
- Ask for permission or purchase the rights to use artwork.
- Buy stock photos instead of simply using images that you find on the web.
- Don't quote song lyrics. Songs are tricky. Even one line might violate copyright law. They're not worth the trouble.

DRM

"DRM" stands for "digital rights management"—or more realistically, "delusions of rights management." It's the concept that large companies can create systems that hackers cannot break. If this is a race, our money is on the hackers.

Most online ebook resellers have their own DRM features built into their systems. Amazon and Apple, however, offer the choice of adding more DRM for your books. Our advice is to decline these offers and err on the side of too little DRM for these reasons:

- DRM inconveniences honest people.
- DRM doesn't stop dishonest people.
- Even if you could stop the dishonest people, they won't buy your book.
- Even dishonest people, if they like your book, may tell other people to buy and read your book.
- You should focus on writing a book that's worth stealing and marketing it so that the world knows about it.

As my mother used to tell me, "Don't worry about stuff that you can't do anything about." Or, as George Carlin said, "Don't sweat the petty things and don't pet the sweaty things."

Loaning and Borrowing Ebooks

I heard a story, perhaps apocryphal, that members of a book club in Colorado Springs, Colorado, lend books to one another by swapping Kindle devices. Besides this simple but effective method, there are several other methods for people to borrow ebooks:

- **Library loans.** A company called OverDrive[†††] provides a loan system for libraries. People can go to its website, enter a ZIP code, and find local libraries that lend ebooks. As a publisher, you can sell your book to OverDrive, which in turn sells it to libraries and schools. People with Kindle or Nook tablets can also use OverDrive's system with public libraries.[†††]

  OverDrive aside, publishers and libraries haven't figured out how to lend ebooks. As we mentioned before, HarperCollins forces libraries to buy another copy once the library has lent the book twenty-six times.

  The problem is that publishers are afraid too many people will borrow the one copy of the ebook. I don't know how this is so different from selling libraries one printed copy of the book, but there are many things publishers do that are hard to comprehend.

- **Person-to-person loans.** Owners of Kindle books can lend them to people for fourteen days.[†††] During this period, the owner cannot read the book, and they can only lend a book once. Publishers decide which of their books are eligible for loans. Owning a Kindle device is not necessary; people can read borrowed books on any tablet with the Kindle app. Barnes & Noble has a similar program called LendMe.

- **Amazon-to-people loans.** The Kindle Owners' Lending Library enables people to borrow books if they own a Kindle device and are a member of Amazon Prime.[†††] Data suggests that people who borrow books go on to buy more books, which may influence you to participate in this program.[†††]

Our attitude is that more lending is better because it generates word-of-mouth advertising. Also, we feel a moral obligation to support libraries because of how they opened up the world for us when we were young.

The upside of library, Amazon-customer-to-person, and Amazon-to-person lending is greater than the downside of too many people borrowing our books instead of buying them. Truly, if thousands of people start borrowing and lending your book, you probably have a huge bestseller on your hands, so don't get paranoid.

Work-for-Hire Agreements

You need to structure your relationships with professional editors and designers to complete your book, so I asked the folks at LawPivot[†††] to explain the key concepts of work-for-hire agreements. Inder Comar, an attorney who works with LawPivot, drafted a template that we provide at APETheBook.com, and Nitin Gupta, founder of the company, provided this explanation:

- The Company receiving the intellectual property (IP) should use a cautionary approach to the IP assignment. In addition to a clause which assigns ownership of the Work to the Company (Section 2.1), other clauses should confirm that the project is a "work-for-hire" (Section 2.2) and that the Contractor is bound to help the Company perfect the assignment in case of any trouble (Section 2.3). In the sample provided, there are at least three contractual provisions the Company can point to that will ensure the Contractor assigns the intellectual property to the Company.

- The Contractor must protect his or her interests by demanding kill fees, such that the Contractor is entitled to compensation even if the project is canceled (half compensation) or after the project is completed (full compensation) (Section 3.1).

- Both sides should agree to settle issues outside of court. An arbitration clause may provide that both sides agree to use an arbitrator in the event of a fee dispute (Section 9.1).

- The Contractor should require that the Company pay legal fees incurred *prior* to any arbitration (Section 9.2.). This gives the Contractor greater protection in the event that the Company walks away without properly compensating the Contractor. In addition, the agreement should permit the Contractor to seek injunctive relief from a relevant court prohibiting the Company from using the Work (Section 9.3).

- Mutual representations and warranties are important. The Contractor should represent and warrant that it owns the Work and can assign the Work upon completion, among other things (Section

5.1). The Company should represent and warrant that it will defend the Contractor from any claims arising out of its use of the Work (Section 5.2). Both sides can and should consider purchasing insurance to protect against litigation or other claims, and perhaps splitting insurance deductibles.

Revisions

No matter how much crowdsourcing and professional copyediting you use, your book will have mistakes in it. The question is what you do once people discover and report the mistakes. There are two schools of thought.

First, there's "Fire and forget." Once you've published a book, you're done. You never want to touch it again. At best, you'll compile a list of mistakes and fix them whenever you get around to it, but like a fish giving birth, you let your young ones swim off to find their own destiny.

Second, there's "Relentless pursuit of perfection." You can't stand the thought of people finding mistakes in your book. Errors embarrass and insult you. You want to update your book every time someone reports a mistake.

I'm a "relentless pursuit of perfection" kind of guy. I hate that people might think I'm incompetent because there are mistakes in my book. Self-publishing is a godsend for people like me because all we have to do is fire up Word, make the corrections, convert the file, and redeploy it to online resellers. In a day or so, the new version is for sale. We can also upload a new file to our print-on-demand supplier, pay a service charge, and print the latest, greatest version on paper, too.

For example, I released *What the Plus!* on March 9, 2012. On April 11, 2012, Google modified the functionality and user interface of Google+. This required me to rewrite approximately 10 percent of the book and replace approximately 105 of the 110 pictures, too. (I replaced most of the pictures because I hate when what a reader sees on a website doesn't match the screenshot in a book.)

In this process of updating *What the Plus!*, Shawn and I learned a few things about revising a Kindle Direct Publishing (Amazon) ebook:

- If you release a revision as a "new" book with a different ISBN, the comments, ratings, and ranking of the original book do not transfer. Amazon considers it a brand-new book, so you lose whatever marketing juice you accumulated.
- When you make "critical" changes to your book, you should contact the Kindle Direct Publishing folks using the "Contact Us" links on the website. Then Kindle Direct Publishing will send e-mail notification of these changes. Customers can choose to update their book by using the "Manage Your Kindle" page on Amazon.com.
- If the changes are not "critical," such as fixing typos, then Kindle Direct Publishing will not send e-mail notification, but customers can still update their books through the "Manage Your Kindle" page.

Summary

Author beware: keep an eye out for companies looking to take advantage of you. Learn copyright laws to protect your work but also to avoid infringing on others. Protect yourself with work-for-hire agreements. And finally, self-publishing gives you the ability to revise your book quickly and efficiently, which is something traditional publishers cannot do.

CHAPTER 21

How to Navigate Amazon

Male Amazon river dolphins will even insert
their penises in each other's blowholes in the
only known example of nasal sex.

David J. Linden, *The Compass of Pleasure: How Our Brains Make Fatty Foods,
Orgasm, Exercise, Marijuana, Generosity, Vodka, Learning,
and Gambling Feel So Good*

Whose World Is It?

This chapter helps you comprehend Amazon's vast empire. When it comes to publishing, this is Amazon's world, and the rest of us (readers, authors, and publishers) live in it. The more I learned about self-publishing, the more I realized that we could have written a book about Amazon alone. To paraphrase the old saying, "It's a rain forest out there."

Most people think of Amazon as an online reseller of books, ebooks, and Kindle devices, plus other items such as shoes, cameras, and gardening equipment. But the company is broader and deeper than that. Amazon wants to sell us everything. The company's total sales in 2011 were $48.1 billion, so this isn't completely facetious. Let's examine the major points of contact for authors.

Kindle

Kindle refers to many goods and services from Amazon. They face both authors and readers:

- **Kindle Direct Publishing** is the service for authors to sell ebooks. It is where you upload your book, manage your author account, adjust prices, and track your earnings.[†††]

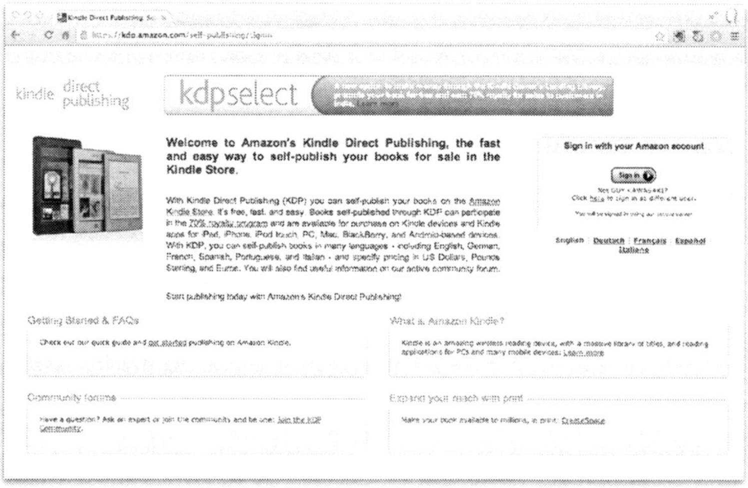

Figure 21.01. Kindle Direct Publishing home page.

- **Kindle Owners' Lending Library.** Members of Amazon Prime who own Kindle devices can borrow books from a collection of approximately 180,000 books called the Kindle Owners' Lending Library. There is a limit of one book per month, with no due date. As we mentioned before, people who borrow books may go on to buy more books, so keep this in mind as a marketing strategy.[†††]

- **KDP Select.** This is a marketing program for self-published authors. In exchange for not selling your ebook through any other reseller, you can put your book in the Kindle Owners' Lending Library, access promotional opportunities, and share in a pool of money called the KDP Select Fund that is distributed to authors based on how many people borrow their book.[|||]

- **Kindle devices.** Amazon sells tablets for reading ebooks that range in price from $69 to $499. As of the end of 2012, the flagship line of these products is the Kindle Fire HD.[†††]

- **Kindle ebooks.** Amazon sells millions of ebooks for Kindle devices, Kindle reading apps, and the Kindle Cloud Reader. This is the entry point of self-publishing for many authors.[†††]

- **Kindle Serials.** Amazon publishes books in a subscription format. Readers pay once and receive future installments automatically. Amazon is looking for unpublished stories for this format.[†††]

- **Kindle Reading Apps.** Amazon provides free apps for Android tablets and phones, iOS tablets and phones, and Macintosh and Windows computers. People do not need to own a Kindle device to use these apps.[†††]

- **Kindle Cloud Reader.** People can read Kindle ebooks without a Kindle device or Kindle reading app by using the Firefox, Chrome, and Safari browsers running on Macintosh, iOS, Windows, Linux, and Chromebook devices.[†††]
- **Kindle Singles.** No, this is not a dating service for book lovers. Kindle Singles is a collection of short books that cost from $0.99 to $2.99. Nonfiction singles often cover current events, such as the discovery of the Higgs Boson particle in the summer of 2012: *Higgs Discovery* by Lisa Randall. Fiction singles often use the same characters in short stories that are in an author's novels—for example, Jack Reacher in *Deep Down* by Lee Child.[†††]
- **Kindle Whispercast.** Amazon provides this service for the management of large-scale deployments of Kindles in schools and organizations. It enables an administrator to register and control Kindles as well as deploy Kindle content.[†††]

Be sure to communicate to your readers that they can read the Kindle version of your book without buying a Kindle device. They can use the free Kindle reading apps on computers, phones, and tablets as well as the Firefox, Chrome, and Safari browsers on their computer to read a Kindle book stored in the cloud.

Amazon Author Central

Amazon Author Central is a combination of your public profile page and analytics of your sales results.[†††] Think of it as your Amazon identity as an author as well as your dashboard. We'll cover it in detail in the next chapter.

CreateSpace

We've already covered CreateSpace[†††] (See chapter 15: "How to Use Author-Services Companies,") but as a reminder, it provides author services such as do-it-yourself tools and a complete suite of services for editing and designing your book. You can order copies of your book through its print-on-demand system as well as have CreateSpace distribute your ebook version.

Amazon Publishing

Think of Amazon Publishing as a traditional publisher such as Penguin, HarperCollins, or Random House.[†††] It signs authors, pays advances, and provides editing, copyediting, cover design, interior design, layout, marketing, and distribution to bookstores as well as Amazon itself. Amazon Publishing books can come in ebook, softcover, and hardcover formats. As of 2012, Amazon Publishing had six imprints:

- **AmazonEncore.** This is the flagship imprint of Amazon Publishing. It uses sales results and customer reviews to identify high-potential self-published books. AmazonEncore then acquires these books and republishes them with the marketing support and sales distribution clout of Amazon.[†††]
- **AmazonCrossing.** This imprint publishes foreign translations of books from around the world.[†††]
- **Amazon Children's Publishing.** Amazon started this imprint with a bang by acquiring the rights to 450 children's titles published by Marshall Cavendish. It focuses on books for "toddlers to teens."[†††]

- **Montlake Romance.** If you like contemporary, suspense, paranormal, and historical romance titles, this is the Amazon imprint for you.[†††]
- **Thomas & Mercer.** The name for this imprint comes from the names of two streets near Amazon's headquarters in Seattle, Washington. It focuses on mysteries and thrillers.[†††]
- **47North.** This imprint publishes science fiction, fantasy, and horror stories. Its name refers to the latitude of Seattle.[†††]

In addition to these imprints, Amazon Publishing acquired Avalon Books as well as the James Bond backlist.[†††]

Audible

Audible sells downloadable digital audiobooks as well as radio shows, podcasts, and speeches. Its selections contain more than 100,000 titles. To use Audible, people select a membership plan to buy credits and then use these credits to buy audiobooks and other offerings.[†††]

Audible also operates Audible Author Services and Audiobook Creation Exchange.[†††] The Audible Author Services program enables authors to receive $1 for each copy of their audiobook sold at Audible. com, obtain samples and links for promotional purposes, and interact directly with Audible marketing personnel. The purpose of Audible Author Services is to "foster direct relationships with more authors."

We've already discussed Audiobook Creation Exchange, but as a reminder, it's where authors can find narrators as well as online ebook resellers for the audio version of their books.

Amazon Advantage

Amazon Advantage is a self-service portal used to control fulfillment and ordering on Amazon.com. This program is optional, and most self-published authors won't ever use it. Amazon Advantage can help you manage pre-orders or fulfill orders yourself—for example, you bought one thousand copies of the print version of your book from a printer and you want to personally sell them on Amazon.[†††]

An Abbreviated Amazon Glossary

But wait, there's more. While we're at it, here's a list of more Amazon sites and services that you may encounter:

- **A9.** This site sells product and visual search technologies as well as ad-delivery technologies.[†††]
- **Alexa.** Amazon sells analytics, metrics, and tools for measuring and increasing web traffic through this site.[†††]
- **Amazon Connect.** This is Amazon Author Central's blog for authors.
- **Amazon Instant Video.** I use Amazon Instant Video with a TiVo. Shawn uses it through his Xbox and Google TV. It rents and sells television shows and movies.[†††]
- **Amazon Mechanical Turk.** You can post tasks that require human judgment and find workers to do them at this website. For example, you may want someone to identify objects in pictures or transcribe recordings.[†††]

- **Amazon MP3.** This is Amazon's music store. It contains over twenty million songs. These songs are cloud-based and playable on Kindle Fire, Android devices, iOS devices, and computers.[†††]
- **Amazon Prime.** If you frequently buy things from Amazon and want them right away, Amazon Prime is for you. It costs $79 per year, and the service provides free two-day shipping and instant streaming of movies and television shows (US-only). Prime members who own a Kindle device can borrow ebooks from the Kindle Owners' Lending Library for free.[†††]
- **Amazon Shorts.** Amazon discontinued publishing short stories, so Amazon Shorts is now discontinued, but Kindle Singles is thriving.
- **Amazon Simple Storage Services (S3).** This service provides online storage infrastructure as part of Amazon Web Services.[†††]
- **Amazon Standard Identification Number (ASIN).** The unique block of ten letters and numbers that identify a product on Amazon's site is called the ASIN. The ASIN for books is the same as its ISBN. Amazon generates an ASIN when it decides to offer non-book items for sale.[†††]
- **Amazon Vine.** This is a by-invitation program for Amazon's "most trusted reviewers," not a precursor to Amazon Wine. Vendors submit products (including books) to Amazon for Vine members to review. We'll show you how to use Amazon Vine in chapter 22: "How to Guerrilla-Market Your Book."[†††]
- **Amazon Wine.** Yup, Amazon now sells wine. The selection is from more than one thousand wineries. Price range from $10 to $100.[†††]

- **Amazon Web Services.** This is a collection of services including storage (Amazon S3), database, network resources, and computing for application hosting, web applications, high-performance computing, and backup.[†††]
- **Amazon Web Store.** Amazon provides website hosting via this website. It provides shopping-cart, credit-card processing, and inventory-management functionality.[†††]
- **CD Now.** You might wonder, "What's a CD?" if you're young. They're the shiny disks that contain music. You can buy them at CD Now.[†††]
- **Internet Movie Database (IMDb).** People use this website to find information about movies, television, actors, production crews, videogames, and fictional characters.[†††]
- **Shelfari.** This is an online community of authors, publishers, and readers. Its mission is to "enhance the experience of reading by connecting readers in meaningful conversations about the published word." [†††]
- **Zappos.** Once a week this Amazon company sends a box to my house. It is the online retailer of shoes, clothing, bags, accessories, and beauty products that pays for shipping both ways.[†††]

Amazon from Cradle to Gratitude

Not too facetiously, let us illustrate the ubiquity of Amazon in an author's life:

- Buy a copy of Microsoft Word from the **Amazon website** to write your book. Since you are a member of **Amazon Prime**, you'll get it in two days with no shipping fees.
- Buy the leading books in your genre for background research and a copy of *The Chicago Manual of Style* from the Amazon website too.
- Listen to music from **CD Now** and **Amazon MP3** while you write. Take a break from writing by watching movies you found in the **Internet Movie Database** and watch it on your TiVo through **Amazon Instant Video**. You do all this, of course, while enjoying some **Amazon Wine**.
- Upload your book to **Kindle Direct Publishing** in order to reach people who use **Kindle** devices as well as tablets, smart phones, and computers.
- Utilize **Author Central** to increase your marketing and promotion efforts.
- Hire people on **Amazon Mechanical Turk** to identify bloggers who could review your book.
- Produce an audiobook version using Audible's **Audiobook Creation Exchange**.
- Create a website to interact with your readers that's hosted at **Amazon Web Services**.
- Use **Alexa** to monitor and increase website traffic.
- Cross the chasm to paper when your fans clamor for a printed version by using **CreateSpace**.
- Cut a deal with **AmazonEncore** to publish your book.
- Buy some shoes and a watch from **Zappos** with your first royalty payment.

- Go to the **Amazon website** to find *APE* and give it a five-star review since it helped you understand the self-publishing game. Maybe even give the authors an Amazon gift card with your smiling face on it via e-mail, Facebook, or snail mail.†††

The only other companies that approach this level of pervasiveness are Google and Apple. The funny thing is that these are three of our favorite companies. Pervasiveness is a good thing.

Summary

Amazon has publishing covered from A to Z (Amazon to Zappos). Self-publishing is an Amazon world, so you'd be foolish to ignore it.

[Entrepreneur]

All writers think of what they do as an art. Smart writers
understand that writing is also a business. Really smart
writers see themselves also as entrepreneurs.

Barry Eisler

This section explains the final role in self-publishing: **Entrepreneur.**
You'll learn how to take a pet project and turn it into a viable product.
Entrepreneuring is the most neglected and hardest of *APE*'s three
roles because it involves marketing and sales, which are foreign
concepts to some authors and despised by the rest.

This section is also valuable to authors who are working with traditional publishers. All authors should take control of their fate and embrace the ideas here in order to maximize their success. Your activities as any kind of author do not end when your book is published. You should market your book for as long as you want people to buy it.

I cover some of the material in this section in my two previous books, *Enchantment* and *What the Plus!* I've included them here because these techniques work in the context of self-publishing.

CHAPTER 22

How to Guerrilla-Market Your Book

The question isn't who is going to let me;
it's who is going to stop me.

Ayn Rand, *The Fountainhead*

Guerrilla Marketing for Authors

This chapter provides a toolkit of tactical and practical guerrilla-marketing tips. You may find this difficult, if not galling, to believe, but having too much money is worse than too little when it comes to marketing.

When people have too much money, they throw launch parties, hire marketing and social-media "experts," buy advertising, and fly around the country on book tours. None of this will help you sell more books in a cost-effective way.

The starting point of guerrilla book marketing is to understand how people discover your book. Consider the ways:

- Friends and colleagues tell them about it.
- They read about it on blogs or websites.
- Amazon or another online reseller suggests it.
- They Googled a term and your book showed up as a result.
- They searched on Amazon for a term and your book showed up as a result.

What do people do after they've found your book? They look at its star rating and read user-generated reviews. Here are guerrilla-marketing ways to make this sequence of events work for you.

Cover the Earth

Ebooks have changed the process of getting books out to influencers and opinion leaders. In the old days, it cost $10 to $15 per book to provide these folks with hardcover books. Now, with e-mail and ebooks, the cost is closer to $0.

Therefore, we recommend using your e-mail address book, e-mail newsletter, and social-media acquaintances to offer the PDF version of your book to anyone who promises to review it. Some people will not fulfill their promise. Others will take advantage of your offer to get a freebie. But so what?

Approximate cost: $0, though, if you're paranoid, there is the theoretical lost revenue from people who would have bought the book but got it for free because you covered the earth.

Make Reviewing Easy

I've reviewed many books, and one of the pain-in-the-ass parts of the process is to find background material such as the author's bio, picture, cover, book specifications (page count, ISBN, price), blurbs, and foreign-rights holders. I put all this stuff in one place to make reviewing *Enchantment* as easy as possible.[†††]

Approximate cost: $0, assuming you have a website or blog to host the files.

Join Help a Reporter Out

Help a Reporter Out (HARO) is a service to help reporters find sources for stories.[†††] For example, suppose that a reporter wanted to write a story about the difficulty of completing a cross-border adoption. He would post a request at the HARO site, and people who are familiar with the adoption process can volunteer to provide information.

All you need to do is sign up at the HARO website.[†††] Then you'll get three e-mails a day with a list of requests. When you see one that matches your expertise, you contact the journalist with a pitch. If you're selected, you may get extensive free publicity.

Approximate cost: $0.

Use "Hangouts on Air"

Covering the earth and making reviewing easy are good starts. Another great way to give away your knowledge is to conduct Google+ "Hangouts on Air."[†††] These are video webinars to broadcast whatever you want to the world. In addition to the live audience, Hangouts on Air are automatically archived as YouTube videos, so share them with others later and you can embed them on your website.

Approximate cost: $0.

Catalyze User-Generated Reviews

You should ensure that there are positive reviews of your book on Amazon within forty-eight hours of when it ships. It's hard to dig yourself out of a hole if the first reviews are lousy. Here are three ethical ways to do this:

- **Ask your beta testers.** One of the benefits of crowd-sourcing editing is that on the day your book ships on Amazon, there are dozens of people who have already read it. Keep track of the readers who liked your book and ask them to post a review on Amazon.
- **Ask the blurbers.** Ask the people who provided you with blurbs to post their blurbs as reviews. This is a quick way to get several great reviews. (Hat-tip to Kristen Eckstein for this idea.)
- **Contact Amazon's best reviewers.** Amazon publishes two lists of the reviewers who have provided the most helpful reviews: Top Reviewer Rankings and Hall of Fame Reviewers.[†††] You can peruse this list to find people who have reviewed books in your genre. (Hat-tip to Maria Murnane for this idea.)

    Another way to find Amazon's best reviewers is to examine the reviews of books in your genre to find reviewers with "Hall of Fame," "Top 50 Reviewer," or "Vine Voice" badges. (Amazon selects people for the Vine Voice program to receive products to review based on the helpfulness of past reviews.)

Approximate cost for all three methods: $0.

Guest Topic: How to Evangelize Amazon's Best Reviewers, by Dr. Bojan Tunguz

Dr. Bojan Tunguz is a theoretical physicist working to change scientific publishing through self-publishing and dynamic peer review. He is also an Amazon "Top 50 Reviewer." In January 2012, Dr. Tunguz is ranked #17 of all Amazon reviewers, with 2,057 reviews and a helpful rating of 95 percent.

Shawn and I met Dr. Tunguz in the Google+ APE community, and he attended a panel that I moderated called "The Future of Publishing."††† When I heard his story, I asked him to explain how to evangelize Amazon's best reviewers. Here is what he wrote for us.

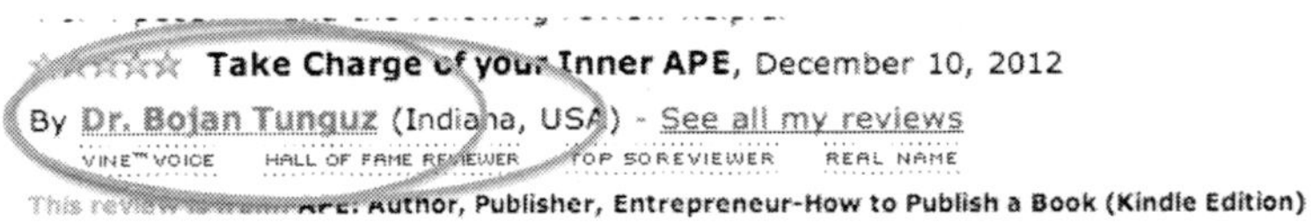

Figure 22.01. Dr. Bojan Tunguz with badges for Amazon's best reviewers

Dr. Bojan Tunguz: I have written reviews for Amazon for almost seven years. What started as a few simple book recommendations has become a hobby and a passion.

Some authors make very basic and avoidable mistakes, causing me to delete their message instantly, or at the very least, subjecting me to a less-than-enjoyable experience. Neither outcome increases the likelihood of a positive review. So here are my top ten tips on how to approach Amazon reviewers to help you.

1. **Start small.** If you're a new or otherwise obscure author, try publishing a shorter work, such as a Kindle Single (thirty to eighty pages). Reviewers are *much* more likely to take a look at your work if it is not a significant time commitment.

2. **Look for reviewers of your genre.** Many authors concentrate on top reviewers, but this is a misguided approach. The reviewer ranking carries weight, but it is better to get a meaningful review from someone who appreciates your book than to get a vacuous review from a top reviewer.

3. **Ensure that the reviewer has published multiple reviews and is still active.** Reviewers with only a few reviews typically enjoyed those particular works and are not interested in reviewing more books. Also, previously active reviewers may no longer be writing reviews.

4. **Use the correct spelling of the reviewer's name in your e-mail.** You'd be surprised how often this mistake is made. Many reviewers don't list their full or real name, so address those with the Amazon handle that they use (again, spelled correctly).

5. **Use proper grammar and spelling in your e-mail.** Bad grammar and spelling are dead giveaways that an author's writing is not very good and is not worth reading.

6. **Offer a free copy of your book—even print.** This is part of your marketing expense, and you don't want to be stingy about it. Few reviewers will pay for a book to review.

7. **Don't boast.** Don't say your novel is the next big thing and that the corrupt publishing world is not recognizing your genius. We're reviewers, not your parents or your psychiatrist.

8. **Break the ice by mentioning specific reviews you liked by the reviewer.** And don't mention a specific review that you liked without marking the review as "helpful." These votes are the only tangible compensation that reviewers get for their effort.

9. **Never offer to pay money for the review.** This is not only unethical and against the policies of Amazon, but it's also tacky, crass, and insulting. We don't review books for the money. We do it to help people find good books to read.

10. **Don't pester reviewers about when they will post a review.** Most reviewers are busy with their own lives, work, and other books. They are doing you a favor, and it may take many months before they can finally get to your work. Be patient.

My last recommendation is that you post a thank-you comment on the review. Do this even if the review is negative. And if a review is negative, don't retaliate by giving it an unhelpful vote and asking your friends and relatives to do the same. Frankly, if you can't deal with negative reviews, don't publish a book.

Optimize Your Title

Amazon and Google aren't clairvoyant. Your book's title and subtitle must contain the keywords people search for. For example, we knew people looking for self-publishing information aren't going to search for "ape." They're "authors" and "publishers" and maybe even "entrepreneurs," and they want to know "how to publish a book" but not "ape."

A great way to optimize your title and subtitle is to use the Google Adwords keyword tool.[†††] This is a site where you can enter keywords, and Google will tell you how many times per month people search for a term.

This is how I learned that people search for "how to publish" 1,500,000 times a month and for "self-publish" 110,000 times a month. Hence, *APE*'s subtitle is "How to Publish a Book" and doesn't contain the phrase "self-publish." (Hat-tip to Michael Alvear for this idea.) Approximate cost: $0.

Optimize Amazon's Author Central

Author Central provides services to Kindle Direct Publishing authors, and it is a key component of your marketing efforts to Amazon customers.[†††] The main sections are:

- **Books.** This is a list of the books you are currently selling on Amazon. You can provide editorial review, book details, and "book extras" such as a "ridiculously simplified synopsis."
- **Profile.** Your profile includes your biography, up to eight photos, up to eight videos, your blog feeds, and a calendar of your events. People see this when they visit your Amazon author page.[†††]

- **Sales info.** You can view the sales history of the print version of your book via major retailers. The sales tracking information is from BookScan, a service of the Nielsen Company.[†††] To see your ebook sales history, however, you need to go to the "Reports" tab of your Kindle Direct Publishing account.
- **Customer reviews.** You can read all the reviews of your book sorted by the date or number of stars.

Approximate cost: $0.

Do Something Fun

There are some additional ideas that you can implement if you have the bandwidth and money. I can't prove that these ideas sell more books, but they are fun.

- **Offer autographed covers.** As I mentioned in chapter 10, "How to Get an Effective Book Cover," you can offer people an autographed cover in exchange for posting a picture of themselves with your book on social-media sites. Approximate cost: $2 per cover.

    When you travel, you can also visit bookstores, ask their permission to autograph your book, and then use Google+, Facebook, or Twitter to tell people which stores have your autographed book. Approximate cost: $0.

- **Stickers and other tchotchkes.** Walls360, a company I advise for, makes fabric stickers that are reusable.[†††] You can print a T-shirt for $7 each. Mugs cost $5 each. Buttons are a few pennies each. If you have a small number of people you'd like to thank, consider these gifts. Approximate cost: $500.

- **Contests.** I ran a contest for the best video of people saying "What the Plus!"[†††] Hosting a contest is a complex task. Luckily there are companies such as Friend2Friend, Strutta, and Wildfire that can help you.[†††] Approximate cost: $500–$1,000, plus prizes.

- **Quizzes.** HarperCollins created quizzes to spark interest in novels. Friend2Friend, Strutta, and Wildfire can help you create quizzes, too. Approximate cost: $1,000.

- **Infographics.** A good infographic communicates ideas faster and better than text. My friends at ColumnFive created infographics called How to Achieve Enchantment and How to Increase Your Likeability.[†††] I ran these charts on my blog as well as provided a link so that anyone else could run them too. Approximate cost: $1,500.

Figure 22.02. Example of an infographic.

- **Badges, buttons, and banners.** The number of people who voluntarily placed *Enchantment* badges, buttons, and even banners on their blogs and websites amazed me.[†††] The key to making this happen is to write a book that people like so much that they want to help you make it successful. Approximate cost: $50 per graphic, although your cover designer can make these for you in fifteen minutes.
- **Wallpapers.** Many people downloaded graphic images of *Enchantment* to use as their desktops on their computers, smart phones, and tablets.[†††] Approximate cost: $50 per graphic, although your cover designer can do these quickly too.

The Grass Is Sometimes Browner

You might wonder what it'd be like if you were working with a traditional publisher as opposed to doing this guerrilla marketing yourself. Surely, life would be good and easy if that were the case.

Here's a slice-of-life exchange for you between Penelope Trunk, author of *The New American Dream*, and the publicity department of her traditional publisher:

> Three months before the publication date, the PR department called me up to "coordinate our efforts." But really, their call was just about giving me a list of what I was going to do to publicize the book. I asked them what they were going to do. They had no idea. Seriously. They did not

have a written plan or any list, and when I pushed one of the people on this first call to give me examples of what the publishers would do to promote my book, she said "newsgroups."

I assumed I was misunderstanding. I said, "You mean like newsgroups from the early '90s? Those newsgroups? USENET?"

"Yes."

"Who is part of newsgroups anymore?"

"We actually have really good lists because we have been working with them for so long."

"People in newsgroups buy books? You are marketing my book through newsgroups?"

I'm not going to go through the whole conversation, OK? Because the person was taken off my book before the next phone call.

At the next phone call, I asked again about how they were going to publicize my book. I told them that I'm happy to do it on my blog, but I already know I can sell tons of books by writing about my book on my blog. So they need to tell me how they are going to sell tons of books.

"LinkedIn."

"What? Where are you selling books on LinkedIn?"

"One of the things we do is build buzz on our fan page."

I went ballistic. There is no publishing-industry fan page that is good enough to sell books. No one goes to fan pages for publishers, because publishers are not household brand names. The authors are. That's how publishing works.

"You know what your problem is?" I said, "Marketing online requires that you have a brand name and a following, and the book industry doesn't build its own brand. But I have my own brand. So I'm better at marketing books than you are. I have a voice online and you don't."

I scheduled a phone call with my editor's boss's boss to tell him that. I told him his business is online marketing and his team has no idea how to do it, and he should hire me.

He told me, "With all due respect [which, I find, is always a euphemism for I hate your guts] we have been profitable every year that I've run this division and I don't think we have a problem."

Sometimes the grass is browner, not greener, so be careful of wishing for a contract with a traditional publisher. Penelope's example is an excellent illustration of the real world of working with a traditional publisher.

Summary

For self-publishers, guerrilla tactics are the way to gorilla-size success. The cost for most of these ideas is $0, and the expensive ones are no more proven than the free ones. This is because the quality of your book and the quantity of your moxie are more important than the amount of money you've spent.

CHAPTER 23

How to Build an Enchanting Personal Brand

If I am not for myself, then who will be for me? And if I am
only for myself, then what am I? And if not now, when?

Rabbi Hillel, *Pirkei Avot*

The Brand Called You

This chapter explains how to create an enchanting personal brand. In the next chapter, we'll examine the tools to spread your brand. The goal of these two steps is to build a "platform" for your book.

"Platform" is marketing-speak for the sum total of people you know and people who know you, including:

- Friends and followers on social-media services
- People in your e-mail address book
- Readers of your blog
- Readers of your previous books
- Bloggers
- Reviewers
- Other authors
- People who have seen you speak

In the old days, authors used the platforms of their publishers. Indeed, this remains one of the reasons to seek a traditional publisher, although I've never come across an author who was happy with the marketing efforts of his publisher.

Many experienced authors consider self-publishing once they have established their own platform beyond their publisher's. However, as a novice self-publisher, you may experience *no marketing* instead of *insufficient marketing* unless you build your own platform.

The process of building a platform takes six to twelve months— the same amount of time it takes to finish a book—but you cannot start the process after your book is done. If you don't have a platform yet, you need to build one as you are writing your book.

Step 1: Trustworthiness

Call me idealistic, but your platform is only as good as your reality. If you suck as a person, your platform will suck too. The three pillars of a personal brand are trustworthiness, likeability, and competence: TLC.

Trustworthiness means that people can depend on you because you are honest, forthright, and effective. Here are seven ways to build trustworthiness:

- **Trust others first.** If you want people to trust you, you have to trust them first. This isn't a chicken-or-egg issue—the sequence is definite: you trust, and then you're trusted. Give people the benefit of the doubt and assume that they are good until proven bad. Then give them another chance.

- **Underpromise and overdeliver.** Do what you say you're going to do, early and under budget. People should be able to depend on you. If you achieve this goal 75 percent of the time, you're better than most people.

- **Deliver bad news early.** If you can't deliver, then tell people as soon as you know there's a problem. Waiting until the last minute in hopes of a miracle doesn't build trust. You should communicate the problem as soon as possible to increase the opportunities for fixing the problem.

- **Bake a bigger pie.** There are two kinds of people: eaters and bakers. Eaters think the world is a zero-sum game: what someone else eats, they cannot eat. Bakers do not believe that the world is a zero-sum game because they can bake more and bigger pies. Everyone can eat more. People trust bakers and not eaters.

- **Tell people what you don't know.** No one knows everything. There's nothing wrong with this. You can build trust by explaining what you don't know. Then people will believe you when you say you do know something. Acting like you're omniscient reduces trustworthiness.

- **Figure out what you don't know.** To take trust to the next level, figure out what you don't know and then provide the answer. For example, you may have never visited Hawaii, but if you see someone ask what the best shaved-ice store is in Honolulu, you can still figure this out with Google or Yelp. This shows your ability to do research and to follow through—both powerful components of trustworthiness.

- **Disclose your interests.** There's nothing wrong with making a living. What's wrong is not disclosing conflicts of interest. For example, when I shared three posts about Microsoft Office templates[†††] for raising venture capital, I added the text "Promotional consideration paid by Microsoft." I took some heat for doing a promotion, but not for trying to hide it.

Step 2: Likeability

Likeability is the second pillar of a personal brand. Jerks seldom build great brands. A great book can overcome an unlikeable author, but why increase the challenge? Likeable people bring a smile to the face of others. They radiate energy—they don't suck it up. Folks look forward to dealing with likeable people—even going out of their way to encounter them. Here are five ways to build likeability:

- **Accept others.** If you want people to like you, you have to like them first. This means accepting people no matter their race, creed, net worth, religion, gender, politics, sexual orientation, or your perception of their level of intelligence. It means not imposing your values on others. (Yes, this even means accepting people who choose a different computing or mobile-phone platform from you.)

It's even better if you delight in people who are different from you, because they add diversity to your life. Many people impede their likeability by rejecting people who don't share the same sensibilities. If you want only your clones to buy your book, you're not going to sell many copies.

- **Add value.** People like people who add value to the world. You don't need to be a Mother Teresa because making the world better can take many forms—for example, technical assistance and pointing out online resources are often enough. Give without expectation of return and, ironically, you'll probably increase the returns that you reap.

- **Default to "Yes."** When you meet people, always be thinking, "How can I help this person?" If they don't make a request, ask them how you can help them anyway. The upside of such a positive attitude far outweighs the downside of people trying to take advantage of you.

- **Stay positive.** If you want a likeable reputation, don't attack folks or denigrate their efforts. Stay positive. Stay uplifting. Or stay silent. Like my mother used to say, "If you don't have anything good to say, shut up."

- **Share your passions.** By sharing your passions, you provide fertile ground to begin conversations and to explore commonalities. My passions are hockey and photography. I've seldom met people who shared these passions and not liked them.

Step 3: Competence

Competence is the third pillar of a platform. The goal is to establish yourself as a trusted source of information, insight, and assistance. When you achieve this status, people will read your book because of your credibility.

Competence is usually associated with nonfiction authors, but it applies to novelists as well. For example, Ray Bradbury achieved competence in science fiction, Patricia Cornwell in forensics, and John Grisham in law. Here's how to develop and demonstrate competence:

- **Own a niche.** Pick a niche that you love and focus on it. The National Living Treasures of Japan provide good examples.[†††] The Japanese Ministry of Education has designated these people as artistic and cultural treasures because they have mastered skills such as papermaking, ceramics, and metalworking. Watch the YouTube video of swordmaker Gassan Sadaichi to appreciate what it means to own a niche.[†††]

- **Let go of niches you can't/don't own.** Owning a niche takes lots of energy. Owning every niche takes infinite energy. You don't have infinite energy. If you want to own a niche, then give up the ones that you can't own or don't care about. Then, to repeat the lesson in the trustworthiness section above, disclose what you don't know.

- **Pay your dues.** When people ask how long it takes to write a book, my answer is "thirty years" because that's how long ago I started my career. While it may take six to twelve months of work at the keyboard to type in a book, the accumulation of knowledge and understanding is the harder and more time-consuming part.

  This is why I throw up a little when a twenty-five-year-old tells me that he believes he should write a book about "all he's learned" by starting his $1 million consulting company.

- **Watch and learn.** You can learn a skill by watching and copying someone who's good at it. This takes the humility to admit that you can learn from others and the open-mindedness to embrace their techniques. Few people seem willing or able to do this—for example, millions of people watched Steve Jobs introduce new products, and yet they still suck at the process.

- **Eat like a hummingbird, poop like an elephant.** Read voraciously outside your area of expertise. Attend conferences and trade shows that have (ostensibly) nothing to do with your niche. Think of ways to apply other niches to yours. And then spread your knowledge—don't keep it to yourself.

  Wondering about the bird and elephant? If humans had the metabolic rate of a hummingbird, we'd ingest 150,000 calories per day, and elephants poop 150 pounds per day. That's how much information you should consume and pass along.

- **Try new methods.** If you want to remain competent, you need to push the edge of knowledge by trying new methods. You'll experience failure, but failure can teach competence as long as you don't give up. It is part of the process of paying your dues. What separates competent from incompetent people is the willingness to try new methods and to learn from failure.

Summary

I'll tell you a story about competence. Shawn and I first met on Google+ when I asked my followers about self-publishing, and I got the eight different answers from five different people.

Shawn told me to use Adobe InDesign while other experts told me InDesign would not work. Then less than ten minutes after I sent him a chapter of *What the Plus!* that included bullets, images, and captions, he sent back a MOBI file and a picture of the chapter displayed on his Kindle.

This is why Shawn is coauthor of *APE*.

CHAPTER 24

How to Choose a Platform Tool

> Finally finished invention. Disappointed to
> find that no one can read.

@JGutenberg, October 3, 1439. *Historical Tweets*[†††]

So Many Tools, So Little Time

This chapter explains the tools for building a platform. Now that you're a TLC (trustworthy, likeable, competent) person, you can move to the next step. Remember: these tools are only as good as the person wielding them. Let's start with the traditional ones.

- **E-mail.** E-mail is the granddaddy of marketing tools, but it is still one of the most effective. If I had a choice between obtaining someone's e-mail address or that person following me on a social-media service, I would pick the e-mail address. From this point on, respond to everyone who sends you an e-mail and save his or her e-mail address for future contact.

- **E-mail newsletter.** An e-mail newsletter is a publication that people subscribe to because they are interested in what you have to say. It requires producing a steady flow of content but not nearly as much as a blog (see below) because you can include items such as announcements and events in a newsletter that are not as appropriate for a blog.

  You can use a service such as MailChimp or Constant Contact to handle subscriptions, campaigns, and analytics.[†††] Diane Capri, author of *Licensed to Thrill*, provides a good model for how to solicit subscribers for an e-mail newsletter on her website.[†††]

- **Website.** We suggest setting up a website as "brochure ware" to provide information that doesn't change often. This is what I've done with GuyKawasaki.com. It's a way to provide detailed information about you and your book, but you should expect people to visit it only a few times (if you're lucky!).

- **Blog.** If you can write thoughtful posts at least once a week, then blogs can help establish your competence. However, it is difficult to keep up this pace. You should assume that fewer than 1 percent of the people who visit your blog will buy your book. Think of how difficult it is to get 100,000 people to visit your blog and then imagine that only 1,000 will buy your book.

  Blogging is good practice for honing your writing skills and keeps you in the flow between books. If you're interested in blogging, check out tools such as WordPress, TypePad, Blogger, and Tumblr.[†††] However, we recommend using Google+ as a blogging platform—see below.

Social-Media Services

Social-media services such as Google+, Facebook, Twitter, LinkedIn, and Pinterest enable you to win the marketing trifecta: fast, free, and ubiquitous. Social media provides the fastest, easiest, and cheapest way to build a platform, but it requires at least an hour or two per day for six to twelve months. Here is a synopsis of social-media options:

- **Google+.** We adore this service because it enables us to write lengthy posts, embed pictures and video, and interact with people who share our passions. You can probably find like-minded people on Google+ for everything you're interested in too. For example, there are circles about science, novice photography, and knitting.[†††]

  If you don't already blog or if you have a blog that few people read, we recommend making Google+ your blogging platform. It is much easier to generate traffic for a Google+ account than for a standalone blog because of the built-in sharing and liking features of the service. (You can read everything I know about Google+ in *What the Plus!*)[†††]

- **Facebook.** This is the McDonald's of social networking, with "over 1 billion served." You should enable people to subscribe to your Facebook profile so that they see all your posts. Then you can choose to share posts with either your subscribers or with your friends and family. To learn more about using Facebook, read *Facebook Marketing: An Hour a Day* by Mari Smith and Chris Treadaway.[†††]

- **Twitter.** Think of Twitter as a river: it can get you places fast, but it can also drown you. It's great for staying on top of current events, soliciting assistance, and expressing your perspectives in 140-character messages. Twitter is also a powerful resource for information, inspiration, and interaction. For example, on Twitter there's a collective of self-publishers, as well as novelists, and children's authors. You can find more people interested in self-publishing on Listorious, too.[†††]

- **LinkedIn.** This website is a place for people to make business connections. It's useful for these purposes for any kind of author. However, the usefulness of LinkedIn to build a platform is limited because the mind-set of LinkedIn is geared toward making connections for job hunting and business development—not establishing a reputation.

- **Pinterest.** People share what they find interesting by "pinning" it at this website. It's analogous to pinning a flyer on an old-fashioned bulletin board in a public venue. For the most part, people are pinning clothing, food, and design articles. If you especially want to build a following with women, Pinterest is useful. However, the level of interaction and exchange of thoughts are lower than on Google+, Facebook, and Twitter.

- **YouTube.** Google's YouTube website is a powerful tool if you can consistently produce interesting videos. However, the amount of time, effort, and luck needed to effectively use YouTube to build a platform is daunting.

We've presented six social-media networks you can use to build a platform. Now we'd like to narrow them down, because you don't have enough time to use all six. If we were starting to build a platform today, we would focus on Google+, Facebook, and Twitter because of their widespread popularity.

As we mentioned, we recommend spending at least one to two hours on them every day for at least six months, starting from the moment you're thinking of writing a book. This is a big effort, and we know it. However, there's no way around the issue: as a self-publisher, you need a platform, and Google+, Facebook, and Twitter are the best tools for building one.

Social Networks for Writers and Readers

In addition to the large, general-purpose social networks, there are social networks that focus on writers and readers. Here are some of the useful ones.

- **BookTalk.** This site enables people to participate in discussion groups about books. It also provides live chats and interviews with authors. The emphasis is on people discussing books chapter by chapter, not authors interacting with readers.
- **Goodreads.** The focus of Goodreads is people discussing the books they are reading and the books they want to read. This enables the community to find books and share their reading experience.
- **KindleBoards.** This is an online discussion board about all permutations of Kindle: ebooks, tablets, accessories, and apps. There are thousands of topics containing millions of comments.

- **MobileRead.** This online discussion board concentrates on reading books using mobile devices. Topics include ebook readers, ebook apps, and various ebook formats.
- **Nothing Binding.** This site provides a social network for authors, readers, publishers, and book buyers. It has an ambitious and lovely goal: "...break the chains of the current publishing dinosaur system that is blocking the great wave of literary progress, learning and enjoyment."
- **Shelfari.** Amazon owns Shelfari and positions it as a "community-powered encyclopedia for book lovers." The central metaphor is a virtual bookshelf that contains books you own, read, or want to read. You can join or create groups and interact with other book lovers. I love that you can import all your Amazon purchases into your Shelfari bookshelf.

Figure 24.01 Part of my Shelfari bookshelf.

Google+ Communities

The Google+ communities[†††] feature is a way to build a social network for your book. It's a free service on Google+, but you don't have to participate in the rest of Google+ to maintain a community—just as you don't have to participate in the rest of Yahoo! to operate a Yahoo! group.

To start, you click your way through an easy process[†††] on the Google+ website. The first decision you'll encounter is whether to make your community public or private. While your first inclination may be to make it public, making it private so that you can control who joins the community is useful.

The next steps involve writing a tagline, picking a photo, providing text for an "About" section, and creating discussion categories. Then you invite people to join and start communing.

You can also join other communities. For example, Shawn, Peg Fitzpatrick, and I operate a community for authors, editors, publishers, and designers called APE if you'd like to join the fun.

Summary

Social media is the trifecta of marketing: fast, free, and ubiquitous. There are general-appeal services such as Google+, Facebook, Twitter, and LinkedIn. Of these, Google+ is our favorite. There are also social networks for readers and writers, and you can build your own social network using Google+ communities. All of these services provide great ways to build your platform.

CHAPTER 25

How to Create a Social-Media Profile

It is better to be hated for what you are
than to be loved for what you are not.

André Gide, *Autumn Leaves*

HotOrNot Versus eHarmony

This chapter helps you create an enchanting social-media profile. Every social-media service enables you to create a "profile" that provides biographical information, and many people view these profiles to decide if you're worth circling, following, or liking.

A useful analogy for social-media profiles is two online dating sites. At HotOrNot, people decide whether they want to meet someone by looking at their pictures.[†††] At eHarmony people complete an extensive questionnaire along twenty-nine dimensions of compatibility.[†††]

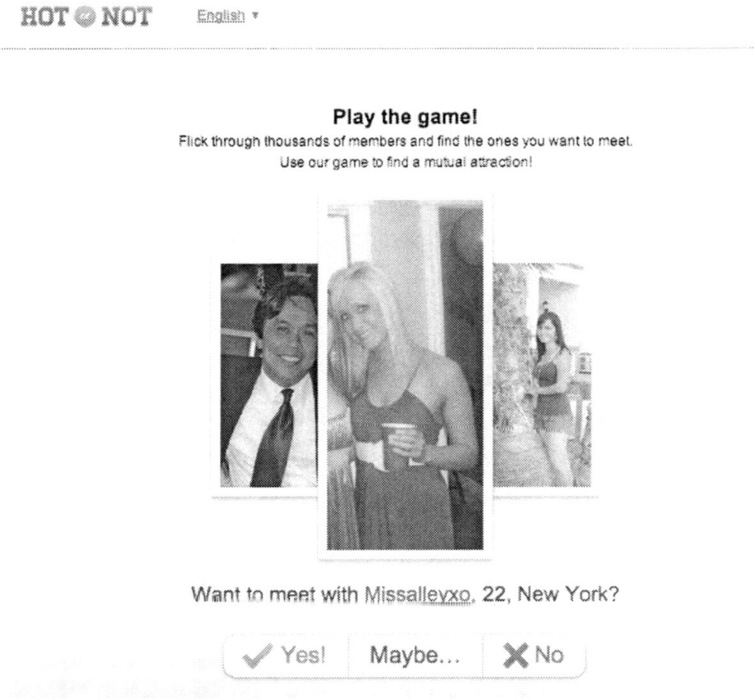

Play the game!

Flick through thousands of members and find the ones you want to meet.
Use our game to find a mutual attraction!

Want to meet with Missalleyxo, 22, New York?

✔ Yes!   Maybe...   ✗ No

Figure 25.01. The HotOrNot home page.

Social media is closer to HotOrNot than eHarmony because people make snap judgments. Your profile is important because you have a few seconds to convince people that you're worth paying attention to and therefore worth circling, liking, or following.

Name

If you haven't registered for a social-media service yet, select a name that is simple. This will make it easier for people to find you and your posts. For example, the simplest and best name for my accounts is "Guy Kawasaki" as opposed to "GKawasaki," "Guy T. Kawasaki," or "GTKawasaki."

Profile and Cover Photo

Your profile photo is a window into your soul. It is usually the first thing people see about you, and they will make an instant judgment about your likeability and trustworthiness.

You may think these tips about profile photos are duh-isms, but I see crappy profile photos every day. Here's how to create a good profile photo:

- **Show your face.** Don't use a logo, graphic, cartoon, pet, or kid. Find or take a photo where you have a "Duchenne smile" (the kind of smile that uses both the jaw and eye muscles, named after French neurologist Guillaume-Benjamin Duchenne).
- **Use a tight shot.** Emphasize your face. It's neither necessary nor desirable to show everyone in your life including your dog and the setting sun.
- **Go asymmetrical.** Don't stick your face exactly in the middle of the photo. It's a lot more interesting off to one side or another. Professional photographers seldom place a face in the middle of a photo.
- **Do it well.** Ensure that your photo is in focus, your face is well lit, and there isn't any redeye. Don't use a cheesy photo from your ten-year-old, one-megapixel camera phone. You don't have to be Yousuf Karsh or Annie Leibovitz, but don't be a clown, either.

Figure 25.02. The profile photo of Mari Smith is just about perfect.

Google+ enables you to display either five small photos or one large cover photo in addition to a profile photo. Facebook enables you to display a cover photo and profile photo. Whether you use five small photos or one big photo, their purpose is different from a profile photo.

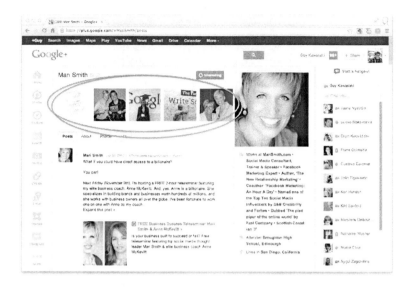

Figure 25.03. Mari Smith's five photos in Google+.

A profile photo should primarily show your face. When people read your posts or your comments, they should feel like they are looking at you across a table. The five small photos or cover photo should tell your story and portray your passions. They provide a pictorial biography that's equal to a thousand words.

Many people don't have a Facebook cover photo; this is a waste of a marketing opportunity. Facebook explains how to add one in its FAQ, so be sure to add one.††† There's also a YouTube video by Terry White that explains how to create a Facebook cover photo—his principles apply to Google+ cover photos too.†††

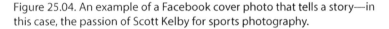

Figure 25.04. An example of a Facebook cover photo that tells a story—in this case, the passion of Scott Kelby for sports photography.

Here's one more resource for creating a good profile photo. The folks at LunaMetrics compiled a cheat sheet of the dimensions for profile photos as well as the photos and videos accompanying posts for Facebook, Twitter, Google+, YouTube, LinkedIn, and Pinterest.[†††]

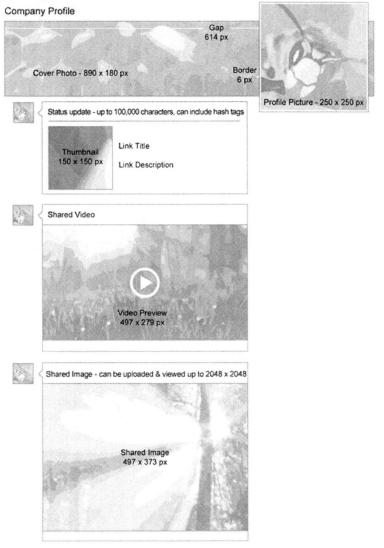

Figure 25.05. Optimal dimensions for Google+ from the Lunametrics cheat sheet.

Biographical Information

Biographical information is not the place to show your sense of humor or uniqueness. Go for the simple and solid: an explanation of your educational background, what you do, and your areas of expertise.

The goal is to personify likeability, trustworthiness, and competence, so resist the two extremes of clever coyness and over-the-top crassness. A good test is whether you would like and trust a person with your biographical information. An even better test is whether you'd want your son or daughter to date someone with your biographical information.

Contact Settings

Give up the notion of people leaving you alone if you want to succeed as an author. Provide your e-mail address or at least an e-mail address that you don't mind getting cluttered with spam—so that reaching you is easy.

I provide my cell phone number in my e-mails—how's that for accessibility? People never call it. You should be so lucky that thousands of people want to get in touch with you—it means you're building a platform.

Summary

These are the essential elements of an enchanting and effective social-media profile. Just keep in mind that your profile has to attract followers in a HotOrNot, at-a-glance world filled with attention-deficient people.

CHAPTER 26

How to Share on Social Media

Creativity is knowing how to hide your sources.

Albert Einstein

Demonstrate Your Competence

This chapter explains how to share enchanting and effective posts. Sharing posts is one of the main ways to build your platform because it increases the number of people who follow you.

There are two kinds of people on social networks: those who want more followers and those who are lying. Gaining more followers shows that people find you interesting, intelligent, and cool—and makes your platform powerful.

Always share posts that add value to the lives of your followers. That value comes in three forms: (1) information—what happened; (2) insights—what does it mean that this happened; and (3) assistance—how to make good things happen or avoid bad things.

This applies to nonfiction writers as well as novelists. Here are examples of content that would help authors in different genres build their platform:

- **Mystery/Thriller.** "Deadly Pandemic Bird Flu Details Finally Are Made Public." Scientists explain how scientists made the deadly bird flu (H5N1) transmissible between ferrets.[†††]
- **Romance.** "Olympic Torchbearer Stops Mid-relay, Proposes." David State, an Olympic torchbearer, stopped midway through his run to propose to his girlfriend, Christine Langham.[†††]
- **Young Adult.** "'Hunger Games' Hits Bull's-eye for Girls and Archery." *The Hunger Games* has sparked interest in archery because girls want to emulate Katniss Everdeen, the heroine of the movie.[†††]
- **Paranormal.** "How to Survive the Zombie Apocalypse Using Science." UC Berkeley neuroscientist Bradley Voytek explains the neuroscience of the zombie apocalypse.[†††]
- **Women's Issues.** "Post-Mastectomy Woman Banned from Swimming Topless by Discriminatory Parks Dept." The Seattle Parks and Recreation refused to let a double-mastectomy cancer survivor swim topless in a public pool.[†††]
- **Science Fiction.** Photos of Ray Bradbury from 1920 to 2012. The *Los Angeles Times* collected pictures of science-fiction writer Ray Bradbury from his childhood to death.[†††]
- **Entrepreneurship.** "What Is Market?" Venture capitalist Jeff Bussgang provides the range of salary and equity compensation for high-tech start-ups.[†††]

Eclecticism is also good, so after you establish a reputation for a particular expertise, you should include posts about your other passions. This will make you more enchanting because you're multidimensional.

Sources of Information

We salute anyone who can regularly generate content that's informative, analytical, helpful, amusing, or amazing. I did it for a few years, but I couldn't sustain it because I have a wife, four kids, one dog, two chickens, two turtles, one guinea pig, and two lizards.

By necessity I became a curator, which means that I find good articles and point people to them. Curation is valuable because there is an abundance of good stories but many people don't have the time to find them. Here are the several sources for stories to share:

- **People you follow.** You followed people for a reason, right? Then their posts should be a rich supply of ideas for you.
- **Alltop.** I am a cofounder of this site. It is an online "magazine rack" of topics ranging from A (Adoption) to Z (Zoology). Our researchers curate RSS feeds from more than 25,000 websites and blogs that cover more than 1,000 topics. I use Alltop to find most of the stories that I post on Google+ and Facebook. As a writer, you may find Writing.Alltop and Publishing. Alltop interesting.[†††]

Figure 26.01. The Publishing.Alltop page.

- **StumbleUpon.** This is a community of approximately twenty million people who "stumble upon" websites and rate them. This enters the websites into the StumbleUpon system for the rest of the community. StumbleUpon has categorized websites so that members can select topics such as gadgets, design, or sports. For example, if you're a crime writer, you might search for stumbles that are relevant to crime (you must be signed in for this link to work).[†††]

Figure 26.02. StumbleUpon categories.

- **NPR.** Every day you can find something worthwhile on NPR. My favorite shows are *TechNation; Fresh Air;* and *Wait, Wait Don't Tell Me.* An easy way to digest NPR is NPR.Alltop.com.[†††]
- **TED.** The TED conferences produce some of the most intellectually stimulating videos in the world. Its eighteen-minute limit forces speakers to get to the point. The expansion of TED to local conferences makes this source even richer.[†††]

The Elements of Posts

Social media has its own unwritten rules of composition and content. Here are the general principles:

- **Be brief.** The sweet spot for posts on Google+ and Facebook is two to three sentences. Twitter, by definition, limits you to 140 characters.
- **Post publicly.** Don't hide your good stuff under a bushel. You need exposure and awareness as far and wide as possible, so let everyone read your posts. There's no such thing as too big a platform.
- **Post regularly.** I often share ten posts in a day, but I'm a few standard deviations above the average. Three to five posts per day on each social-media service is the right number. No one complains about getting too few posts, but if you share too much, you'll hear about it, or you'll lose readers. If this happens, adjust your volume.
- **Link to the source.** Link to the source of your information, analysis, or assistance. The goals are three-fold: First, enable readers to learn more about the subject; second, send traffic to the source as an act of gratitude; third, develop the habit of citing sources.
- **Give credit.** When others point you to something that you share, acknowledge them by mentioning their name. This shows that you have class and that you know how the game works. You'll also rack up karma points, so remember: ABC ("Always Be Crediting").

- **Include a photo or video.** Pure text posts don't cut it in the highly visual world of social media. Every post should contain eye candy in order to attract attention. Be sure to give credit to the source of the photo or video if it's not yours.

- **Use the active voice.** "Apple announced a new iPhone today" is more powerful than "A new iPhone was announced by Apple today." Brevity and the active voice are two sides of the same coin.

- **Add a hashtag.** Hashtags enable people to find your posts about a popular topic on Google+ and Twitter. For example, if you're sharing a post about bacon, add "#bacon" to the post.

- **Share when your audience is awake.** This sounds simple, but share your posts when your target audience is awake. If your audience is spread around the world, my advice is share posts from 8:00 a.m. Pacific to 10:00 p.m. Pacific because that's when the spammers in Southeast Asia are asleep. Tools such as Hootsuite, Buffer (disclosure: I advise for Buffer), and Do Share can schedule your posts. (More on these tools in the next chapter.) SocialBro and Tweriod can help you figure out when your Twitter followers are online.[†††]

- **Repeat your tweets.** I repeat my tweets four times, eight hours apart. I can prove that this increases click-throughs by a factor of four. I don't repeat posts on Google+ or Facebook because this practice isn't accepted there. The assumption that everyone sees your posts no matter what time you share them is wrong—this is like believing CNN should show a news clip only once.

Guest Topic: How to Pin Your Way to Success, by Peg Fitzpatrick

Peg Fitzpatrick is the director of marketing and social media for Kreussler Inc., founder of #MyBookClub, and managing partner of 12 Most.[†††] She's passionate about blogging and social media, with a special love for Google+ and Pinterest.

When she read this chapter of *APE*, she didn't think that I did justice to Pinterest. Guilty as charged! So I put the ball back in her court by asking her to explain how authors can best use Pinterest.

Peg Fitzpatrick: Guy and Shawn are guys, so they don't get Pinterest yet, but did you know that it was the fourth largest traffic referrer for all US websites in 2012? It's time for authors to get with the program and start pinning!

The good news is that Pinterest requires less effort than Google+, Facebook, Twitter, and LinkedIn, because you don't need to respond to comments. By spending ten to fifteen minutes a day pinning new content or repining other pins, you can establish a presence. This makes Pinterest great for writers who don't have time to spend on social media.

Here are best practices for authors to observe when using Pinterest:[†††]

1. **Build a foundation.** Start by completing your Pinterest profile. Use your name, not the name of your book, to create your Pinterest account, because you might write more than one book. Add links to your Google+, Twitter, Facebook, and LinkedIn accounts as well as your website to your Pinterest profile. Also, include keywords such as "author," "book," "writing," and words that describe your genre, such as "romance," "mystery," or "entrepreneurship."

2. **Start a collection.** Pinterest is different from other social-media sites where one's timeline contains everything that you post. On Pinterest, you create multiple boards for specific topics, such as reviews, interviews, ideas, and resources.

3. **Rename your boards.** Board names should communicate what people will find. Do not keep the default board names. Make sure you use all the real estate available by completing the description for each board, and use good keywords to help people find your pins and boards.

4. **Pin pretty stuff.** Pinterest has the highest aesthetic standards of any social-media platform, so ensure that your pins stand out by using bright and interesting photos. The maximum width of a photo is 554 pixels, but you can add images that are taller than that.

5. **Write an original description.** Each pin has a section where you can add a description or comment. This content provides the text for shared pins, so think in the form of a tweet: brief, interesting, and funny.

6. **Customize your boards.** Take advantage of Pinterest's custom board-cover option. Choose interesting photos for the cover and drag to put them in the perfect position.

7. **Repurpose your content.** Pin your blog posts so that your Pinterest followers will read your blog. You can also pin your longer, more involved Google+, Facebook, and LinkedIn posts too. The big picture is that you're trying to present a personal brand that is interesting, intelligent, and enchanting.

8. **Cross-pollinate content.** One of the biggest challenges in using social media to build a marketing platform is finding good content every day. Here's a little secret: if a post is hot on a service such as Google+, it will probably be popular on Pinterest, too. Thus, a viable strategy is to monitor what's hot on other social-media websites and then pin the hot stories with nice pictures to Pinterest.

9. **Use your secret boards.** You can create three boards that are private. Use them wisely to curate content, save ideas for future projects, and keep time-sensitive items that you'll want to make public later for a bigger splash.

10. **Be subtle.** Don't pin only things about your book. Pinterest is for sharing ideas and inspiration, not selling your wares. Like all social media, you shouldn't talk only about yourself. Focus on attracting followers because of your content and curation in order to earn the privilege of promoting your book to them.

11. **Collaborate.** Use a board to collaborate with other pinners and crowdsource ideas. Don't blindly accept board invitations, because that board will appear on your Pinterest page. If these boards feature inappropriate content or spam, your participation in them, no matter how small, will harm your reputation.

12. **Show your personality.** Pinterest is a great place to highlight some of the things that make you unique. Show your hobbies, places you've lived, or your travel bucket list.

Pinterest has broken into the mainstream and should be a part of your social-media marketing mix for your book. Being a writer gives you an advantage over less creative folks, so use this space to help build momentum for your book and stretch your social-media efforts. Before you know it, you'll actually be having fun there. Check out the *APE* Pinterest board to see what I mean![†††]

Summary

Finding, writing, and sharing high-content posts involves a great deal of time and effort, but this is essential to developing your platform. These tips will make you as efficient as possible, but you will have to pay your dues. The fact that building a platform is hard means that many authors won't do it, so you'll stand out from the crowd.

CHAPTER 27

How to Comment and Respond on Social Media

Love all, trust a few, do wrong to none.

William Shakespeare, *All's Well That Ends Well*

Commenting

This chapter explains how to engage people on social-media sites in order to establish your reputation and attract more followers. There are two forms of engagement: commenting on people's posts and responding to comments on your posts.

There are four reasons to comment on other people's posts:

- Provide positive feedback to the author of a post.
- Increase the value of the post with additional information, insight, and assistance.
- Interact with influencers, authorities, and leaders who probably wouldn't answer your e-mail.
- Position yourself as an interesting and credible person worth circling, following, or liking.

Many people comment on posts to spark a controversy, attack others, or generate spam. Never, ever comment on people's posts for these reasons if you want to build a platform.

"This Is What I Think"

A good model for comments is that you are talking to people at a dinner in their home. As a guest, you should show a high level of civility and class and behave, but you should also express what you think about topics. Here's how to be a great commenter.

- **Add value.** Good comments make a post even better. This doesn't mean that people should only say positive things—negative feedback that is honest, supportive, and respectful is as valuable as positive feedback.
- **Help people.** When you see a person who needs help, step up and volunteer. This will expand your reputation as someone who is trustworthy and likeable—not someone who's only using social media to sell more books. Here's a power tip: Google makes everyone an expert, so you can probably search for the answer and provide a useful link to questions outside your area of expertise.
- **Stay on topic.** You can provide supplemental information and even add color and drama, but you must stay on topic. If I share a post about hockey, God bless you if you want to talk about other sports or even about your non-sports passions. But don't start telling people to donate money to the Republican National Committee. A link to your website is in poor form, unless it has something to do with hockey.

- **Show some class.** Refrain from profanity and the big three "-isms": racism, sexism, and ageism. If the world doesn't know you don't have class, don't remove all doubt. Remember: you're a guest in someone's home.

Responding

Responding to people's comments on my posts—even the negative ones—is one of the pleasures in my life. It's the best way to show that you believe in two-way communication, and that you're not simply blasting out propaganda.

You should respond to 100 percent of the comments that require answers. Here's how to make responding work for you:

- **Take the high road.** No matter how negative the comment, don't lower yourself by getting into a fight. You won't "defeat" the commenter, and lurkers will think less of you.
- **Understand the numbers.** If Mother Teresa were on Google+, Facebook, or Twitter, some people would complain about her posts. The vast majority of people probably like what you're posting, so don't let a few orifices ruin your day or cause you to lash out.
- **Delete, block, and report orifices.** Don't hesitate to get rid of jerks. Think of your posts as your swimming pool. Get rid of the people who pee in the water, and move on.

- **Answer, don't pontificate.** Answer the question with as few words as possible. People's attention spans are too short to read long essays. Remember the three C's you learned in school: Clear, Concise, and Complete.

- **Maximize notification.** On Google+, you can "+ mention" people you're responding to by typing "+" and then their screen name. On Facebook, you only need to type in their name (assuming the person follows you). This will cause both services to notify the responders that you've written a message to or about them. The convention on Twitter is to "@mention" them by typing the "@" symbol plus their screen name. Many Twitter users search for @mentions of their names, so they may see your notification.

- **Respond within a few hours.** The life of a post and its comments is two to four hours. You need to answer comments within a few hours to appear attentive. You can lengthen the life of a post by using the + mention method because notification will pull people back to the post.

- **Limit arguing.** The best (and worst) interactions often occur between commenters on your posts. It's fascinating to watch strangers develop relationships and take posts in deeper and serendipitous (albeit related) directions. That's the good news. The bad news is that commenters sometimes get into knock-down fights and post mean-spirited comments that they would never utter in person.

My suggestion is to embrace the rules of amateur boxing and fight for only three rounds. The opening bell is when the author shares a post. Round 1: Person A posts a comment. Round 2: Person B responds to the comment. Round 3: Person A responds to the response. This is the end of the fight—even if Person B responds again. If Person A and B want to go more rounds, they can start their own thread and fight someplace else.

Social-Media Goodies

There is an ever-increasing array of goodies to help you manage sharing, commenting, and responding at multiple social-media sites. Here are our favorites:

- **Buffer.** If you'd like to schedule your Facebook, Twitter, and LinkedIn posts in advance, Buffer is for you. You set the starting time and ending time for posts plus the interval between posts. Then you add posts to the "buffer," and they go out first-in, first out. (Disclosure: I advise for Buffer.)[†††]
- **Do Share.** If you'd like to schedule your Google+ posts in advance, this Chrome extension will do the trick. It requires that you're using Chrome, and it must be running at the time that you want the posts to get shared.[†††]

- **Google+Blog.** This is a WordPress plugin that shares your Google+ posts into a WordPress blog. This means you can use Google+ as your primary social-media channel while still maintaining a blog presence. However, it works in one direction: Google+ to blog, not blog to Google+.[†††]
- **Hibari.** One of the ways to tame the Twitter river is to use a dedicated application instead of website access. Hibari is one of these apps.[†††]
- **Hootsuite.** This service enables you to manage Facebook, Twitter, Google+, and LinkedIn from one website. You can draft and schedule posts as well as monitor mentions of your accounts. Unfortunately, Hootsuite works only with the company pages of Google+ and LinkedIn. You probably have a personal page, not a company page, so Hootsuite won't help you on much on those two services.[†††]
- **Tweetdeck.** Like Hibari, Tweetdeck is a dedicated Twitter application. Whereas Hibari is a one-column format, Tweetdeck uses multiple columns of tweets to display different search conditions.[†††]

This is an abbreviated list of social-media tools. If in doubt, search for the kind of functionality that you want—for example, "scheduling tweets," and you're likely to find an app or utility for that.

Summary

Commenting and responding on social-media services is what separates a good platform builder from an average one. Don't think of a comment or response as one-to-one communication. They are ways to demonstrate your openness and humanity to everyone who's watching, too.

CHAPTER 28

How to Pitch Bloggers and Reviewers

Are you kidding? That guy was a mystery wrapped in an enigma and crudely stapled to a ticking fucking time bomb. He was either going to hit somebody or start a blog.

Lev Grossman, *The Magicians*

Life's a Pitch

This chapter explains how to successfully pitch your book to bloggers, reviewers, and thought leaders. For a self-publisher, marketing is a constant pitch to get these folks to mention your book.

Whom to Pitch

Step one is to identify to whom you should pitch. Here are starting points that cover self-published books and ebooks:

- **BookReviewBlogs.** Blog Nation maintains a directory of blogs. People add blogs of all kinds to this directory, and then BookReviewBlogs displays only blog posts that are book reviews.[†††]

- **Ereader News Today.** Tips, tricks, and free and bargain ebooks for Kindle is the focus of this website.[†††]

- **Indie Book Reviewer.** This website provides a compilation of the blogs and websites that review indie books, organized by genre.[†††]

- **IndieReader.com.** This website focuses on self-published books, and it has a publishing partnership with the *Huffington Post* and *USA Today.* You can guarantee a review by entering the IndieReader Discovery Awards contest.[†††]

- **Kindle Daily Nation.** People who are looking for free Kindle books as well as Kindle tips, news, and commentary visit this website.[†††]

- *Kirkus Reviews.* Kirkus helps resellers and readers to discover new books. It is one of the most prestigious places to get your book reviewed.[†††]

- **Midwest Book Review.** This organization gives "priority consideration to small publishers, self-published authors, academic presses, and specialty publishers." You need to send it two finished books, a cover letter, and a media kit.[†††]

- *Publishers Weekly.* This is one of the most important sources of publishing-industry news. It operates a program called *PW Select,* which is a quarterly supplement to the regular edition for the book trade.[†††] Most of the self-published books only get a listing, but the organization also reviews approx- imately 25 percent of submissions. The publication also selects a handful of authors for interviews in the publication.

These organizations and websites are a subset of the online resources available for self-publishers and ebook authors. I created a resource to enable you to see as many as I could find at Publishing. Alltop. Lisa Kalner Williams also provides a list of bloggers who interview authors and writers that is very useful.[†††]

Pitching on Steroids

NetGalley can help you market and deliver your book to a database of 85,000 professional reviewers, bloggers, journalists, librarians, and booksellers.[†††] You upload your PDF or EPUB file, and then you control access, including whether people can share, copy, and distribute your book.

A single-title listing lasts six months and costs $399. Recipients can read your ebook in a plethora of ways, including browsers, Kindle devices, Kindle apps, Nooks, iPads, and Android devices. NetGalley provides multiple methods for promoting your book:

- **Catalog.** You can upload your book to a catalog where registered NetGalley members can peruse titles and request books that interest them.[†††]
- **"NetGalley Roundup" newsletter.** NetGalley sends e-mail newsletters to members according to genre. The cost of this placement ranges from $60 to $75.
- **"NetGalley at the Library" newsletter.** NetGalley also sends a monthly newsletter to librarians. The cost of this placement also ranges from $60 to $75.

- **"Feed Your Reader" featured-title e-mails.** NetGalley can send e-mails to members according to genre or to its entire membership. NetGalley identifies these as paid advertisements. The cost is $25 per 1,000 names per genre or $500 to all members.

- **Widget.** NetGalley creates an embeddable widget that contains a link to your book. You can include this widget on your website or in your e-mails.

Figure 28.01 Example of a NetGalley catalog listing.

There are also programs specifically for self-published titles or small presses, and, as we mentioned earlier, NetGalley has a partnership with the Independent Book Publishers Association (IBPA) that provides discounts to IBPA members. This is a no-brainer if you can also take advantage of the other benefits of joining the Independent Book Publishers Association.[†††]

DIY Pitching

I receive a pitch a day to review or blurb books, and it's depressing to see how clueless most of these pitches are. This section explains how to make effective pitches to reviewers and bloggers. Step one is to build a relationship before you need it.

- **Get a referral.** If you haven't met the person, try to get a referral from someone who knows both of you. LinkedIn is useful to make this kind of connection if it's within one generation—that is, a friend of a friend as opposed to a friend of a friend of a friend.[†††]
- **Go to events.** The best relationships start by meeting people in person, so go to networking events and work the crowd. Take it from someone who knows, it's much harder to turn down someone you've met in person. One of the most target-rich events is SXSW Interactive; it's held every March in Austin, Texas, if you can make it.[†††]
- **Circle/like/follow them on Google+, Facebook, and Twitter.** Many people pay strict attention to who has circled/liked/followed them, so it's helpful to do this to get on the radar of bloggers and reviewers.

- **Comment on their Google+, Facebook, Twitter, or blog post.** They also read all the comments on their posts, so place something there that's positive, helpful, and insightful.
- **Share/retweet their posts/tweets.** Finally, reviewers and bloggers notice who has spread their posts and tweets, so do this for the posts/tweets that you like. The process is all about their getting familiar with your name.

Don't misunderstand: you need to suck up, but you need to suck up with subtlety. All these activities lead us to step two: making contact via e-mail.

- **Aim.** Contact only people who cover your genre of book by doing research on their previous reviews. For example, don't pitch your science-fiction book to a romance blogger. And ensure that your recipient reviews books—not every blogger and journalist does.
- **Personalize.** Never begin an e-mail with "Dear Reviewer" or anything that indicates you don't know the person's name. Don't even bother sending the e-mail if you don't know the person's name. You're doomed if you are this lazy anyway.

  You should customize the body of your pitch, too, even though most of your pitch is the same for everyone. For example, if you were pitching me to review your book, mentioning that you read my books, use a Macintosh, or play hockey is very effective.

- **Do it yourself.** I hate pitches that PR flacks send along these lines: "Did you know that Joe Schmoe of Schmoe Industries has written a new book? He is available for an interview with you." The only time this works is when I already know the PR person or Joe Schmoe has accomplished something that I've heard about. If these conditions don't exist, make contact by yourself.

- **Keep it short.** The ideal length for an e-mail is five sentences: Who you are; what the name and subject of your book is; what the gist of the book is; what you would like me to do; and how to get a copy if I'm interested. That's it. No more, no less. I don't want your life story. Remember: HotOrNot, not eHarmony.

- **Make contact when others aren't.** If you want to break through the noise, send your e-mail during the weekend or first thing in the morning (recipient's time). You want your e-mail to hit the person's inbox when fewer e-mails are arriving, so your recipient is more likely to respond to you.

Step three is to follow up on your e-mail. A reasonable time to wait (for both parties) is two to three days. Send an even shorter e-mail to ask if he received your previous e-mail and if he would consider reviewing your book. A week later, send one more e-mail. Then give up. It wasn't meant to happen.

How to Write a Good Press Release

In addition to your e-mail pitch, you should enclose a press release about your book. The purpose of a press release is to provide all the basic information about your book in one or two pages. Here are the components of a press release:

- **Header.** This is the top portion of the press release. It contains the text "For Immediate Release" plus a headline and subhead.
- **First paragraph.** The first paragraph should answer the five basic questions: Who, What, Why, When, and Where.
- **Body.** The body of the press release contains more information about your book and a quote from you, plus a quote or two from outside experts.
- **Contact info.** Always include your e-mail and mobile phone number, so people can easily reach you. God forbid that a reviewer or blogger wants to interview you about your book, but she can't find you.

Assume that people won't read beyond the first paragraph unless you've titillated their interest. Imagine that the person has received a dozen press releases that day—why does yours stand out? This isn't as bad as it sounds because reviewers and bloggers are continuously looking for something to write about.

There are two ways to make your press release stand out. First, your book is relevant. For example, sending a book about iOS programming to a romantic-novel blogger is a total waste of time—and a stain upon your intelligence. Second, there is a news hook in your press release that helps the reviewer or blogger serve her readership by providing information, analysis, or assistance.

Don't Forget Traditional PR

When I released *What the Plus!*, I relied solely upon my social-media accounts on Google+, Facebook, and Twitter. I offered an electronic copy to people who said they would review it. I announced it at a keynote session with the head of Google+, Vic Gundotra, at SXSW in March 2012.††† What more did I have to do? I "knew" that I could introduce a book solely by going direct to people.

With hindsight, I knew wrong. Six months after my cover-the-earth introduction, McGraw-Hill published a softcover version of the book, and Pamela Peterson, the McGraw-Hill publicist, pitched more than two hundred reviewers, journalists, and publications. This is a list of the coverage she obtained:

- The 60-Second Marketer
- BlogTalkRadio University
- The Content Wrangler
- *EContent* magazine
- *Entrepreneur*
- eWeek
- *FastCompany*
- GeekWire.com
- *Huffington Post*
- *InformationWeek*
- *Kirkus Reviews*
- Lendio.com
- Likeable Media
- Silicon Age/*Forbes*
- Social Buzz TV
- Social Media Examiner
- *The Social Media Monthly*
- Society for Technical Communication

Let me ensure that you understand what I'm saying. Six months after I released the ebook version of *What the Plus!*, approximately twenty news outlets covered the release of the softcover version because of a traditional PR launch by a traditional publisher.

The lesson is that you need to conduct an introduction campaign that reaches out to hundreds of publications as well as your social-media following. I'm not suggesting firing a shotgun into cyberspace, but there are probably two hundred relevant targets for any genre.

In my case, I should have used a PR agency because I didn't have the time or energy to professionalize the pitching, and I was wrong about the impact of traditional PR. This is why we hired a PR team to introduce *APE*.

Virtual Book Tours

In the old days, publishers paid for author "book tours." This involved visiting ten cities in fourteen days. Authors would fly in at night, appear on a morning-drive radio show, record a television interview, meet with the local newspaper's book-reviews editor, and then do a signing at a local bookstore.

Book tours don't happen anymore unless you're already a well-known, mega-successful author or celebrity affiliated with a big publisher. Book tours are too expensive, and it's difficult to sell enough books in each city to justify the travel expenses. However, Jackie Morse Kessler, author of young-adult books, reinvented the book tour and turned it into a "blog tour."

In an article titled "Launching a Successful Blog Tour" by Alan Rinzler, Jackie explained that she got bloggers to agree to host her at their blogs by publishing a guest post or an interview and giving away some kind of prize on that day. This is a great idea because it makes the blogger commit to a specific day, and you can make ten to twenty "appearances" without leaving your home.

In addition to blog appearances, you should also pursue podcast interviews on BlogTalkRadio, Facebook chat sessions, Twitter chat sessions, and Google+ Hangouts on Air. You can conduct all of these without leaving your home or office, at little expense.

Goodreads

Goodreads is a community of people who love books. You can see what books people are reading and what they think of them. You can also post your own reviews and list what you're currently reading and what you intend to read.

As you rate books, Goodreads learns about your literary taste and makes recommendations for other books to read. There are also discussion groups and book clubs that you can form or join. This is a lovely concept for everyone involved.

You need to fill two roles to get the most out of Goodreads. First, you act as a reader and member of the community. Start at the Goodreads home page, where you create an account and start discussing the books that you've read.

Second, you act as an author using the Goodreads Author Program. Create an account, search for your own name, and click on it. This will take you to an author-profile page. As a member of the author program, you can do these things:

- Add your picture and bio.
- List what your favorite books are.
- Create a blog.
- Publicize events.
- Share excerpts and samples of your writing.
- Create a quiz about your book.

- Share videos.
- Advertise to the ten million members of Goodreads.
- Give away your book to build buzz.
- Lead a discussion group.
- Participate in group discussion and forums about your book.

There's a lot to like about Goodreads, but using it is an investment in the same way that Google+, Facebook, and Twitter are. You reap what you sow. The beauty of Goodreads is that you know you're sowing in a field where everyone, by definition and self-selection, loves to read.

Summary

My old boss at Apple, Jean-Louis Gassée, once told me, "Do you know what the difference is between PR and advertising? Advertising is when you say how great you are. PR is when other people say how great you are. PR is better." Jean-Louis was right: when other people talk about your book it's better and cheaper, so take this information and start pitching.

CHAPTER 29

How We APEd This Book

When you've worked hard and done well
and walked through that doorway of opportunity,
you do not slam it shut behind you.

Michelle Obama, at the 2012 Democratic National Convention

Do As We Did

This chapter explains how Shawn and I authored, published, and entrepreneured *APE*. When people face a big legal, financial, or medical decision, they often ask a lawyer, accountant, or doctor, "What would you do if you were me?" This is especially true if the expert has laid out multiple options with advantages and disadvantages, so that the person making the decision is more confused than ever.

We hate confusion, and we have asserted that we are experts in self-publishing by having the chutzpah to write this book. Big assertions mean big responsibilities, so this is how we APEd *APE*.

Author

- **Hardware.** We wrote *APE* on MacBook Airs and twenty-seven-inch iMacs.
- **Software.** We wrote *APE* with Microsoft Word. We used Dropbox to maintain backups and share versions, and Evernote to store sources and notes. I used Snapz Pro X and Preview to take screenshots.
- **Reviewing.** I used a Samsung Galaxy Note 10.1 running Adobe Reader††† to review drafts in an ebook format. Shawn used his iPad and Adobe Reader too. Don't tell Shawn, but real men use ~~Android, not~~ iOS. (What Guy fails to realize is that because I'm the one who creates the final ebook and print files I can change this statement and get the last word, and he can't do anything about it! *-Shawn*)

Publisher

- **Layout.** Shawn used Adobe InDesign CS6 to design and produce MOBI (Kindle), EPUB (iBookstore, Nook, Google Play), print-ready PDF (Lightning Source and CreateSpace) files and an interactive PDF for direct sale and distribution. We did not do a Kobo version.
- **Cover design.** We hired Holly Thomson, independent artist, to design the cover.

- **Crowdsourced editing.** I shared a post on Google+, Facebook, and Twitter asking for volunteer beta testers. They applied by filling out an online registration form. Approximately 250 volunteered, and I sent them the Word manuscript. Approximately 60 returned the manuscript with comments. I would estimate that they made 500 to 1,000 suggestions and corrections.

- **Professional copyediting.** We hired Rachelle Mandik, independent editor, to copyedit *APE*. She also made one pass through *APE* as a content editor.

- **Online resellers.** We signed up for Kindle Direct Publishing for ninety days, so that Amazon would include *APE* in the KDP Select Program.

- **Print versions.** We used both CreateSpace and Lightning Source for the print versions of *APE*. CreateSpace handles all of the print orders from Amazon.com (and international Amazon sites). Lightning Source handles all print orders through wholesale and Ingram. Our profit was the spread between the printing costs and what resellers paid for *APE*.

    Using two printers allows us to accomplish two things: First, because Amazon owns CreateSpace, there are fewer mouths to feed on Amazon.com orders; this means more profit per book compared to Amazon selling a Lightning Source book. Second, we recognize that not all brick-and-mortar stores enjoy giving Amazon business (not that we agree with this perspective), so we added Lightning Source and its Ingram distribution to make booksellers happy.

Entrepreneur

- **Blog reviews.** One week before the shipping date, I asked all my followers on social media to complete an online form if they would like a review copy of *APE*. This generated approximately 700 leads.
- **NetGalley.** We paid for an e-mail blast by NetGalley to its 85,000 bloggers and journalists. This generated another 551 downloads, and there were also 338 requests from people who came to the NetGalley site to download the book too. These efforts resulted in sixteen reviews, though people may have reviewed *APE* and not reported back to NetGalley.
- **Amazon reviews.** The call for blog reviews and NetGalley efforts meant that approximately 1,600 people read *APE* before we released it. At 7:00 p.m. on December 9, 2012—five hours before people could receive *APE* via Amazon—I sent an e-mail to approximately 250 beta-test sites and the 700 bloggers who had received a review copy: a total of approximately 950 people.

  I told them that Amazon was going to permit people to post reviews at midnight and asked them to post a review as soon as they could. When I woke up the next morning, there were approximately forty-five reviews—most of them with five stars.
- **Social media.** We promoted *APE* using both of our Google+, Facebook, Twitter, and LinkedIn accounts, as well as my blog and HolyKaw.
- **PR.** We hired a PR team led by Tara Kusumoto to launch *APE* even though Shawn and I have many relationships with the press and bloggers.

- **Press interviews.** The outreach to bloggers and Tara's PR efforts generated ten to fifteen interviews, podcasts, and/or webinars per week. More than thirty days after launch, this pace continues, with no end in sight.
- **Live events.** Shawn and I (with the help of our friend Peg Fitzpatrick) conduct Twitter chat and Google Hangout events to promote *APE* at the rate of two per week.
- **Google+ community.** We set up an *APE* Google+ community[†††] that encourages the exchange of ideas between authors, publishers, and entrepreneurs.

Summary

During a trip to Sydney, I spoke to the employees of Google Australia. At several points during the presentation I urged the audience to not overthink their posts and to "let it rip." I noticed loud laughter each time I used the phrase until I finally had to ask them what was so funny.

After an awkward period of silence, one employee explained that "let it rip" in Australia does not mean "go for it" as it does in America. Instead, it means, roughly, "It's OK to fart."

I was going to tell you that it's time to let it rip, but I feel bad for the people near Australian readers. Therefore, Shawn and I want to tell you to go **APE: Author** a great book, **Publish** it quickly, and **Entrepreneur** your way to success. Self-publishing isn't easy, but it's fun and sometimes even lucrative. Plus, your book could change the world.

By the way, if you want to buy five hundred copies of the ebook version of *APE*, we can most assuredly take care of you in several mutually satisfactory ways.

[Glossary]

Anyone who is too lazy to master the comparatively small
glossary necessary to understand Chaucer deserves to
be shut out from the reading of good books forever.

Ezra Pound, *ABC of Reading*

[#]

47North

An imprint of Amazon Publishing that offers science-fiction,
fantasy, and horror novels.

[A]

A9

An Amazon company that develops search and advertising technology, specifically product search, cloud search, visual search, advertising technology, and community question-answering.

Adobe Digital Editions

Software that lets users view and manage ebooks and other digital content; supports industry-standard ebook formats including PDF and EPUB.

Adobe InDesign

See InDesign.

Adobe Reader

Software that allows users to view and annotate PDF documents.

Advance

An amount paid to an author before the completion of a book. The purpose is to provide working capital in order to permit an author to write a book. The advance is "paid back" through deductions in royalties once the book is published.

Affiliate links

Special links between websites that can be tracked by online stores to identify where a buyer was directed from so the online store can pay that affiliate a commission on any resulting purchases.

Agent

A person who helps clients identify editors and craft a book proposal, and then pitches editors to acquire a book.

Alexa

An Amazon service that provides analytics, metrics, and tools for measuring and increasing web traffic.

Alltop

A website dedicated to keeping users up to date about "all the topics" via a collection of RSS feeds from websites and blogs.

Amazon Advantage

A self-service portal used to control fulfillment and ordering on Amazon that helps authors manage preorders or fulfill orders themselves.

Amazon Author Central

An Amazon portal that allows authors to control their bio page as it appears on Amazon.com, including information such as related work, biographies, photos, blogs, videos, and tour events. Author Central also provides analytics such as sales tracking through BookScan, book rankings on Amazon.com, and author rankings on Amazon.com

Amazon Children's Publishing

An Amazon imprint that focuses on books for young people, toddlers to teens.

AmazonCrossing

An Amazon imprint that publishes foreign translations of books from around the world.

AmazonEncore
An Amazon imprint that acquires self-published books that have sold well.

Amazon Hall of Fame Reviewer
In the list of Amazon's top reviewers (*See* Amazon Top 50 Reviewer) someone is given the Hall of Fame title when they rise to the 10th ranking, or better.

Amazon Instant Video
An Amazon service that provides television shows and movies for purchase or rental that can be viewed on such devices as TiVo, Xbox, and Google TV.

Amazon Look Inside
A free program offered by Amazon that allows customers to preview a small portion of a book before purchase.

Amazon Mechanical Turk
A marketplace where people post tasks that require human judgment and workers complete these tasks, such as identifying objects in pictures or transcribing a recording.

Amazon MP3
An online store where customers can browse twenty million songs that can be downloaded and played on a Kindle Fire, Android device, PC, Mac, or iPhone/iPad.

Amazon Prime
A membership program ($79 per year) that provides free two-day shipping on all qualified purchases as well as inexpensive one-day shipping rates and access to free streaming of a selection of Amazon Instant Videos.

Amazon Publishing

The publishing arm of Amazon that acts like a traditional publisher by acquiring books. Its imprints include: AmazonEncore, AmazonCrossing, Amazon Children's Publishing, Montlake Romance, Thomas & Mercer, and 47North.

Amazon Simple Storage Service

A service, also known as Amazon S3, that provides data storage infrastructure for storing and retrieving any amount of data, at any time, from anywhere.

Amazon Standard Identification Number (ASIN)

A unique block of ten letters and numbers that identify a product on Amazon's website.

Amazon Top 50 Reviewer

Amazon's top 50 reviewer list is a list of individuals who have consistently provided high-quality, helpful reviews on Amazon. com product listings.

Amazon Vine

A by-invitation program for Amazon's "most trusted reviewers" in which vendors submit new or pre-release products (including books) to Amazon for Vine members to review.

Amazon Vine Voice

A reviewer in the Amazon Vine (*See* Amazon Vine) program. Reviewers are invited to be an Amazon Vine Voice by Amazon based on the quality and performance of past reviews left by that individual.

Amazon Web Services

A web infrastructure platform that encompasses computing, content delivery, database, deployment and management, application, software, networking, payments and billing, storage, support, web traffic, and workforce products and services.

Amazon Webstore

A service that offers website design, shopping-cart functionality, credit card processing, ecommerce hosting, inventory management, and other features that enable individuals and organizations to build online businesses.

Analytics

Tools that help authors track various data points of their book, thus providing insight into the success of sales and marketing promotions, as well as pricing experiments. In self-publishing, these analytics can be provided in near real-time, while traditional publishers only provide sales figures in a semi-annual, or quarterly, royalty statement.

Android APK

A file format used to distribute and install application software and middleware onto Google's Android operating system.

Annotating

The act of adding notes to a text or picture that explain or comment on the subject.

App

The abbreviation for "application."

Apple Book Proofer

An Apple developed application (Mac OS X required) used to preview EPUB-based iBooks as they would appear in the iBookstore.

Apple Pages

See Pages (Apple).

Artisanal publishing

The concept of authors writing, publishing, and lovingly crafting their books with complete artistic control in a high-quality manner.

Audible

An Amazon company that markets a collection of approximately 100,000 audio versions of books.

Audible Author Services

An online portal for authors to connect with Audible and its services. This program can only be used by authors listed on a book; a publishing company or other legal entity cannot sign up for Audible Author Services on an author's behalf.

Audiobook Creation Exchange

A service provided by Audible that enables authors to post their books where producers and narrators can bid for the audio rights to the works.

Author (the *A* in "APE")

The writing stage of self-publishing.

Author House

An author-services imprint of Author Solutions.

Author-services companies

Organizations that help authors self-publish their books by providing services such as editing, cover design, and management of resellers.

Author Solutions

The parent company of multiple self-publishing imprints including: iUniverse, Wordclay, AuthorHouse, Xlibris, AuthorHive, Trafford Publishing, Palibrio, and Hollywood Pitch. Penguin recently acquired Author Solutions.

[B]

Back flap

The back, inside flap of a dust jacket covering a hardcover book.

Backlighting

The light in an ebook that appears behind the text and enables people to read in dark conditions.

Barnes & Noble

The worldwide bookseller/store that created the Nook ebook device.

Beta testers

People who read the books before the commercial release and offer feedback to the author.

Blog

A website where individual people or groups record information and their opinions on subjects.

Blogger
A person or journalist who writes articles or posts for a website (*See* Blog).

Blurb
A short, promotional description that appears on the back cover or inside of a book.

Blurbers
People who provide blurbs.

Book half title
A page in a book that contains only the title.

BookBaby
A company that manages an author's Amazon, Apple, and Barnes & Noble accounts, charges a one-time fee based on service level, and pays 100 percent royalties.

Bookmarking
A feature that enables readers to tag important pages in an ebook.

Books on Tape
A division of Random House that sells unabridged audiobooks.

BookScan
Part of the Nielsen ratings company, a data analytics provider for the book-publishing industry. Its reports include the sales results of book retailers in the United States.

BookSurge
An early author-services company that is now part of CreateSpace (*See* CreateSpace).

BookTalk.org
An online community in which people discuss books chapter by chapter and take part in live chats and interviews with authors.

Bulleted list
A way of organizing long sections of text by pointing out the most important aspects of the writing.

Buffer
A website to schedule Twitter, Facebook, and LinkedIn posts.

Buzz
Speculative or excited talk that centers on generating good (or bad) word-of-mouth publicity for a book.

[C]

Calibre
A free, open-source ebook-management tool available for Macintosh, Windows, and Linux that can import and export many formats.

CD Now
An Amazon online retailer that sells music.

The Chicago Manual of Style
A comprehensive, authoritative source on writing style and process for writers, editors, and publishers.

Chrome
A web browser created by Google.

Circling

The act of establishing a connection between two people on Google+. Roughly synonymous with "following," and "friending" on Twitter and Facebook, respectively.

ClickBank

An online retailer that enables authors to sell ebooks directly by creating an account, uploading the files, pricing them, and selling them.

Commenting (on social-media websites)

The act of responding to other people's posts.

Content editing

The process of reviewing a manuscript to make it more appealing by suggesting changes to the content, organization, structure, and style.

Conversion

The process of transforming a book from one format to another.

Copyediting

The process of improving the spelling, grammar, usage, style, and factual accuracy in a manuscript.

Copyright

The exclusive legal right to reproduce, publish, sell, or distribute the matter and form of something (as in a literary, musical, or artistic work).

Copyright page

The page in a book containing information about the current edition.

CreateSpace
An Amazon author-services company that acts as an intermediary between authors and online and brick-and-mortar resellers.

Critique Circle
A free online collaborative-writing workshop for all genres with an extensive array of features.

Critters Workshop
A member of the Critique.org family of online workshops/critique groups for writers of science fiction, fantasy, and horror.

Crowdfunding
The collective effort of individuals who network and pool their resources online to support efforts initiated by other people or organizations.

Crowdsourcing
A process that involves outsourcing tasks to a group of people online and offline.

[D]

DAISY
A global consortium of organizations that works to ensure that all published information is available to people with print disabilities, at the same time and at no greater cost, in an accessible, feature-rich, navigable format.

Dellarte Press

A company that provides the opportunity for women's fiction writers and romance authors to self-publish their books.

Democratization

A fundamental change in publishing in which anyone with a computer and a word-processing application can publish a book and anyone with a computer, tablet, or smart phone can buy a book.

Desktop publishing

The production of printed material by way of a personal computer, laser printer, and publishing software.

Dictionary/Wikipedia access

The integrated dictionary and Wikipedia links in an ebook that make it easy for readers to get clarification about things they don't understand.

Digital rights management (DRM)

The concept of adding special code to digital products to prevent illicit copying and distribution.

Direct sales (digital)

A system in which authors sell their ebooks or printed books directly to readers.

Disintermediation

The idea that entities that do not add value to a process eventually get removed. Traditional publishers must fight disintermediation in a world where self-publishers can produce books of equal or better quality.

Distribution
The process of making a book available to the reader.

Do Share
A Chrome extension to schedule Google+ posts.

DOC
A Microsoft Word file format.

DOCX
A newer version of DOC.

DRM
The acronym for digital rights management; *see* digital rights management.

Dropbox
An online service that lets the user sync photos, documents, and videos to a cloud-based file system while making those files available on multiple computers and devices.

Dumb apostrophe
An apostrophe that appears as a vertical stroke (') rather than as an open (') or closed (') mark.

Dumb dash
An em dash that appears as two hyphens (--) or as one hyphen (-) rather than as an em dash (—) or an en dash (–), respectively.

Dumb quotation marks
Quotation marks that appear as two vertical strokes (") rather than as open (") or closed (") marks.

[E]

Ebook

A book-length publication in digital form, consisting of text, images, or both, and produced on, published through, and readable on computers or other electronic devices.

Ebook reseller

A merchant who acquires rights from authors to sell their ebooks; major online ebook resellers include Amazon (Kindle Direct Publishing), Apple (iBookstore), Barnes & Noble (Nook), Google (Google Play), and Kobo.

Edit911

A website where authors can hire editors and proofreaders who are experts in book editing, dissertation editing, and other document, copy, and text editing.

Editorial assistant

A person who helps an editor fulfill his or her role at a traditional publisher.

E-Junkie

A website that helps authors sell books directly and charges according to the number of files and amount of storage space used, while the number of downloads is unlimited.

Elance

A website that helps authors find independent contractors.

E-mail newsletter

A digital publication distributed via e-mail that informs readers about an author's latest business ventures.

Em dash

A long dash, the width of the letter "m," which can replace commas, semicolons, colons, and parentheses in order to signal emphasis, an interruption, or an abrupt change of thought.

En dash

A dash that indicates a closed range of values such as dates, times, and numbers, or acts as a hyphen connecting adjectives or prefixes to open compounds.

Enchantment

A *New York Times* and *Wall Street Journal* best selling book by Guy Kawasaki that explains how enchantment fits in today's world through the pillars of likability, trustworthiness, and a great cause.

Encryption

The process of encoding information for security purposes.

Entrepreneur (the *E* in "APE")

The final stage of self-publishing where an author turns a project into a business through marketing and sales efforts.

Epigraph

A phrase, quotation, or poem placed at the beginning of a book or beginning of a chapter.

EPUB

A popular ebook format standard used by most online resellers and ebook readers (except Amazon and Kindle), based on a ZIP archive and HTML files.

EpubCheck

A tool to validate EPUB files, version 2.0 and later; it can detect many types of errors in EPUB.

EPUB converter site

A website that transforms a Microsoft Word document into an EPUB file, thus allowing the user preview a book on an actual Kindle or Nook before uploading to major ebook resellers.

EPUB file

An ebook file that is formatted according to the EPUB standard with the file extension .epub.

ePub Zip

A program used to create an EPUB file from a directory structure containing properly formatted files as defined by the EPUB standard.

eReaders

Devices designed specifically for the use of reading ebooks.

Ereader News Today

A website that offers free books, tips, and tricks for Kindle readers. This is a good place to start for self-publishing authors looking to pitch their book to bloggers and reviewers at the beginning of a guerilla-marketing campaign.

Espresso Book Machine

A self-contained unit that prints and binds a softcover book.

Extension

A small software program that extends the functionality of a software application.

Evernote

A website that enables users to store digital tidbits by sending documents to their unique system e-mail address, clipping websites, and scanning documents.

[F]

Facebook

A social-media website whose more than one billion users can create personal profiles, post status updates and photos, add other users as "friends," exchange messages, and more.

Figment

A niche community that enables writers to share their works with readers of primarily teen fiction.

File formats

A standard way of encoding information for storage in a computer file.

Following

The act of establishing a connection between two people on Twitter. Roughly synonymous with "circling," and "friending" on Google+ and Facebook, respectively.

Footnote
A reference, explanation, or comment placed below the text on a page.

Foreign rights
The right to publish a book in a foreign country. Foreign rights are usually sold by an author's publisher to other publishers in different countries. As a self-publisher you can publish in your native language worldwide and maintain foreign rights, but selling rights to a foreign publisher often involves the foreign publisher translating the book to the local language as well.

Foreword
Prefatory words by someone other than the author.

Freemium
A business model in which a product is provided free of charge, but a premium is charged for advanced features, functionality, or virtual goods.

Friending (on social-media websites)
The act of adding someone to your list of associations on Facebook. Friending requires both parties to agree to the connection and allows both users to see information, photos, and posts that are categorized under the "friends only" privacy setting. This is different from subscribing, *See* Subscribing (on social-media websites).

Front flap
The front, inside flap of a dust jacket covering a hardcover book

Front matter
Pages of a book that precede the first page of the text, and may include the half title, frontispiece, title page, dedication, table of contents, acknowledgments, list of illustrations, and list of tables.

Frontispiece
A decorative illustration that appears in the front matter of a book, usually facing the title page.

Fujitsu ScanSnap S1500M
A scanner that works particularly well with Evernote.

[G]

Ganxy
A website that enables authors to sell ebooks directly to readers.

Ghostwriter
A writer who writes books, articles, stories, or any other form of texts that are formally credited to another person.

Global distribution
The process of making a publication available for purchase in many countries worldwide. For example, Kindle Direct Publishing lists an ebook in one hundred countries and iBookstore in fifty countries.

Glossary
A list of terms in alphabetical order located at the end of a book that includes important terms.

Goodreads

A social networking site for writers and readers that lets people share what books they are reading and what books they want to read.

Google AdWords keyword tool

A site where users can enter keywords and find out how many times per month people search Google for those terms.

Google Checkout

An online payment-processing service provided by Google, aimed at simplifying online purchases.

Google Docs

A cloud-based word processor that is useful for sharing an outline or short sections of a book.

Google Play

Google's content business that sells music, books, magazines, video, games, and applications.

Google Uploader

A Google application that lets users upload books as EPUB or PDF files that are larger than ten megabytes.

Google+

Google's social network.

Google+Blog

A WordPress plugin that enables a Google+ post to become a WordPress blog post.

Google+ community

A feature of Google+ that enables people to form public and private groups to share common interests.

Guerrilla marketing

A marketing strategy that uses low-cost, unconventional means.

Guideposts

Elements of a book that writers use to help readers work their way through the text.

Gumroad

A website that enables authors to sell ebooks directly to readers.

Hall of Fame reviewer

See Amazon Hall of Fame reviewer.

Hangouts on Air

A Google+ feature that enables groups of up to ten users to create live broadcasts that can be viewed publicly.

Hardcover

A book bound with unbending protective covers that may have flexible, sewn spines.

HarperCollins

One of the world's leading English-language publishers.

Hashtag

A symbol (#) used on Twitter and Google+. Using a hashtag enables people to find posts about a popular topic.

Hibari

A standalone software application for Twitter featuring a one-column orientation.

Highlighting

A feature of ebook reading apps that lets the reader mark important text.

Hootsuite

A social media tool that acts as a hub in managing social-media efforts across multiple platforms including Google+, Facebook, and Twitter.

HTML

A standardized system for tagging text files to achieve font, color, graphic, and hyperlink effects on web pages; the acronym for Hypertext Markup Language.

The Huffington Post

A news website covering topics such as politics, business, entertainment, environment, technology, popular media, lifestyle, culture, comedy, healthy living, women's interests, and local news.

Hyperlink

A link from a hypertext file or document to another location or file, typically activated by clicking on a highlighted word or image on the screen.

[I]

iBooks Author

A software application that authors can use to create Multi-Touch ebooks for iPads.

iBookstore

Apple's platform to sell traditional eBooks as well as Multi-Touch ebooks.

Imprint

A sub-brand or label of a publisher. For example, Portfolio is an imprint of Penguin.

IMDb

See Internet Movie Database.

Independent Book Publishers Association

A trade association of independent publishers.

Independent contractor

A person who is not an employee but is hired to perform a specific task on a specific project (such as copyediting, cover design, or interior design).

InDesign

An Adobe software application that lets the user create works such as books, brochures, flyers, magazines, newspapers, and posters.

Index

An alphabetical record at the end of a book containing names or subjects with references to the pages where they appear.

Indie Book Reviewer

A compilation of blogs and websites that review indie books, organized by genre.

Indiegogo

A crowdfunding site where users can raise money for cultural projects such as films, music, art, and books.

IndieReader

A website that focuses on self-published books.

IndieReader Discovery Awards

Awards given to new indie writers by a panel of accredited reviewers; sponsored by IndieReader.com.

Infographics

Visual representations of information or data.

Ingram Content Group

A service provider to the book-publishing world. A distributor of content to retailers, libraries, schools, and other partners.

Inkubook

An author-services imprint of Author Solutions.

Input format

The starting file format used when converting from one format to another. As an example, when converting from a Word DOC file to an EPUB file, the input format is a Word DOC file.

Intellectual property

A work in which the creator is granted exclusive rights of ownership, reproduction, and distribution. A book is considered the intellectual property of the author, protected by intellectual property laws.

Interactive PDF

See Portable Document Format.

Internet Movie Database (IMDb)

An online database of information about movies, television, actors, production crews, videogames, and fictional characters. Owned by Amazon.

iPad

A tablet designed and marketed by Apple.

ISBN

International Standard Book Number; a number is assigned to every publication including printed books, ebooks, and audiobooks.

iTunes Producer

A desktop app by Apple that enables authors to upload and manage their books; available as a free download to registered iBookstore content providers.

iUniverse

An author-services imprint of Author Solutions.

[J]

JPEG
A standard file format for images.

Juvenile fiction
Fiction written for children, adolescents, and young adults.

Juvenile nonfiction
Nonfiction written for children, adolescents, and young adults.

[K]

KDP Select
See Kindle Direct Publishing Select.

Kickstarter
A crowdfunding platform where authors can create an online campaign to financially support their projects.

Kindle
Amazon's brand of ebooks, tablets, eReader apps, and websites.

Kindle Cloud Reader
A service that enables people to read ebooks without a Kindle device or Kindle reading app by using the Firefox, Chrome, and Safari browsers on Macintosh, iOS, Windows, Linux, and Chromebook devices.

Kindle Daily Nation
A website that provides free Kindle books as well as Kindle tips, news, and commentary.

Kindle Direct Publishing
Amazon's self-publishing service and one of the major ebook resellers.

Kindle Direct Publishing Select (KDP Select)
A marketing program in which, in exchange for selling exclusively through Amazon, self-published authors can offer books for free for up to five days, put them in the Kindle Owners' Lending Library, access promotional opportunities, and share in a pool of money distributed to authors based on how many people borrow their book.

Kindle Fire HD
The flagship line of Amazon's tablet products characterized by a color touch screen and powered by Android OS.

Kindle Owners' Lending Library
An online library that enables Amazon Prime members who own a Kindle device to borrow ebooks.

Kindle Paperwhite
Amazon's line of backlit ebook readers.

Kindle reading apps
Free, installable apps offered by Amazon that can be used to read Kindle ebooks with tablets, phones, and computers.

Kindle Serials

An Amazon service that publishes books in a subscription format; readers pay once and receive future installments automatically.

Kindle singles

Short books (usually short stories, novellas, or nonfiction works about current events) offered by Amazon that cost from $0.99 to $2.99.

Kindle devices

Dedicated reading devices sold by Amazon, ranging in price from $69 to $499; the flagship line of these products is the Kindle Fire HD.

KindleBoards

An online discussion board that focuses on all forms of Kindle: ebooks, tablets, accessories, and apps.

Kindlegraph

A service that enables authors to "autograph" ebooks by inserting a personalized message and digitized signature.

Kirkus Reviews

A service that helps readers and resellers discover new books; it also provides editing services.

Kobo

One of the major sellers of ebooks and ebook readers.

[L]

LaTeX
A word processor (or "document preparation system") that emphasizes content over appearance; output is usually high-quality technical and scientific publications.

Library loans
See OverDrive.

LibreOffice
A free, open-source productivity suite that includes a word processor and spreadsheet program, among other applications.

Lightning Source
A print-on-demand company that offers authors low printing costs; owned by Ingram.

Liking (on social-media websites)
A method of showing approval for a post or brand on Facebook.

LinkedIn
A social network oriented toward job hunting and business development.

Look Inside
See Amazon Look Inside.

Lulu
An author-services company that offers copyediting, cover design, and distribution to self-publishing authors.

[M]

MacBook Air

A Macintosh laptop, notable for being particularly light, thin, and sexy.

MailChimp

A service for handling subscriptions, campaigns, and analytics for e-mail newsletters.

Manuscript

The text of a book in a word-processor format. The manuscript is typically refined, polished, and reworked until it is ready for the publishing stage.

Metadata

Ancillary information embedded in an ebook file, including the cover, title, author, copyright, and ISBN of an ebook.

Microsoft Word

Microsoft's word-processing software, and the most prevalent one in use.

Midwest Book Review

An organization that reviews books while giving "priority consideration to small publishers, self-published authors, academic presses, and specialty publishers."

MOBI

A standard ebook file format used by Amazon and Kindle.

MobileRead

An online discussion board focusing on the reading of books using mobile devices; topics include ebook readers, ebook apps, and ebook formats.

Montlake Romance

An Amazon imprint that publishes contemporary, suspense, paranormal, and historical romance titles.

Multimedia content

Features such as those found in Multi-Touch books, including graphics, photos, links, movies, animations, and user-interaction elements such as self-assessment quizzes.

Multi-Touch ebook

Books available for iPads that contain multimedia content.

[N]

National Public Radio (NPR)

A multimedia news organization that focuses on unbiased and in-depth journalism.

NetGalley

A service that lets authors and publishers market and deliver their ebooks to professional reviewers, bloggers, and journalists.

Nexus 7

A tablet offered by Google.

Nook

Barnes & Noble's brand of tablets and ebook readers.

Nothing Binding

A social network for authors, readers, publishers, and book buyers with the goal of breaking "the chains of the current publishing dinosaur system that is blocking the great wave of literary progress, learning and enjoyment."

[O]

Online ebook reseller (digital)

A service that sells ebooks on behalf of an author. The major online ebook resellers are: Kindle Direct Publishing (Amazon), the iBookstore (Apple), PubIt (Barnes & Noble), Google Play (Google), and Kobo.

OpenOffice Writer

An open-source word processor that comes included in the OpenOffice productivity suite.

Open Source

Software products that are available for free and can be used in any way.

Optimal images

The ideal image size for document pages, determined according to the screen size of the reading device used.

Orphan

A hallmark of poor page layout. (1) The first line of text in a paragraph is separated from the rest of the paragraph by a page break or new column; (2) A word or part of a word that is not long enough to clear the indent of the following paragraph is by itself on the last line of a paragraph.

Output format

The file format produced during conversion. As an example, when converting from a Word DOC to an EPUB file, the output format is an EPUB file.

OverDrive

A digital-content distributor of ebooks and audiobooks that focuses on the school and library market.

[P]

Pages (Apple)

Apple's word processor and page-layout application.

Palibro

An author-services imprint of Author Solutions.

Paragraph styles

A feature of word processors used to tag paragraphs with specific style options such as font, size, color, and alignment. Changes to the paragraph style automatically affect all paragraphs in the document tagged with that style.

PayPal

An online service that lets people pay, get paid, or transfer money safely.

PDF

See Portable Document Format.

Pinterest

A social network where people "pin" things they find interesting, especially food, clothing, and design pictures.

Pitch

A summary of a manuscript created for the purposes of marketing, especially to potential publishers or reviewers.

Platform

Marketing-speak for the sum total of people you know and who know you, including, among others, friends and followers on social-media websites, e-mail contacts, readers of your blog or previous books, bloggers, reviewers, other authors, and people who have seen you speak.

Plugin

A small software program that extends the functionality of a software application.

Point of sale

The location where a transaction occurs in exchange for a product or service.

Portable Document Format (PDF)

A static-page file format designed to mimic a printed page.

Interactive PDF

A PDF intended to be distributed as a digital book. Common characteristics of an interactive PDF include hyperlink text underlined and colored to distinguish it from the surrounding text and a table of contents cross-linked to chapters and sections in the PDF.

Print-ready PDF

A PDF intended to be submitted to an author-services company or print-on-demand company, used to produce printed books. Common characteristics of a print-ready PDF include hyperlink text that is neither underlined nor colored differently from the surrounding text, and front matter consistent with *The Chicago Manual of Style.*

Print-on-demand

A service offered by companies such as Lightning Source, which enables authors to quickly print copies of their manuscript for distribution at relatively low cost.

Print-ready PDF

See Portable Document Format.

Print-to-Order

The Lightning Source program in which Lightning Source sells a book on an author's behalf and pays him or her the difference between the wholesale price and printing costs.

Print-to-Publisher

The Lightning Source program in which an author orders copies of his or her book from Lightning Source, which then ships copies of a manuscript to the author, wholesalers, retailers, and warehouses; these books appear to come from the author, who pays the company for printing, handling, and shipping; the author bills and collects from the recipients of the books.

Print-to-Warehouse
The Lightning Source program in which Lightning Source prints a book for a publisher and then ships it to the publisher's warehouse for inclusion with books from other sources (also known as "cross-docking).

PR Newswire
A global provider of multimedia platforms that enable marketers to leverage content to engage with all their key audiences.

Proof pages
A mock-up of the typeset version of a book, sent to authors by publishing companies near the end of the publishing process.

Proofreader
A person who reads proof pages either cold or against a copy-edited manuscript and marks any further corrections.

PubIt
The reseller system of Barnes & Noble's Nook e-readers.

Publicist
The "vice president of marketing" for a book who interacts with the sales force, editor, book reviewers, bloggers, and resellers; the publicist, not the editor, typically controls the marketing budget for the book.

Publisher (the *P* in "APE")
The stage of the self-publishing process that involves editing, copyediting, layout creation, uploading, and printing in order to get a manuscript ready for distribution.

Publishers Weekly
A news magazine directed at publishers, librarians, booksellers, and literary agents.

Publishing Spring
The turning point in early 2012 when tablets and eReaders grew beyond an early-adopter fad and Christmas present and became a mainstream product.

Pubslush
A crowdfunding website dedicated to books.

Pure-text novel
A novel that is composed entirely of text and no graphics.

PW Select
A quarterly supplement to the regular edition of *Publishers Weekly* focused on self-publishing and containing listings and reviews of self-published books.

[Q]

There are no Q words in this glossary because you should never quit. Writing is a long, hard journey, but it is also one of the most rewarding experiences of your life. So don't give up, and keep going.

[R]

Reseller
A company that acts as an intermediary between an author and his or her readers by stocking, marketing, and selling the author's work.

Retail price
The price customers see and pay for the final version of a consumer product.

Review Fuse
An online peer-review site for writers.

Revisions
Changes and corrections made to a complete draft of a manuscript or set of proofs.

Royalty
The author's share (usually 10 to 15 percent) of the net revenue that a publisher receives from selling his or her book.

[S]

Scribes
People who were employed to copy text before the advent of printing technology.

Scrivener
Word-processing software that focuses on outlining, structuring, taking notes, and tracking research sources.

Sector expert

An author who specializes in writing works on a certain topic or in a specific genre or field.

Self-publishing

The process by which an author publishes a book using his or her own resources without the assistance of an established publisher.

Serial comma

The final comma in a sentence listing items; specifically, the one immediately preceding the coordinating conjunction. Helps avoid ambiguity.

Series title

A part of the front matter of a book, when that book happens to be part of a larger series. Specifically, the part of the front matter that contains the title of the work, volume, the name of the general editor, and the titles of previous works in the series.

Sharing (on social-media websites)

The act of posting links or material on a social-networking site in a way that communicates it to friends, fans, followers, or other members of the network.

Shelfari

Amazon's online community of authors, publishers, and readers whose mission is to "enhance the experience of reading by connecting readers in meaningful conversations about the published word."

Site license

A license to use a book or software within a facility that provides authorization to install the software on all or some number of servers for a specified number of users at specified locations as well as make copies of the book or software for distribution within that jurisdiction.

Skype

An online service that enables users to make video calls and phone calls and to send instant messages.

Smart apostrophe

An apostrophe that is curled (' ') as opposed to a straight line (' ')

Smart dash

A dash that is elongated to denote its specific meaning: em dash (—); or en dash (–).

Smart quotation marks

A quotation mark that is curled (" ") as opposed to straight lines (" ").

Smashwords

An author-services company and distributor working on a 15 percent commission; focuses on ebook resellers such as Apple, Barnes & Noble, Kobo, Sony, and Diesel—but not Amazon.

Social media

The term for interactive online platforms like Google+, Facebook, Twitter, or LinkedIn that allow users to share posts, pictures, and comments.

Softcover
A book bound in a flexible paper cover and sold at a lower price than hardcover.

Special characters
Symbols, punctuation marks, and other characters that are neither numbers nor letters such as "*," "&," "%," and "#."

Spine (book)
The part of a book to which the pages are attached and on the outside of which usually appear the book title, the author's name, and the publisher's name and logo.

StumbleUpon
An online community of people who "stumble upon" websites and rate them and, in so doing, enters the websites into the StumbleUpon system for the rest of the community.

Styles (Microsoft Word feature)
A feature in the Format menu of Microsoft Word that lets users apply various sets of formatting choices to paragraphs.

Subhead
A heading within a chapter that identifies and separates topics within that chapter.

SXSW Interactive
An annual conference in Austin, Texas, focusing on emerging technologies and new media.

[T]

Table of contents
A section in the front matter of a book where its various chapters (and possibly subheadings) are listed along with their page numbers.

Tablet
A type of personal computer with a touchscreen that can be operated with fingertips, a stylus, or both; a popular device for reading ebooks.

Technical editing
The process of making corrections and revisions to a book about a technical topic, both for technical errors and for errors involving the use of language (spelling, grammar, and so on).

TED
A collection of conferences where highly qualified speakers discuss their passions and expertise.

Thomas & Mercer
An imprint of Amazon Publishing that specializes in mysteries and thrillers.

TIFF
A standard image file format commonly used by publishers for cover images and interior images.

Time to market
The time between when a manuscript is completed and when it becomes available for consumer purchase.

Title page
The page in the front matter of a book that contains the full title of the work, the subtitle, the name of the author, and the name and location of the publisher.

Top 50 Reviewer
See Amazon Top 50 Reviewer.

Trade book
A book intended for general readership, as opposed to academic or technical readership.

Traditional PR
Publicity methods other than social-media marketing, especially those that rely on older approaches such as reaching out to major news outlets.

Traditional publishing
The alternative to self-publishing, and the process of publishing works through major publishing houses such as Penguin and HarperCollins.

Trafford
An author-services imprint of Author Solutions.

TrialPay
One of the payment methods customers can use on E-Junkie, along with PayPal, Authorize.net, and Google Checkout.

Trustworthiness, likeability, and competence (TLC)
The three pillars of establishing an enchanting personal brand.

Tumblr

One of the four major blogging platforms, along with Blogger, TypePad, and WordPress.

Tweet

A message no longer than 140 characters, sent by users to their followers on Twitter.

Tweetdeck

A standalone software application for Twitter featuring a multi-column orientation.

Twitter

A major social networking website that revolves around 140-character messages called tweets; users can send these messages to their followers, or follow other users (friends, celebrities, favorite brands, and so on) to receive those messages.

TypePad

One of the four major blogging platforms, along with Blogger, Tumblr, and WordPress.

[U]

Unbound

A crowdfunding website dedicated to books.

URL

The address of an Internet resource; it can be any type of file stored on a server, such as a web page, a text file, a graphics file, or an application.

USA Today
One of the most widely read American daily newspapers.

User-generated reviews
Reviews created by ordinary users of a product, as opposed to those created by professional reviewers.

Utilities
Tools for writers to back up manuscripts, store tidbits of information, and transfer large files.

[V]

Vanity publishing
An alternate term for self-publishing, with derogatory connotations; it implies that authors self-publish only after being rejected by mainstream publishers.

Version control
The tracking and storing of drafts of a project over various stages of its creation in order to allow backtracking or the revisiting of older versions for reference.

Vine Voice
See Amazon Vine Voice.

Virtual book tour
A book tour conducted through electronic media, such as guest appearances on blogs or podcasts.

[W]

Wattpad
An online community, primarily for writers and readers of novels and poetry, that focuses on feedback and collaboration.

What the Plus!
Guy's guide to Google+ and his first attempt at self-publishing.

Wholesale price
The price at which a product is initially sold to a reseller, as opposed to retail price, which is the final price a consumer pays for the product.

Widget
A small piece of prebuilt, self-contained code that can be easily embedded in existing applications or websites.

Widget (iBooks Author)
Small interactive components used in Apple's Multi-Touch iBooks that provide a rich media experience.

Widow
A hallmark of poor page layout. A widow is when the last line of a paragraph appears by itself on the following page or in the next column.

Wikipedia
A multilingual, web-based, free-content encyclopedia project operated by the Wikimedia Foundation and based on an openly editable model.

Word (Microsoft)
See Microsoft Word.

Wordclay
An author-services imprint of Author Solutions.

WordPress
One of the four major blogging platforms, along with Blogger, Tumblr, and TypePad.

Word processor
A software design for producing typewritten documents with automated and usually computerized typing and text-editing equipment.

Word styles
See Styles (Microsoft Word feature).

Workaround
A plan or method to circumvent a problem without eliminating it.

Work-for-hire document
A legal agreement that provides intellectual-property protection when an author hires an independent contractor.

Writers' conference
A networking event where writers go to meet agents, editors, and other writers.

WritersCafe.org
An online community where writers can post their work, get reviews, and connect with other writers.

[X]

Xlibris
An author-services imprint of Author Solutions.

[Y]

YouSendIt
An online service that provides a way to transfer large files.

YouTube
A website that lets people discover, watch, and share originally created videos.

[Z]

Zappos
An online retailer of shoes, clothing, bags, accessories, and beauty products run by Amazon.

ZIP
A file that contains one or more files that have been compressed into the ZIP format, which saves storage space.

Thank you. Now go write a book!

—*Guy and Shawn*